BLACK WRITING FROM CHICAGO:
IN THE WORLD, NOT OF IT?

EDITED BY RICHARD R. GUZMAN
WITH A FOREWORD BY CAROLYN M. RODGERS

SOUTHERN ILLINOIS UNIVERSITY PRESS / CARBONDALE

Publication of this book was partially underwritten by
a grant from Southern Illinois University Carbondale
through its Reflective Responsive University Grants
Program.

Library of Congress Cataloging-in-Publication Data

  Black writing from Chicago : in the world, not of it? /
edited by Richard R. Guzman ; with a foreword by
Carolyn M. Rodgers.
     p. cm.
  Includes bibliographical references.
  1. American literature—African American authors.
2. American literature—Illinois—Chicago. 3. African
Americans—Literary collections. 4. Chicago (Ill.)—
Literary collections. I. Guzman, Richard.

PS508.N3B45 2006
810.8'0896073077311—dc22
ISBN-13: 978-0-8093-2703-4 (cloth : alk. paper)
ISBN-10: 0-8093-2703-1 (cloth : alk. paper)
ISBN-13: 978-0-8093-2704-1 (pbk. : alk. paper)
ISBN-10: 0-8093-2704-X (pbk. : alk. paper)
                                    2005031338

Printed on recycled paper. ♻

The paper used in this publication meets the minimum requirements of American National Standard
for Information Sciences—Permanence of Paper for
Printed Library Materials, ANSI Z39.48-1992. ∞

FOR HAKI R. MADHUBUTI

Fierce and Gracious. Warrior, Nurturer.

Contents

Foreword
  Carolyn M. Rodgers **xi**

Acknowledgments **xiii**
Introduction **xv**

J.W.M. (Colored) **1**
  The "Colored Question"

John Jones (1816–1879) **3**
  From *The Black Laws of Illinois, and a Few Reasons Why They Should Be Repealed*

W. Allison Sweeney (1851–?) **9**
  From "The Other Fellow's Burden"

James David Corrothers (1869–1917) **14**
  "At the Closed Gate of Justice" and from *The Black Cat Club*

Lucy Parsons (1853–1942) **17**
  From "On Anarchy"

Ida B. Wells (1862–1931) **20**
  From *The Reason Why the Colored American Is Not in the Columbian World Exposition*

Robert S. Abbott and the *Chicago Defender* **29**
  March 24, 1917: "Big Dailies Worried by Recent Migration" by R. T. Sims

  January 14, 1939: "The Plight of the Jewish Minority" by Kelly Miller

  February 20 and 27, 1943: "The American Negro Press" by W. E. B. DuBois

  April 27, 1946: "Simple and the Heads" by Langston Hughes

Fenton Johnson (1888–1958) **38**
  "Tired," "Prelude," "Questions," and "A Fragment"

1927 *Intercollegiate Wonder Book, or The Negro in Chicago (1779-1927)* **42**
  From "Organized Students Are Powerful," "Entering Chicago," and "The New Negro"

Rev. John L. Tilley (1898–1971) **46**
  "When Day Is Done"

Frank Marshall Davis (1905–1987) **48**
  "Four Glimpses of Night" and "Frank Marshall Davis: Writer"

Leonidas M. Berry (1902–1995) **52**
  From *I Wouldn't Take Nothin' for My Journey*

Era Bell Thompson (1907–1986)   60
From *American Daughter*

Alice Browning (1907–1985)   66
"Old Mis' Cane"

Richard Wright (1908–1960)   74
From "I Tried to Be a Communist"

Cyrus Colter (1910–2002)   92
"Overnight Trip"

William Attaway (1911–1986)   102
From *Blood on the Forge*

St. Clair Drake (1911–1990) and Horace R. Cayton (1903–1970)   106
From *Black Metropolis*

John Hope Franklin (b. 1914)   110
From *Racial Equality in America*

Margaret Danner (1915–1984)   116
"These Beasts and the Benin Bronze" and "Beautiful? You Are the Most"

Richard Durham (1917–1984)   119
From "Premonition of the Panther"

Margaret T. Burroughs (b. 1917)   127
"For Eric Toller"

Gwendolyn Brooks (1917–2000)   129
"To Don at Salaam," "Walter Bradford," and from *Maud Martha*

Dempsey J. Travis (b. 1920)   133
From *I Refuse to Learn to Fail*

Hoyt W. Fuller (1923–1981)   138
From *A Journey to Africa*

Herman Cromwell Gilbert (1923–1997)   147
From *The Negotiation: A Novel of Tomorrow*

Frank London Brown (1927–1962)   155
"McDougal"

Lerone Bennett Jr. (b. 1928)   158
From *Before the Mayflower: A History of the Negro in America*

Lorraine Hansberry (1930–1965)   163
From *To Be Young, Gifted and Black*

Sam Greenlee (b. 1930)   168
From *The Spook Who Sat by the Door*

Ronald L. Fair (b. 1932)   175
From *Hog Butcher*

Useni Eugene Perkins (b. 1932) 181
"A Poem for Jazz Lovers and People Who Hate Wars"

Dick Gregory (b. 1932) 185
From *Nigger!*

Conrad Kent Rivers (1933–1968) 191
"Four Sheets to the Wind and a One-Way Ticket to France, 1933,"
"Underground," "A mourning letter from Paris," and "In defense of
black poets"

Johari Amini-Hudson (b. 1935) 195
"Black Expressions: circa chicago state (& othr state institutions)" and
"(Untitled)"

Clarence Major (b. 1936) 198
"Discovering Walt Whitman," "Read the Signs," "A Guy I Know on 47th
and Cottage," and "The Syncopated Cakewalk"

Sterling Plumpp (b. 1940) 203
From *Blues Narratives* and from *Horn Man*

Haki R. Madhubuti (b. 1942) 208
From *Black Men: Obsolete, Single, Dangerous?*

Carolyn M. Rodgers (b. 1945) 215
"Prodigal Objects," "Sheep," "In the Shadow of Turning: Throwing Salt,"
and "Jazz: Mood Indigo"

Clarence Page (b. 1947) 220
From *Showing My Color*

Charles Johnson (b. 1948) 226
"The Education of Mingo"

Fred Hampton Sr. (1948–1969) 238
From "You Can Murder a Liberator, but You Can't Murder Liberation"

Warren Foulks (d. 1980) 243
"#5 The Courts"

Michael Warr (dates unavailable) 245
"Not Black Enough" and "Something's Got to Go"

Angela Jackson (b. 1951) 248
"Journey to Africa"

Leanita McClain (1952–1984) 250
"The Middle-class Black's Burden" and "How Chicago Taught Me to
Hate Whites"

Sandra Jackson-Opoku (b. 1953) 259
From *Hot Johnny and the Women Who Loved Him* and "Ancestors: In Praise
of the Imperishable"

CONTENTS

D. L. Crockett Smith (b. 1954)   262
"Cowboy Eating His Children"

Marvin Tate (b. 1959)   264
"Soulville Revisited" and "The Ebony Mannequin in the Marshall Fields State Street Store Window"

Rohan Preston (dates unavailable)   266
"This One" and "Dreams in Soy Sauce"

Barack Obama (b. 1961)   269
From *Dreams from My Father: A Story of Race and Inheritance*

Elizabeth Alexander (b. 1962)   277
"The Josephine Baker Museum" and "Blues"

Quarysh Ali Lansana (b. 1965)   282
"hyphen," "seventy-first & king drive," "rogers park," and "fat-free"

Tyehimba Jess (b. 1965)   286
"Magic" and "We Live"

Regie Gibson (b. 1966)   289
"prayer" and from "blooz man"

Angela Shannon (dates unavailable)   293
"Doris"

Audrey Petty (b. 1967)   295
"Gettysburg"

Tara Betts (b. 1974)   305
"Two Brothers on 35th Street" and "A Mixed Message"

Ken Green (b. 1964)   310
"Debate" and "One Man Parade"

Afterword   317
Credits   325

Foreword

Carolyn M. Rodgers

This is an extraordinary book, and it goes without saying that it is long overdue. As editor Richard Guzman points out in his afterword to this unique collection, only *Jump Bad* (published more than thirty years ago!) and *NOMMO* (published in 1987) preceded this one. Neither previous anthology has the scope or the versatility of the present one. This anthologist takes on the mammoth task of assembling a completely diverse group of Black writers, welded together by the most probably, improbable, fragile, and tenable bond: a Chicago experience gained by either passing through or staying on. Richard Guzman has definitely succeeded at this, and what we have here is a scholarly book of great importance, and a sheer delight to read as well.

It does not seem as if it has been thirty years and more since *Jump Bad* came out. I can still remember, as if it were yesterday, sitting in Gwendolyn Brooks's living room on Seventy-fourth and Evans. We were discussing the birth of the anthology, and she had told us that Dudley (that's what she called him, so that what we called Dudley Randall, founder of Broadside Press) was going to publish the book. I remember Gwendolyn saying, "What shall we call it?" and I promptly replied, "jump bad," because a couple of days before, I had seen in my neighborhood a little boy throw his coat and books on the ground, make fists, and challenge another young boy: "You wanna jump bad with me?" he'd said. "Come on!" And they had started circling each other.

For obvious reasons, it had impressed me. The children, so pure and direct in their acts and feelings, I thought, knew how to defend what they felt needed defending. They knew how to fight, and not only with words! When they became angry enough, they showed little fear. I told Mrs. Brooks about it.

Gwendolyn Brooks laughed and said, "All right, we'll call it that, but *you* have to write the book jacket notes for that!" I agreed to, happily.

I remember how Chicago was a focal place for Black authors, during the 1960s and '70s. I truly believe that there was something very special, perhaps even magical, about being a Black Writer in Chicago then, and most likely even before then. We all felt that. Maybe, it was something like being in

Harlem during the 1920s Harlem Renaissance, only it was like 1920s Harlem in Chicago all the time.

During the 1970s, I met James Baldwin at Mrs. Brooks's home, when he swept into the windy city, stopped off at her house—the first Black Pulitzer Prize winner in poetry—and she and her husband threw a party for him. And not once, during the entire evening, did I see him without a drink in one hand and a cigarette in the other. Later on, I met Alex Haley when he came to a meeting of the Organization of Black American Culture (OBAC) at Margaret Burroughs's home, which at that time was also serving as the first home of the DuSable Museum of African American History. We used to hold our weekly meetings there, and Hoyt W. Fuller was our writing workshop sponsor and leader. He was also the editor of *Negro Digest/Black World,* published by John H. Johnson.

Hoyt had invited Alex Haley, who had published *The Autobiography of Malcolm X,* to come and read portions of an unpublished *Roots* to us. I met Conrad K. Rivers, Theodore (Ted) Ward, Margaret Danner, Margaret Walker, Lerone Bennett Jr., and of course, Margaret Burroughs, and so many others it is impossible to name them all here. Giants. Many of them had already become living legends. Some of them passed through Chicago and some stayed. We claimed them all.

It must have taken hours and hours of research and reading to compile this collection of over fifty Black authors who came to Chicago, and either stayed or passed through Chicago's ivory and Benin doors on their way somewhere else. The result is this magnificent African American piece quilt of writings; this mosaic of fear, hope, desperation, triumph, love, laughter, and joy; essays, poems, short stories, bits and pieces of novels and plays. It's all here.

When you read this book, you will be inspired; you will be moved to tears and laughter and anger; and you will come away with this sure knowledge:

All the Black writers in this book have in no uncertain terms let the world know that they are definitely in the world, even if they are not *of* it.

Acknowledgments

Thanks first and foremost to Third World Press for its generosity and to Rose L. Perkins for her assistance there. Thanks to Northwestern University Press and Rachel Delaney, and to the many writers who not only gave encouragement but were so generous with their works. Chris Beskid helped with the initial research, and my son Bryan Guzman with the early production work on the manuscript. North Central College's Faculty Development Committee provided two grants, and colleague Ann Keating much encouragement. This project started many years ago at the urging of June Sawyers, who connected me with Karl Kageff at Southern Illinois University Press. Both are wonderful editors. Thanks also to Kathy Kageff for her careful work with the manuscript. My wife, Linda Bonifas-Guzman, thought this project important, and possibly daring, from the beginning—something that kept me going.

Introduction

This objection of mine to the designation African-American is not popular. Nevertheless! The phrase is *ISLANDING*. The phrase is limiting. The phrase is weak . . . Almost a honeyed *music: AF-ri-can A-MER-i-can.* (As opposed to B-L-A-C-K! Which comes right out to meet you, eye to eye.)

—Gwendolyn Brooks, *Report from Part Two*

As might be expected, the writing collected here is sometimes less refined. It's Chicago writing. Instead it is "more." Describing the daring of the city's Black writing, Hoyt W. Fuller said it was like Ray Charles's music: more gritty, more blunt and aggressive, more raw and free-wheeling than most American writing.[1] Some of it is more hopeful—Era Bell Thompson's writing, for example. But Fenton Johnson, one of the city's earliest literary stars, expressed more despair and more fatalism than any Black writer ever had before. He stunned turn-of-the-century America, just as Chicago, the "City of the Century," stunned America with an explosive growth and grinding materialism, which always threatened to crush the human spirit. The arts, too, had to struggle harder, get scrappier, grittier, and when artists survived here, they expressed more triumph, and sometimes more sentimentality, than elsewhere.

Race added that much more to the struggle. In part, this collection attempts to follow the complex, often clashing, currents of a crucial race theme. My subtitle turns a phrase of Jesus' into a question. His followers, he said, were certainly *in* the world, but were not to be *of* it, were not to be "worldly." It has always been a pivotal question for Black Americans: the extent to which they could be, should be, or should *want* to be part of the world of American culture and society at large. On the one hand, Black culture has contributed in incredible disproportion to what makes the United States so distinctive culturally, politically, and spiritually. It has made the United States what it is to such an extent that every American could be said to be one-third Black at the very least. Why wouldn't Blacks want to be integrated into something they have so largely made? Racism blocked such integration, of course. And it is obvious that American culture has always manipulated Black culture, swallowed it, commodified it, profited from it, while shutting Black people out. Because of this, separatism and integration become opposite poles of a continual spectrum of tension that has played out more powerfully in Chicago than virtually anywhere else.

Rather humble appeals to "play fair" and to let Blacks be fully part of America characterize much of the rhetoric of the earliest pieces in this collection, which pieces an academic might place in the so-called "Antebellum" period of Black writing in America (1800–1865).[2] These give way to more aggressive appeals to reason in the "Reconstruction" period (1865–1900). But after the forging of distinctly Black styles in the "Negro Renaissance" (1900–1940), the "Protest" period (1940–1959) and the "Black Arts Movement" (the 1960's), Black writing almost obsessively foregrounds the question of assimilation—of how much Blacks should ever want to be part of a larger society that continues to mistreat them. The answer, shouted in Chicago probably louder than anywhere else, was often: *Not much, Not in ANY way if it can be helped.* In Chicago from the 1960s to the 1980s, the Organization of Black American Culture, OBAC, was a megaphone for this shout, as well as a major world site for the ferment of Black styles and themes.

In his seminal 1970 essay "The New Black Literature: Protest or Affirmation," Hoyt W. Fuller wrote: "The trouble with black literature in America is—and always has been—the white literary establishment." "Even James Baldwin," he continues, "bought the assimilationist philosophy and proceeded to launch a brilliant literary attack against the works of Richard Wright in particular and all 'protest' literature in general. He lived to regret it."[3] Indeed, shortly after such "assimilationist" attacks, Baldwin began articulating a kind of reverse assimilation, saying that Blacks needed to forget about integrating with whites. Whites, in fact, needed to integrate into Blackness.[4] Ralph Ellison voiced it another way, saying it was time for whites to ask how Black *they* were, instead of Blacks always having to struggle with being absorbed into whiteness.[5] These attempts to see assimilation in reverse is one of many strategies that map a hazy middle ground between a separatist and an integrationist Black ideology.

Many of the pieces in this collection can be heard talking to each other along this separatist-integrationist spectrum. Some writing focuses on figures who have become icons of that hazy middle ground: Colin Powell, for example—or, more intriguingly, Josephine Baker, who held herself at such a distance from white America even as much of the white world here and elsewhere idolized her. The *Intercollegiate Wonder Book* can be seen as a handbook for Blacks who want to step fully into American society, while Haki Madhubuti's *Black Men: Obsolete, Single, Dangerous?* can be seen as a handbook for separatist Blacks, just as his Third World Press championed business, writing, and education by Blacks for Blacks.

The flows across this spectrum are complex. The *Chicago Defender* newspaper manifested a radicalism that demanded full equality and, perhaps, integration. Yet its habit of referring to African Americans not as "Blacks" or "Negroes" but as "The Race" maintained a strong separatism. In contrast, the writing coming from Chicago's Johnson Publishing moved clearly towards an integrationist ethic, not only in the way its *Negro Digest* was styled largely after *Readers Digest,* or *Ebony* magazine after *Life* magazine, but also in its increasing championing of less radical, middle-class values. Yet the content of *Negro Digest* and *Ebony* was often very radical, particularly when Hoyt W. Fuller himself worked for Johnson. However, as the excerpt included here makes plain, Fuller's break with Johnson was largely over the more middle-class direction of *Ebony,* along with Fuller's empathy for the Palestinians. A clearer contrast would be Johnson's protégé Era Bell Thompson, whose sunny optimism stands in contrast to Richard Wright's pessimism, just as her *American Daughter* was deliberately named to stand in contrast to Wright's *Native Son.* Yet here, too, Wright cannot be said to be wholly separatist, only hyperconscious of the difficulties of integration at any level.

It often comes down to attitudes about middle-class-ness. That theme runs through selections from Sam Greenlee and many others. Hoyt W. Fuller and Ronald L. Fair excoriate the Black middle class, while Dempsey J. Travis, Leonidas Berry, and others laud it. The controversy continually flares, in recent times most famously over Bill Cosby's May 2004 "lectures" on the problems of Black youth. A 2005 ABC *Nightline* special on the controversy featured Shelby Steele touting individual responsibility and initiative as the key to full opportunity in American society. But Michael Eric Dyson said it was disingenuous to put the burden so squarely on "the poor." Not only is the problem more systemic, he said, but the Black middle class who abandon their brothers and sisters is even more to blame.[6] In this book, perhaps the most interesting formulation of the tension occurs when Barack Obama notes a church brochure that says it is all right to seek "middle-incomeness" but not middle-class-ness. The emotional center of this book, however, is Leanita McClain's writing. To read her pieces—and Rohan Preston's poem, which alludes to her suicide—is to understand how the question of middle-class-ness can victimize; how she, like many others, can career from one end of the integration-separation spectrum to the other.

The story by Cyrus Colter shows that the degree to which one embraces the world also depends on the subtleties of personal relationships and the interior landscapes of regret and fear related to, but also beyond, race and class. For Gwendolyn Brooks, I chose not those more readily available classics like "The Chicago *Defender* Sends a Reporter to Little Rock," which would have well represented her contributions to the Protest phase of Black writing, but rather pieces that also show how very personal choices shape our decisions to be less "of the world," as Maud Martha decides. Then again, her wonderful poems to Haki Madhubuti (then Don L. Lee) and Walter Bradford reflect, successively, a delight in a certain kind of "being in the world," and a determination to "Stay" and not to be beaten down by it. As I have said, the flows across the spectrum of this theme are extraordinarily complex.

So too is the reality of cultural flow that has made Chicago such a central *site* of Black writing in America, a site flowed to and criss-crossed over and over by thousands of migrants, and by the words, images, spirits, and bodies of the greatest Black artists in the United States and the world. Some writers included here, like Charles Johnson and Elizabeth Alexander, have moved on from Chicago. Can we call them Chicago writers? I looked for a certain tone, such as I alluded to in the first paragraph of this introduction, but also for significance of time spent and works published. In Alexander's case, for example, I included poems from *Body of Life,* published in Chicago by Tia Chucha Press. But the reverse scenario is much, much more the case: why not call *more* Black writers Chicago writers? Arna Bontemps, Langston Hughes, Jean Toomer, Chester Himes, Margaret Walker, Carter G. Woodson, James Alan McPherson, even Harlem's James Baldwin—it was tempting to claim these and many, many others as "Chicago writers," so central was the site of Chicago to their careers. For example, Baldwin's titanic struggle with the father figure brought him to Chicago to seek out Elijah Muhammad, a story he told first in *The Fire Next Time;* and one of McPherson's first big writing breaks came when the *Atlantic Monthly* published his pieces on Chicago's Blackstone Rangers. For example, perhaps the biggest of them all, Margaret Walker, claimed proudly by Louisiana, wrote *For My People,* her most famous work and winner of the Yale Younger Poets Prize, while she was with the Federal Writers' Project in Chicago and participated as a key figure on the Chicago writing scene.

It has become common to acknowledge a Chicago Renaissance (1932 to 1950) flowing across the traditional line between the Negro Renaissance and the Protest Movement mentioned earlier. This renaissance was led by individuals like Richard Wright and Gwendolyn Brooks, but perhaps as much by a powerful community, Bronzeville, a site stretching seven miles from Twenty-second to Sixty-third Streets between Wentworth and Cottage Grove. The home of Elijah Muhammad, leader of the Nation of Islam, of Johnson Publishing and the *Chicago Defender* (initially at least), of Brooks and many other writers, and of such luminaries as Joe Louis and Mahalia Jackson, Bronzeville supplanted Harlem as the center of Black culture in American during the 1940s.

Chicago was also the site at which so much about the "modern, urban Negro" came to be constructed. Charles S. Johnson, the first Black president of Fisk University, coauthored *The Negro in Chicago*, considered a landmark in sociology, as was *Black Metropolis*, a study of Chicago by Horace Cayton and St. Clair Drake, the first in-depth study of Black urban life. And inevitably there is Richard Wright, whose Bigger Thomas, the center of *Native Son* (a national sensation in 1940), created a mythic kind of Black consciousness that defined decades of thinking about Blackness that continues to this present day. "The scene of modernism for Blacks," writes Houston A. Baker Jr.,

> was to be a Chicago of the intellect and imagination, an urban space in which an archetypal "Bigger" Black consciousness was to find itself caught in a nightmare of acquisitive real estate owners, callous labor leaders, corrupt political officials and morally blind social welfare workers. Bigger in the electric chair might well have been emblematically and realistically enacted by the Black Panthers' leader, Fred Hampton, who was murdered by the [Chicago] State's Attorney's office in 1969.[7]

These social and mental constructs emanating from Chicago have been central to Black culture worldwide. But culture is also *literally* published forth, and Chicago was the site of some of the most important publishing ventures in Black history. Robert S. Abbott's *Chicago Defender* first appeared in May 1905 and went on to become the largest Black-owned paper in the world, at one time claiming an international readership of over 500,000 a week. Running editorials, cartoons, and train schedules, the *Defender* fueled the Great Northern Migration, which brought over a million Blacks north, over 100,000 of them to Chicago. Among its regular commentators were W. E. B. DuBois and Langston Hughes. Reading a collection of letters between Hughes and Arna Bontemps, it is easy to notice the *Defender* mentioned more often than any other publisher. Hughes is represented in this collection because the *Defender* was the site of his first regular column and the birth place of Jesse B. Semple and all the "Tales of Simple" that followed.[8]

In 1996, John H. Johnson received the Presidential Medal of Freedom, primarily for starting the Johnson Publishing Company in 1942, a signal event in American history. Besides publishing *Ebony* and *Jet,* Johnson, especially when the fiery Hoyt W. Fuller edited for him, had an enormous influence on Black writing through the publication of the *Negro Digest* (later *Black World*). Then in 1967, Haki Madhubuti, with the help of writers like Carolyn M. Rodgers and Johari Amini, started Third World Press, another publishing institution of incalculable significance to Black writing in Chicago and the world.

Robert S. Abbott with an initial investment of 25 cents and a press run of 300, John H. Johnson with a $500 loan against his mother's furniture, Haki Madhubuti with $400 and an old mimeograph machine—that's how these three great sites of Black publishing began. This collection intends to honor these achievements, as well as hint at the importance of dozens of Chicago writers to the history of Black writing in America.

I have arranged the book roughly in chronological order by author's birth. I have not divided it into the standard literary periods mentioned above (Reconstruction, Negro Renaissance, etc.) because I did not necessarily represent a given writer by the classic works from the periods with which he or she might have been most closely associated. I have chosen, for example, more recent work from Carolyn M. Rodgers, whose work today seems to me as fine as her work in the Black Arts Movement in the 1960s and early '70s. I have not chosen the most fiery '60s poems of Haki Madhubuti, but rather later work, which turns that distinctive fire inward for the sake of rejuvenating the Black community from the inside out. As I've mentioned, I thought it quite important to show the unfolding and persistence of the integrationist-separatist tension. That too sometimes wrinkles chronology. Leonidas Berry, for example, was never seen as a literary type, and his work was written decades after the place it occupies in the contents. I have put it close to selections from the *Intercollegiate* and Era Bell Thompson, however, not only because of his birth date, but also because it carries a similar tone towards and a similar take on the in-the-world-not-of-it theme.

Given exceptions like these, however, reading this book cover to cover reveals a story that roughly reflects literary periods. The history of Black writing in America is usually divided into *seven* periods, of which I mentioned the middle *five* above. These five are flanked on the front end by the so-called Colonial Period (1746–1800) and on the back end by the Neo-Realist Movement (the 1970s and on). Writers from Chicago have played a major role in every period except the Colonial, for obvious reasons. In this collection, John Jones's *The Black Laws of Illinois* represents the Antebellum Period (1800–1865); and Ida B. Wells's pamphlet against participation in the 1893 World's Fair is a major document of the Reconstruction Period (1865–1900). Among the most important authors of the Negro Renaissance (1900–1940, of which the Harlem Renaissance was just a part) are Fenton Johnson and Frank Marshall Davis, although Davis is often seen as a key player in the next movement, too. Davis, along with Richard Wright, Frank London Brown, Lorraine Hansberry, and Gwendolyn Brooks were central to the Protest Movement (1940–1959), though Brooks is also seen as central to the next movement. This Black Arts Movement (BAM) of the 1960s was fueled by Haki Madhubuti, Carolyn M. Rogers, Johari Amini, Angela Jackson, Hoyt W. Fuller, and many other Chicago writers, some of whom—like Sandra Jackson-Opoku—have gone on, with the likes of Chicago-area native Charles Johnson, to produce important works in the Neo-Realist Movement, which began in the 1970s and, under the powerful influence of Toni Morrison and others, dominates Black writing today. This writing shares the stage, however, with still-vibrant 1960s influences, some of which show up in the resurgence of performance poetry. Chicago performance and Slam poets like Tyehimba Jess, Tara Betts, Regie Gibson, and Marvin Tate are among the most exciting in the nation and read almost as well on the page as they play on the stage.

Choosing works that aptly represent different literary periods; that trace the complex flows of a theme; that capture the gritty, occasionally sentimental tone of Chicago Black writing: besides these criteria, I have also tried to choose writing that I by-and-large enjoyed for its use of language, its honesty, its probing logic. In her foreword to Johari Amini's collection of poems *Let's Go Somewhere*, Gwendolyn Brooks sums up so much of what writing can do and be all at once in terms of language, form and feeling, and social and thematic significance. She also identifies a uniqueness, along the lines of what I also tried to express at the beginning of this introduction. There is no better way to end an introduction to Black writing from Chicago than to quote Gwendolyn Brooks, who always preferred "Black" to African-American:

There is such freedom in what the "new" Black poets are doing now. They feel FREE to do what they want to do, to commit Sins against any of the Academies, against any of the musty Musts. To use—as they experiment, feel out, grope toward their various kinds of Way—Too many capitals, Too many dots and slants and dashes, Too much alliteration. They feel free to run words together, or pull them impudently and unprecedentedly away from each other. To make a squalling harmony. Johari's poems are of the essence of this constructive impudence, this endorsement of chainlessness, this singular blend of confidence and awe.[9]

I am haunted by the many who have been left out—Leon Forrest, for example—and try to make some small amends in my afterword. But I hope enough have been included to give some glimpse of Chicago Black writing's *more* quality, a quality compounded of "squalling harmony" and "constructive impudence," of "confidence and awe" blended in a singular way indeed.

Notes

The epigraph is from Gwendolyn Brooks, *Report from Part Two* (Chicago: Third World Press, 1996), 133.

1. Hoyt W. Fuller, "Towards a Black Aesthetic" in *The Black Aesthetic*, ed. Addison Gayle Jr. (New York: Anchor Books, 1972), 9.

2. For an example of the standard divisions of Black literary history see the table of contents in *The Prentice Hall Anthology of African American Literature*, ed. Rochelle Smith and Sharon L. Jones (Upper Saddle River: Prentice Hall, 2000).

3. Hoyt W. Fuller, "The New Black Literature: Protest or Affirmation," in *The Black Aesthetic*, ed. Addison Gayle Jr. (New York: Anchor Books, 1972), 330, 336. This essay, along with the one mentioned in note 1 above, is considered a seminal essay in Black cultural critique.

4. See James Baldwin, "My Dungeon Shook," the first part of *The Fire Next Time*, in *Collected Essays* (New York: Literary Classics of the United States/Library of America, 1998), 293.

5. In his essay "Junior and John Doe," in *Lure and Loathing: Essays on Race, Identity, and the Ambivalence of Assimilation*, ed. Gerald Early (New York: Allen Lane/Penguin Press, 1993: 175–76), James Alan McPherson quotes Ellison as saying: "I tell white kids that instead of talking about black men in a white world or about black men in white society, they should ask themselves how black *they* are because black men have been influencing the values of the society and the art forms of the society. How many of their parents fell in love listening to Nat King Cole?"

6. "Controversial Cosby," ABC *Nightline*, May 26, 2005.

7. Houston A. Baker, "Critical Memory and the Black Public Sphere," in *The Black*

Public Sphere: A Public Culture Book, ed. Black Public Sphere Collective (Chicago: University of Chicago Press, 1995), 31.

8. See Langston Hughes, Arna Bontemps, *Arna Bontemps–Langston Hughes Letters, 1925–1967,* ed. Charles H. Nichols (New York: Paragon House, 1990).

9. Gwendolyn Brooks, introduction to *Let's Go Somewhere,* by Johari Amini (Chicago: Third World Press, 1970), 7–8.

BLACK WRITING FROM CHICAGO

J.W.M. (Colored)

Little is known about the actual identity of "J.W.M. (Colored)," though it might be reasonable to suppose that J.W.M. could be related to Mary E. Mann. The letter, though short, manages to range widely over the major themes of Black advocacy writing of the time, including the nobleness of the African and pride in the fact that the first person to die in America's revolutionary war was Crispus Attucks, a Black man. The piece also ends with startling thoughts concerning miscegenation. The letter's most immediate purpose, however, was to argue for Mary E. Mann's admission to a Chicago high school. Mann had graduated from Dearborn elementary school with the necessary marks but was originally denied admission because she was "of Negro birth." The controversy divided the Chicago school board, though Mann was eventually admitted, becoming the first Black to attend an Illinois high school. She graduated tenth in the Normal program, which prepared girls for teaching in the city's school, but was not allowed to sit with her classmates on stage or march forward to receive her diploma. She was appointed to a colored school that had opened June 15, 1863, and though the school was constantly troubled and closed after only twenty-two months, Mann's pioneer status remains.

The "Colored Question"

Chicago *Tribune*, August 1, 1861

SIRS—I noticed in the *Evening Journal* of the 30th inst., an article headed, "Colored Children in the Normal Department." The writer concedes to the African his "capacity"—that he is a *man;* that he is endowed alike with his more favored Caucasian. But while conceding these oft denied endowments, they, like all other providential gifts to the African, *must come* in their *turn* and in the "proper *time* and *manner.*" When is "the proper time?" Shall it come when *vice, injustice,* and *barbarism* shall have ceased to walk boldly hand-in-hand over the rugged graves of *Washington, Right, Truth, Justice* and *Humanity?* Shall the "proper manner" be after night in the writer's kitchen, or at the white Sabbath Schools, where he is sometimes denied that blessed privilege? Ah, yes! these are the "immunities" meted out to the oppressed African while he gropes his gloomy way through the unpleasant pit of *insult, prejudice* and *inequality.* How long shall doughfaces with Southern proclivities continue to heap injury upon the benighted African, unequaled only among the Pagans? But the African is aware that all this filthy water emanates from the gory pools of Democracy. Sir, if the African "child" and the young American can sit in the same pew in the common schools, why is he unfit to sit in higher schools, since they started together for the same high object—education? If the *poor* American citizen's vote is equal to that of his *rich* brother, why is he unfit for the Presidency? Oh! the long and gloomy night of the African! when shall it be ended? When shall *man* cease to preach doctrines that modern Christianity and civilization ought to have long since dispersed? In the same issue I noticed another, bearing the following caption: "Colored Teachers," in which the writer says in Chicago the colored people have more privileges than the State laws extend to them. That I admit. Every man in Illinois ought to vote in favor of repealing those Black Laws that stigmatize the fair name of Illinois. The writer also hopes that the colored people of Chicago may ever be treated with justice and right. Oh! that word *right!* Who are its recipients? The descendants of Hannibal and Attucks have too long waited for its reception. Sirs, academies and high schools were instituted for the rearing up [of] society, for diffusing the arts and sciences throughout the great family of mankind, irrespective of color, caste or clime. I, too, am opposed to mingling the races. Who are the abettors and controllers of amalgamation if not the slaveholders and the Northern bloodhounds? Is it the African? Ah, no. Those gentlemen who preach so loudly against it, may be designated as its *daily foes* and its nightly abettors!

Yours for the right,
J.W.M. (Colored)

John Jones (1816–1879)

Born in Greene County, North Carolina, around 1816, John Jones moved to Chicago in 1845 and established a tailor shop, which eventually had many wealthy, white Chicago customers. By the 1870s, it had made Jones perhaps the wealthiest Black in the Midwest. But Jones is best known as the author of the pamphlet *The Black Laws of Illinois*, part of his tireless crusade against laws that, among other things, prohibited Blacks from testifying in courts and purchasing property. Jones became the first Black to hold elected office in the state when, in 1872, he was elected to a three-year term on the Cook County Board of Commissioners. In a 1905 letter to the Illinois Historical Society concerning the 1875 celebration of Jones's thirty years in Chicago, his daughter Mrs. L. J. Lee says that, "The whole life of Mr. Jones has been spent in devotion to the welfare of his race . . ." For example, he was "instrumental in sending hundreds of fugitives to Canada on the day after the signing of the Fugitive Slave law," but he regarded "none of his labors . . . with more satisfaction than his warfare upon the Black Laws of this State." Jones died on May 27, 1879, and is buried in Graceland Cemetery, Chicago's most famous resting place.

Mention should also be made of his wife, Mary Jones. In 1955, his granddaughter Theodora Lee Purnell wrote to the Illinois Historical Society, Chicago, noting that the society had an oil painting of her grandfather. "I have," she writes, "the mate of this portrait, an oil painting of Mary Jones . . . which was painted at the same sitting . . . They belong together." She continues:

> My Grand-mother, Mary Jones was at his side in his every endeavor and accomplishment as a citizen of the United States, the State of Illinois and Chicago in particular. . . .
>
> In her own field she made Chicago history.
>
> She was mistress of the home where Nathan Freer, John Brown, Frederick Douglass and Allen Pinckerton visited. She harbored and fed the fugitive slaves that these men brought to her door. In fact she stood at my Grand-father's side . . . when their early Chicago home became one of the Underground Railway Stations. . . .
>
> She was a pioneer in the . . . Suffrage Movement and was hostess to Susan B. Anthony, Carrie Chatman Catt, Emma Chandler and Mrs. John Brown.
>
> In later years after her husband's death, she contributed generously to the now famous Hull House Social Service Center, Phylis Wheatley Home for Unfortunate Girls, to Provident Hospital . . .

Mrs. Purnell was then eighty-four years old and seeking assurance that history would be remembered more fully. In the excerpts below from *The Black Laws*, one sees that John Jones's argument is also based on reading history more fully—Black and white entwined, as if Black history is American history itself.

The Black Laws was a sixteen-page pamphlet published by the Tribune Book Company in 1864. Passages of Jones's text are given below along with my summaries of the omitted parts. After this I have placed some sections of a speech Jones delivered in 1872. Also published as a pamphlet, it consisted of much of the same material and, in many ways, represents a more rousing expression of the heart of the original pamphlet, most of which was a section by section rebuttal of the Black Laws. In the "speech pamphlet," Jones extends his plea to read history more fully into a call to vote the right people into office.

From *The Black Laws of Illinois, and a Few Reasons Why They Should Be Repealed*

Gentlemen, Editors of the *Chicago Tribune:*

Your humble petitioner (though a colored man) most respectfully asks space in your valuable paper, sufficiently large to publish the Black Laws of this our beloved State, together with some of the reasons why they should be repealed. I wish to publish them by sections, accompanying each section with arguments and facts as I may be able. . . . People of the State of Illinois, I appeal to you, and your Representatives, who will assemble in the city of Springfield in a few weeks, to legislate for a noble and generous people. We ask you in the name of the Great God, who made us all; in the name of Christianity and Humanity, to erase these laws commonly called Black Laws. We know that thousands of you do not know the effect these laws have upon the colored inhabitants, and you, in your relations with them . . .

"AN ACT CONCERNING NEGROES AND MULATTOES

"SECTION 1. No black or mulatto person shall be permitted to reside in this State, until such person shall produce to the County Commissioners' Court where he or she is desirous of settling, a certificate of his or her freedom . . . . And until such person shall have given bond, with sufficient security . . . for the use of the proper county, in the penal sum of one thousand dollars, conditioned that such person will not, at any time, become a chard to said country . . . and that such person shall, at all times, demean himself or herself in strict conformity with the laws of this State . . ."

This section is in direct violation of the Constitution of our State, which declares that *all* men are born free and independent, and have an indefeasible right to enjoy liberty and pursue their own happiness. . . . It is also a gross violation of the Constitution of the United States, the second section of the fourth article of which declares, that the citizens of each State shall be entitled to all the privileges and immunities of citizens of the several States... such as the rights of protection, of life and liberty, to acquire and enjoy property, to pay no higher impositions than other citizens, and to pass through or reside in the State.

Now it may be said by our enemies, that we are not citizens, and therefore have no such rights as above mentioned. If being natives, and born on the soil, of parents belonging to no other nation or tribe, does not constitute a citizen in this country, under the theory and genius of our government, I am at a loss to know in what manner citizenship is acquired by birth. Fellow citizens ... within the meaning of the United States Constitution, we are American citizens; by the facts of history, and the admissions of American statesmen, we are American citizens; by the hardships and trials endured; by the courage and fidelity displayed by our ancestors in defending the liberties and in achieving independence of our land, we are American citizens ...

[At this point Jones quotes lengthy speeches and proclamations given in the Senate, in Congress, and as calls to arms. Moving on to section 2, he appeals partly to practicality, noting that colored men are employed in all vocations, yet anyone employing a "negro or mulatto" without a bond or certificate would be fined $500. He notes the inhumanity of sections 3 and 4, which detail the degree to which Blacks and mulattos must register every member in their families, and section 5, which deems every Black or mulatto without the proper papers a "runaway slave or servant." Section 5 also violates constitutional protections against unjustified seizure, etc. Sections 6 to 22 detail such things as how far a slave or servant can stray from his masters "tenement" without a pass, how slaves may be beaten for laziness, and (section 19) how "No negro, mulatto, or Indian shall at any time purchase any servant other than of his own complexion.]

As to sections sixth to the twenty-second ... had they been written in the dark ages, they would have been worthy of comment, but as they were approved in the nineteenth century by a Christian Legislature, they speak for themselves. Are you willing they should remain on your statute book? ... the above named sections are the only portions of the black code which are a dead letter. I know that many friends think the black laws are a dead letter altogether, but I propose to show, before I get through publishing these laws, that they are a *living*, active reality, with the exception of the above named sections.

[Jones goes on to show how these laws have seeped into the Revised Statutes of the State, in particular a statute forbidding any Black, mulatto, or Indian "to give evidence in favor or against any white person whatsoever." He notes that the statute incorrectly defines a mulatto as a person with "one-fourth part or more negro blood," whereas Webster defines mulatto as half white, half Negro.]

But enough of this. It is not the complexion or shades of men that we are discussing; it is the rights of all inhabitants of the State . . . the white, the black, and the colored. The interest of one, is the interest of all. We are inseparably and rightfully connected, in our business relations, with each other, and for this reason, if no other, we ought to be allowed to testify . . .

[The pamphlet ends with formal and humble appeals to the people of Illinois, to Governor Richard Yates, to the Legislators. Near the end he writes:]

. . . allow me to say, my white fellow-citizens, God being our helper, we mean to remain on American soil with you. When you are in peace and prosperity, we rejoice; and when you are in trouble and adversity, we are sad. And this notwithstanding, proscription follows us in the school-house, and, indeed, drives us out; follows us in the church, in the lecture-room, in the concert-all, the theatre . . . follows us to the *grave;*—for I assure you, fellow citizens, that today a colored man cannot buy a *burying lot* in the city of Chicago for his own use. All of this grows out of the proscriptive laws of this State. . . . And more than this, the cruel treatment that we receive daily at the hands of a portion of your foreign population, is all based upon these enactments. They, seeing that you, by your laws, have ignored us . . . therefore take license to insult and maltreat us every day. . . . They think we have no rights which white men are bound to respect, and according to your laws they think right.

[From the "speech pamphlet":]

On the 22d day of September, 1862, Abraham Lincoln flung out a declaration, or prelude, to our ultimate emancipation, notifying the world that upon certain contingencies a Proclamation of Freedom would be issued . . . and we stand here today, fellow countrymen, as freemen disenthralled, with all the political rights that are enjoyed by any other citizen in this glorious republic of ours—clothed with eligibility to any political position within the gift of the people.

The effort of our enemies has been to prove to the civilized world that we were without history, therefore not entitled to share the respect of the civilized world; because, they say, it makes no difference how profound their thinkers may have been, or how eloquently their orators may have declaimed, without history behind them they are not entitled to respect. My purpose now is to show that we have history . . .

[As the transcriber notes, "Here the speaker recited many events in which the colored man was conspicuous, naming as the most prominent, the part he took in the mobs of Boston . . ." Indeed, John Jones spends much time extolling Crispus Attucks, the legendary Black man who was the first to die in America's revolutionary war. Jones quotes from the Declaration of Independence and from speeches given to Congress testifying to the contributions of Black soldiers. He recounts "The glory of the defense of Red Bank," where every member of a Black regiment was killed "after a terrible and sanguinary struggle" in repulsing fifteen thousand Hessian troops.]

These were times that tried men. They had no time to talk about the North and South. Massachusetts and South Carolina, black or white, the object was to keep the enemy out of the house and off of the hearthstone. At the close of the revolutionary war, John Hancock presented the colored soldiers, called the Bucks of America, an appropriate banner (bearing his initials) as a tribute to their courage and devotion in the cause of American liberty . . .

[Jones turns next to the War of 1812, quoting other speeches, as well as Andrew Jackson's urging free people of color to take up arms. "Soldiers!" says Jackson, "the President of the United States shall hear how praiseworthy was your conduct in the hour of danger and the Representatives of the American people will give you the praise your efforts entitle you to."]

It was not until 1863 that we were declared free in this land that had so long boasted of freedom. Our record is [too] well known in the war of the Rebellion to require a recital in my remarks today. Fellow citizens, up to twelve years ago this country had five millions of slaves—the most subject system of slavery the sun ever shone upon. By examining the political history of this country for the last fifty years, it will be seen that the two great parties of the country were the Democratic and Whig parties. We, my fellow citizens cannot lay our shackles at the altar of either of these parties. Neither can we lay our manacles upon the altar of the Church. I would to God that we could have laid them before the pulpit and there thanked God for the instrumentality of the ministry and the gospel. It was said of Wilberforce that when he took his flight for the heavens he carried with him a thousand manacles as an evidence of a well spent life upon the earth. Oh that the ministry could have sent to heaven the five million broken manacles of the slaves of this Republic. But they could not. Then where shall we lay our chains? Where? Where? Upon the altar of the Republican Party. Thank God for the Republican Party! . . . The Hon. Henry Clay said in the Senate of the United States that he "rejoiced to say to the honorable body that neither of the two great parties had any intention of abolishing slavery in this country; that he knew there was a visionary dogma that there could not be property in man; that two hundred and fifty years had sanctioned and sanctified Negro slaves as property, therefore what the law decrees to be property *is* property." Fellow citizens, this great party of freedom has not only given the colored man his freedom, but has set the white man free also. . . .

My colored countrymen, the Republican party has lifted us up from the degradation of slavery and put us upon an equal footing with themselves. . . . One of the first acts after the abolition of slavery was the recognition of the independence of Hayti and Siberia. . . . From the time this party of ours came into power it has met at every turn the hostile opposition of that old proslavery, Negro-hating party, who has styled itself the Democratic party. . . . I deny that a proslavery party can be Democratic. [I]t is to the Republican party that we are indebted . . . and to that party we, in my judgment, ought to cast our first vote, and God being my helper I mean to vote for its candidates in November . . .

W. Allison Sweeney (1851–?)

A passing reference in the Cavalcade of the American Negro assembled in 1940 by the WPA Writer's Program identifies W. Allison Sweeney as one of the "Chicago Poets," and his poem "The Black Man's Burden," published in the *Chicago Daily News* in early December 1913, as "the first Negro free verse." Known more as one of the pioneering Black journalists, Sweeney started in Indiana and became associated with the *Chicago Defender* as contributing editor, and as an editor for the *Chicago Daily News*. He also authored one of the first extensive Black histories, the 1921 *History of the American Negro in the Great World War,* which carries the extensive subtitle: *His Splendid Record in the Battle Zones of Europe, Including a Resume of His Past Services to His Country in the Wars of the Revolution, of 1812, the War of the Rebellion, the Indian Wars on the Frontier, the Spanish-American War, and the Late Imbroglio with Mexico.* His poem, titled in this volume "The Other Fellow's Burden," is included as an appendix and prefaced by this letter of appreciation from Booker T. Washington, dated December 24, 1913, from the Tuskegee Institute, Alabama:

> To the Editor of the *Chicago Daily News:* I have read with sincere interest and appreciation W. Allison Sweeney's poem, "The Other Fellow's Burden." All through Mr. Sweeney's poem there is an invitation put in rather a delicate and persuasive way . . . for the white man to put himself in the negro's place. . . . I believe Mr. Sweeney's poem will go a long way toward bringing about better and more helpful conditions.
>
> Mr. Sweeney is, of course, a member of the Negro race and writes from what might be called the inside. He knows of Negro aspirations, of Negro strivings and of Negro accomplishments. . . . The poem . . . possesses intrinsic merit and I feel quite sure that Mr. Sweeney's appeal to the great American people for fair play will not fall upon deaf ears.

From "The Other Fellow's Burden"

The "white man's burden" has been
   told the world,
But what of the other fellow's—
The "lion's whelp"?

Lest you forget,
May he not lisp his?
Not in arrogance,
Not in resentment,

But that truth
May stand foursquare?

This then,
Is the Other Fellow's Burden.

***

Brought into existence
Through the enforced connivance
Of a helpless motherhood
Misused through generations—
America's darkest sin!—
There courses through his veins
In calm insistence—incriminating irony
Of the secrecy of blighting lust!
The best and the vilest blood
Of the South's variegated strain;
Her statesmen and her loafers,
Her chivalry and her ruffians.

Thus bred,
His impulses twisted
At the starting point
By brutality and sensuous savagery,
Should he be crucified?
Is it a cause for wonder
If beneath his skin of many hues—
Black, brown, yellow, white—
Flows the sullen flood
Of resentment for prenatal wrong
And forced humility?

Should it be a wonder
. . . That ravished motherhood—
So pitiful, so helpless,
Before the white hot,

W. ALLISON SWEENEY

Lust fever of the "master"—
Has borne its sure fruit? . . .

***

The wonder is—the greater one—
That from Lexington to San Juan Hill
Disloyalty never smirched
His garments, nor civic wrangle
Nor revolutionary ebullition
Marked him its follower,

A "striker"? Yes!
But he struck the insurgent
And raised the flag,

An ingrate?
Treacherous? A violator?
When—oh, spectacle that moved the world!
For five bloody years
Of fratricidal strife—
Red days when brothers warred—
He fed the babe,
Shielded the mother,
Guarded the doorsill
Of a million southern homes?

Penniless when freedom came? Most true;
But his accumulations of fifty years
Could finance a group of principalities.

***

. . . Hunted, burned, hanged,
The death rattle in his throat
Drowned by shouts and laughter
And—think of it!—

W. ALLISON SWEENEY

11

The glee of little children.
Still he pressed on, wrought,
Sowed, reaped, builded.

His smile ever ready,
His perplexed soul lighted
With the radiance
Of an unquenchable optimism,
God's presence visualized,
He has risen, step by step,
To the majesty of the home builder,
Useful citizen,
Student, teacher,
Unwavering patriot.

This of the Other Fellow.
What of you, his judges and his patrons?

. . . Has not the hour of his deliverance,
Of your escape from your "other selves"
Struck?

***

Should not his boys and girls,
Mastering the curriculum of the schools,
Pricked on to attainment by the lure
Of honorable achievement,
Be given bread and not a stone
When seeking employment
In the labor mart,
At the factory gate
Or the office door?

Broadened by the spirit of the golden rule,
Will you not grant these children of Hagar
An even break?

W. ALLISON SWEENEY

Is the day not here, O judges,
When the Other Fellow
May be measured in fairness,
Just fairness?

It is written men may rise
"On their dead selves to higher things;"
But can it be that this clear note of cheer
To sodden men and smitten races
Was meant for all save him?

Chants an immortal:
"He prayeth best who loveth best
All things both great and small;
For the dear God who loveth us,
He made and loveth all."

James David Corrothers (1869–1917)

As a young man, James David Corrothers entered the ministry, and he stayed in it his whole life. He also wrote poetry and in his day was, among Black poets, second in popularity only to Paul Laurence Dunbar. Like Dunbar, he wrote many popular dialect poems, most notably "An Indignation Dinner," and, like Dunbar, several classic poems about Blacks, whites, and racial injustice. In "In the Matter of Two Men," Corrothers says that because the white man "seeks the soft, fat place," the Black man grows stronger as he works and studies so hard. Because of this, Corrothers says, "I know which man must win at last, / I know! Ah, Friend, I know!" Such confidence was matched by a keen sense of injustice, as in his most quoted poem "At the Closed Gate of Justice," included below. Besides two books of poetry (the 1907 *Selected Poems,* and the 1914 *The Dream and the Song*), Corrothers published an autobiography, *In Spite of Handicap,* in 1916, and *The Black Cat Club,* a collection of humorous sketches that originally appeared in Chicago newspapers. The fictional club met to read poems and discuss issues of the day, and the excerpt below, which satirizes "De Eddicated Cullud," shows yet another side of Corrothers's wide-ranging, sometimes contradictory, output. While "In the Matter of Two Men" valorizes education, does the sketch below really ridicule it? Certainly, it proposes a vision of self-sufficiency that has deep roots in the Black struggle to protect itself from the white world.

At the Closed Gate of Justice

To be a Negro in a day like this
   Demands forgiveness. Bruised with blow on blow,
Betrayed, like him whose woe dimmed eyes gave bliss,
   Still must one succor those who brought one low,
To be a Negro in a day like this.

To be a Negro in a day like this
   Demands rare patience—patience that can wait
In utter darkness. 'Tis the path to miss,
And knock, unheeded, at an iron gate,
To be a Negro in a day like this.

To be a Negro in a day like this
   Demands strange loyalty. We serve a flag
Which is to us white freedom's emphasis.
Ah! One must love when Truth and Justice lag,
To be a Negro in a day like this.

To be a Negro in a day like this—
    Alas! Lord God, what evil have we done?
Still shines the gate, all gold and amethyst,
    But I pass by, the glorious goal unwon,
"Merely a Negro"—in a day like this!

From *The Black Cat Club*

FROM THE PREFACE

This book is intended as a series of character studies of Negro life as it may be observed in the great cities of the North. The scene has been laid in Chicago because there—more than anywhere else in the North—may be found every type of the American Negro and nearly every phase of his social life. For the Negro is *himself* everywhere, whether educated or uneducated.

Believing that the world needs smiles instead of tears, it has been my desire to present the humorous side of Negro life, as I have observed it. I have endeavored, from a humorist's point of view, to paint the Negro as he is.

FROM CHAPTER 4, "DE EDDICATED CULLUD MAN"

At the next meeting, President Jenkins, delivered a lecture on "De Eddicated Cullud Man."

After a little preliminary business, the dusky throstle of the levee stepped forward. He was clad in a new black dress suit, patent-leather shoes, with light over-gaiters, spotless linen, diamonds, and a self-satisfied grin. He carried a shining silk plug hat and a gold-headed umbrella, both of which he laid tenderly on the table before him. He spoke without notes, in a clear, decided voice which showed that in his own mind, at least, he was master of his subject. He began in a measured, dignified tone, but soon he was gesticulating and fuming in indignant fury and perspiring with emotion, as he warmed up to his subject.

He held his hearers spell-bound, but when he ceased to flood the room with the effulgence of his palpitating intellect, he was perspiring like a man in a harvest-field. His clothing was disarranged, his hat and umbrella were lost, and his wilted collar was dangling by one end. All that remained unchanged about him were his diamonds and his grin. But Sandy had unburdened his soul and was happy.

"Genamuns," he began, "de thriftless eddicated cullud man whut de colleges am scatterin' promiscuous' th'u' ouh lan', as some lan'-po' fahmah tu'ns his cattle out to pick a libbin' foh deyse'fs, whahevah dey kin fine it, am de subjeck ob de disco'sement 'at I 'vites yo' 'tention to dis ebe'nin'. Whilst de college may have tu'n'd out some useful cullud folks, it hab sont out heaps uv 'em 'at have been mo' no accountah den befo'. De kine o'dahkey I'se talkin' 'bout am de feller whut's done bumped his head up ag'inst some college 'tel he cain't talk nothin' but Greek an' Latin, an' cuss you in Trinogometry. Whut's dat chap good foh?—Nothin'!—nothin' whutsomevah!" And Sandy, brought his fist down on the table with a whack that nearly smashed in the crown of his plug hat!

"Dey's many a graddiate," continued Sandy, "'at sticks his d'plomer down into his trunk, an' lets his mammy take keer o' him. No *genamun* would do dat! A *genamun* is a man!—'plomer er no 'plomer! I ain't got no use foh dem 'plomers! An' any member uv de 'Black Cat Club' whut's cotch wid one o' dem 'plomers on 'im 'll be fined an' suspended f'om de society! De shif'less graddiate gen'ly wakes up aftah his po' ole mammy's done washed huhse'f to deff—tryin' make a genamun outen 'im; an' he sneaks off some'ahs, aftah she's in de groun', 'n' gits his se'f a waiter job in some hotel a-nothah. An' when he's off watch, he stan's 'roun' on de con'ah, wid a cigah in his mouf—happy as a big sunflower!—makin' mashes on de yellah gals, an' braggin' 'bout de 'vancement uv his people!

"You kin allus tell 'at feller when you sees'im. He's dressed lak a *genamun*! He looks po'tant, an' he's allus hol'in' indignation meetin's an' resolutin' 'g'in' de lynchin'. An' evah time he resolutes, dey's ten mo' niggahs killed! But de eddicated shade is a-makin' a repertation outen it, an' putty soon he'll be wantin' to run foh Congress, an' boss his white imployah. Dat feller is a fool, an' ef 'twusn't foh him de cullud race 'ud hab mo' peace ob mine. It don't do no good foh to 'buse de Southern white folks; an' to tell 'em whut God's goin' to do to 'em ef dey don't stop lynchin' de niggahs. Dat only makes 'em mad. De thaing foh to do is to be a *genamun* an' git yo' pocket full o' check books, fust mo'gages an' cash.

"Now, s'posen dey wuz a lynchin' 'bout to take place, an' de curly-headed brunette whut was to be de pahty acted upon hel' a fust mo'gage on de home uv evah man in de lynchin' pahty. An' s'posen mose o' dem mo'gages wuz 'bout due er ovah due; an' s'posen jes' 'fo' dey lit de fiah er strung 'im up, de cullud man wuz to say: 'Genamuns, ef you lynches *me*, ma *son* 'll fo'close all ma mo'gages t'morrer! *Dis am ma ultimatum!* Do you thaink dey would have any lynchin'-bee 'at day? No sah! Now, whut could de college dahkey do?—Nothin' but say his prayers. All de big wo'ds in de dictionary couldn't save 'im!" (*Thunderous applause by the club.*)

JAMES DAVID CORROTHERS

16

Lucy Parsons (1853–1942)

Born into slavery in Texas, Parsons sometimes shunned her African American identity, claiming her Native and Mexican American heritage for self-protection instead. However, her marriage to the white Albert Parsons so clearly defied Southern antimiscegenation society that they were forced to flee, winding up in Chicago in 1873, where their anarchist and labor activism reached its height, particularly in the infamous Chicago Haymarket riots of 1886. Albert was one of the men eventually hanged for allegedly being part of a conspiracy, and Lucy Parsons herself barely escaped execution. A mighty opponent of poverty, racism, and capitalism all her life, Lucy Parsons was known as a fiery orator and a skillful organizer of workers, and into her late seventies, she lectured throughout the country championing free speech and fair working conditions. She was also a writer, but most of her work and her library quickly and mysteriously disappeared immediately after the house fire that killed her, and rumors linger that they were confiscated by the government authorities that had always kept close watch on her. In 1889, she wrote *The Life of Albert Parsons, with Brief History of the Labor Movement in America,* a biography that indicted the injustices that led to her husband's execution. Her most famous writing is the essay "To the Tramps," which advocates direct violence against the state for the redress of wrongs against workers and the poor. It ends with the famous imperative: "Learn to use explosives!" Because it is readily available in places like the Lucy Parsons Project web site (www.lucyparsonsproject.org), I have chosen instead a passage from Albert Parsons's *Anarchism: Its Philosophy and Scientific Basis,* published in 1887. In a brief editorial introduction to this piece, really an interview Parsons gave to the New York World, he calls Lucy's speech—transcribed in his collection and appearing here—"the most succinct account we have ever seen" of the philosophy and goals of anarchism. The speech was made "in reply to" a "reporter's inquiry as to the prospects of anarchy in this country and the world in general." As Albert's piece relates, "the woman anarchist dropped her eyes for a moment in deep thought" before beginning:

From "On Anarchy"

"This is the evolutionary stage of anarchism. The revolutionary period will be reached when the great middle classes are practically extinct. The great monopolies and corporations and syndicates met with on every hand are now rapidly extinguishing the middle classes, which we regard as the one great bulwark between the monopoly or wealthy class and the great producing or working class. There will come a time when there will be in this world only two classes—the possessing class and the non-possessing but producing class, the middle classes have been forced into the wage class, owing to the enormous capital now needed to remain in the field of production.

These two classes will therefore find themselves arrayed against each other; a struggle, the revolutionary stage will come and the order of things in the world will be changed by the people themselves."

"Will the change come peaceably?"

"I think not, for all history shows that every attempt to wrest from the wealthy and powerful that which they have, has been made by force. The vanguard of this struggling army will be found in America, because Americans will never submit to being forced to the conditions of the European masses. All the signs of the times show that the fight will begin here. Witness the strikes without number that have swept up and down this broad land like a grand cyclone. Millionaires are made here in one generation, whereas it takes centuries in Europe, and that is a fact that proves that Americans will respond to the call the quicker. The wage system in this country has now reached its full development. It no longer satisfies the needs and wants and aspirations of the people, facts which are illustrated by the poverty and starvation to be met with in the midst of plenty."

"When this struggle comes and culminates in the sovereignty of the people, what then? What sort of a state will follow under anarchism?"

"Well, first let us look at the derivation of anarchy. It means without rule. We pre-suppose that the wage system has been abolished. There wage-slavery ends and anarchy begins, but you mustn't confuse this state with the revolutionary period, as people are in the habit of doing. We hold that the granges, trade-unions, Knights of Labor assemblies, etc., are the embryonic groups of the ideal anarchistic society. Under anarchy the different groups, including all the industrial trades, such the farmer, the shoemaker, the printer, the painter, the hatter, the cigar-maker, etc., will maintain themselves apart and distinct from the whole. We ask for the decentralization of power from the central government into the groups or classes. The farmers will supply so much of the land products, the shoemaker so many shoes, the hatters so many hats, and so on, all of them measuring the consumption by statistics which will be accurately compiled and published. Land will be in common, and there will be no rent, no interest and no profit. Therefore there will be no Jay Goulds, no Vanderbilts, no corporations and no moneyed power.

"Drudgery, such as exists to-day, will be reduced to a minimum. The children will be taken from the factories and sent to museums and schools. The number of hours of labor will be reduced, and people will have more time for pleasure and cultivation of the mind. We base all these results on natural reasons, believing that nature has implanted in every man, in common with all his fellows, certain instincts and certain capacities. If a man won't work nature makes him starve, so in our state, you must work or starve. But we claim that the sum of human happiness will be increased, while the drudgery and poverty and misery of the world of to-day, all due to the powerful concentration of capital, will be done away with. It will be impossible for a man to accumulate Gould's wealth, because there would be no such thing as profit, and no man could get more for his work than he produces. There would be no over-production, because only enough of anyone article would be produced to meet the demand. There will be no political parties, no capitalists, no rings, no kings, no statesmen and no rulers."

"How is this change to be brought about?"

"That comes in the revolutionary stage and will happen, as I said, when the final great struggle of the masses against the moneyed powers takes place. The money and wages now found in the possession of the wage class represent the bare coarse necessaries of life, nothing over when the bills from one week to another are paid. The rest goes to the profit-taking class, and that is why we call the system wage-slavery."

"What criticism of the present form of government do you make?"

"All political government must necessarily become despotic, because all government tends to become centralized in the hands of the few, who breed corruption among themselves, and in a very short time disconnect themselves from the body of the people. The American republic is a good illustration. Here we have the semblance of a republic, of a democracy, but it has fallen into the hands of a powerful few, who rule with a despotism absolutely impossible in Europe. I have but to refer you to Carter Harrison's interview not long ago in the *World,* in which he remarked that the atrocities committed on the anarchists in Chicago would not have been suffered in any monarchy."

Ida B. Wells (1862–1931)

Born into slavery in 1862, Wells first gained national attention in 1887 when she sued the Chesapeake and Ohio Railroad for not allowing her to sit with whites. The case, which she lost, drew her away from school teaching in Memphis and into a career in journalism and crusading for Black rights that is among the most important in American history. She helped establish the African American newspaper the *Free Speech* in Memphis in 1891, and the following year, the death by lynch mob of several of her friends impelled her to begin her famous international campaign against lynching. What drew her to Chicago, which eventually became her home base, was controversy over the "White City" of the 1893 World's Fair. Blacks were being poorly represented in virtually all aspects of the fair, from underemployment to stereotypical exhibits featuring watermelon and Aunt Jemima. Controversy focused on whether Blacks should actually attend a "Colored People's Day" proposed for August 25. Wells and many other Black leaders opposed attendance, and Wells spearheaded a drive to publish a pamphlet to be titled *The Reason Why the Colored American Is Not in the World's Columbian Exposition.* After the rigors of raising sufficient funds for publication, enormous local and national debate on the project's merit in the first place, and many complicated intrigues (mainly concerning whether the venerable Frederic Douglass would or would not participate in the boycott and in the pamphlet's writing), *The Reason Why* finally did appear—and on time, too, though Wells had had to scrap several ideas for it, including its publication in several languages. She had time only to print French and German translations of her preface. The pamphlet included Wells's preface and her essays on class legislation, the convict lease system, and lynching. Douglass contributed an impassioned introduction. I. Garland Penn contributed "The Progress of the Afro-Americans Since Emancipation." Finally, it was left to Ferdinand L. Barnett to write "The Reason Why." A Chicago lawyer who had started the Black newspaper the *Conservator,* and who was one of the original leaders of the opposition to segregated exhibits, he and Ida B. Wells fell in love during the course of these World Fair struggles and married in 1895. Here is what her future husband wrote at the pamphlet's conclusion:

> In consideration of the color proof character of the Exposition Management it was the refinement of irony to set aside August 25th to be observed as "Colored People's Day." In his wonderful hive of National industry, representing an outlay of thirty million dollars, and numbering its employees in the thousands, only two colored persons could be found who occupations were of higher grade than that of janitor, laborer and porter, and these two only clerkships. Only as a menial is the Colored American to be seen—the Nation's deliberate and cowardly tribute to the Southern demand "to keep the Negro in his place." . . . it remained for the Republic of Hayti to give the only acceptable representation enjoyed by us as the Fair. That republic chose Frederick Douglass to represent it as Commissioner through which the Colored American received from a foreign power the place denied him at home. . . .

The World's Columbian Exposition draws to a close and that which has been done is without remedy. The colored people have no vindictiveness actuating them in this presentation of their side of this question, our only desire being to tell the reason why we have no part nor lot in the Exposition. Our failure to be represented is not of our own working and we can only hope that the spirit of freedom and fair play of which some Americans so loudly boast, will so inspire the Nation that in another great National endeavor the Colored American shall not plead for a place in vain.

The actual status of Black participation in the fair, the success of Colored American Day, and of the pamphlet itself remain controversial, and Wells herself is said to have admitted to Douglass that her youth might have caused her to over react. Nonetheless, *The Reason Why* remains a landmark in Black writing. Excerpts from Wells's contributions to it appear below.

From *The Reason Why the Colored American Is Not in the Columbian World Exposition*

PREFACE

TO THE SEEKER AFTER TRUTH

Columbia has bidden the civilized world to join with her in celebrating the four-hundredth anniversary of the discovery of America, and the invitation has been accepted. At Jackson Park are displayed exhibits of her natural resources, and her progress in the arts and sciences. But that which would best illustrate her moral grandeur has been ignored.

The exhibit of the progress made by a race in 25 years of freedom as against 250 years of slavery, would have been the greatest tribute to the greatness and progressiveness of American institutions which could have been shown the world. The colored people of this great Republic number eight millions—more than one-tenth the whole population of the United States. They were among the earliest settlers of this continent, landing at Jamestown, Virginia, in 1619 in a slave ship, before the Puritans, who landed at Plymouth in 1620. They have contributed a large share to American prosperity and civilization. The labor of one-half of this country has always been, and is still being done by them. The first credit this country had in its commerce with foreign nations was created by productions resulting from their labor. The wealth created by their industry has afforded to the white people of this country the leisure essential to their great progress in education, art, science, industry and invention.

Those visitors to the World's Columbian Exposition who know these facts, especially foreigners will naturally ask: Why are not the colored people, who constitute so large an element of the American population, and who have contributed so large a share to American greatness, more visibly present and better represented in this World's Exposition? Why are they not taking part in this glorious celebration of the four-hundredth anniversary of the discovery of their country? Are they so dull and stupid as to feel no interest in this great event? It is to answer these questions and supply as far as possible our lack of representation at the Exposition that the Afro-American has published this volume.

CHAPTER 2: CLASS LEGISLATION

The Civil War of 1861–5 ended slavery. It left us free, but it also left us homeless, penniless, ignorant, nameless and friendless. Life is derived from the earth and the American Government is thought to be more humane than the Russian. Russia's liberated serf was given three acres of land and agricultural implements with which to begin his career of liberty and independence. But to us no foot of land nor implement was given. We were turned loose to starvation, destitution and death. . . .

The original fourteen slaves which the Dutch ship landed at Jamestown, Virginia, in 1619, had increased to four millions by 1865, and were mostly in the southern states. We were liberated not only empty-handed but left in the power of a people who resented our emancipation as an act of unjust punishment to them. They were therefore armed with a motive for doing everything in their power to render our freedom a curse rather than a blessing. In the halls of National legislation the Negro was made a free man and citizen. . . . Since "reconstruction" these amendments have been largely nullified in the south, and the Negro vote reduced from a majority to a cipher. This has been accomplished by political massacres, by midnight outrages of Ku Klux Klans, and by state legislative enactment. That the legislation of the white south is hostile to the interests of our race is shown by the existence in most of the southern states of the convict lease system, the chain-gang, vagrant laws, election frauds, keeping back laborers' wages, paying for work in worthless script instead of lawful money, refusing to sell land to Negroes and the many political massacres where hundreds of black men were murdered for the crime of casting the ballot. . . .

The South is enjoying today the results of this course pursued for the first fifteen years of our freedom. The Solid South means that the South is a unit for white supremacy, and that the Negro is practically disfranchised through intimidation. . . . Every National Congress has thirty-nine more

white members from the South in the House of Representatives than there would be, were it not for the existence of her voiceless and unrepresented Negro vote and population. One Representative is allowed to every 150,000 persons. What other States have usurped, Mississippi made in 1892, a part of her organic law.

The net result of the registration under the educational and poll tax provision of the new Mississippi Constitution is as follows.

OVER 21 YEARS.		REGISTERED VOTES.
WHITES	110,100	68,127
NEGROES	147,205	8,615
TOTAL	257,305	76,742

Yazoo County, with 6,000 Negroes of voting age, has only nine registered votes, or one to each 666. . . . In Lowndes there is one colored voter to each 310 men. . . .

Depriving the Negro of his vote leaves the entire political, legislative, executive and judicial machinery of the country in the hands of the white people. The religious, moral and financial forces of the country are also theirs. This power has been used to pass laws forbidding intermarriage between the races . . .

CHAPTER 3: THE CONVICT LEASE SYSTEM

The Convict Lease System and Lynch Law are twin infamies which flourish hand in hand in many of the United States. They are the two great outgrowths and results of the class legislation under which our people suffer today. Alabama, Arkansas, Florida, Georgia, Kentucky, Louisiana, Mississippi, Nebraska, North Carolina, South Carolina, Tennessee and Washington claim to be too poor to maintain state convicts within prison walls. Hence the convicts are leased out to work for railway contractors, mining companies and those who farm large plantations. These companies assume charge of the convicts, work them as cheap labor and pay the states a handsome revenue for their labor. Nine-tenths of these convicts are Negroes. There are two reasons for this.

(1) The religious, moral and philanthropic forces of the country—all the agencies which tend to uplift and reclaim the degraded and ignorant, are in the hands of the Anglo-Saxon. Not only has very little effort been made by these forces to reclaim the Negro. but he has always been and is now rigidly

excluded from the enjoyment of those elevating influences toward which he felt voluntarily drawn. In communities where Negro population is largest and these counteracting influences most needed, the doors of churches, schools, concert halls, lecture rooms, Young Men's Christian Associations, and Women's Christian Temperance Unions, have always been and are now closed. . . . Only as a servant or inferior being placed in one corner is he admitted . . . they have deliberately shut him out of everything which tends to make for good citizenship.

To have Negro blood in the veins makes one unworthy of consideration, a social outcast, a leper, even in the church. Two Negro Baptist Ministers, Rev. John Frank, the pastor of the largest colored church in Louisville, Ky., and Rev. C. H. Parish, President of Exstein Norton University at Cane Spring, Ky., were in the city of Nashville, Tennessee, in May when the Southern Baptist Convention was in session. They visited the meeting and took seats in the body of the church. At the request of the Association, a policeman was called and escorted these men out because they would not take the seats set apart for colored persons in the back part of the Tabernacle. Both these men are scholarly, of good moral character, and members of the Baptist denomination. But they were Negroes, and that eclipsed everything else. . . .

(2) The second reason our race furnishes so large a share of the convicts is that the judges, juries and other officials of the courts are white men who share these prejudices. They also make the laws. . . . Possessing neither money to employ lawyers nor influential friends, [Negro criminals] are sentenced in large numbers to long terms of imprisonment for petty crimes. The *People's Advocate,* a Negro journal, of Atlanta, Georgia, has the following observation on the prison showing of that state for 1892. "It is an astounding fact that 90 per cent of the state's convicts are colored; 194 white males and 2 white females; 1,710 colored males and 44 colored females. Is it possible that Georgia is so color prejudiced that she won't convict her white law-breakers. Yes; it is just so, but we hope for a better day."

CHAPTER 4: LYNCH LAW

"Lynch Law," says the Virginia Lancet, "as known by that appellation, had its origin in 1780 in a combination of citizens of Pittsylvania County, Virginia, entered into for the purpose of suppressing a trained band of horse thieves and counterfeiters whose well concocted schemes had bidden defiance to the ordinary laws of the land, and whose success encouraged and emboldened them in their outrages upon the community. Col. Wm. Lynch drafted the

constitution for this combination of citizens, and hence "Lynch Law" has ever since been the name given to the summary infliction of punishment by private and unauthorized citizens."

This law continues in force today in some of the oldest states of the Union, where courts of justice have long been established, whose laws are executed by white Americans. It flourishes most largely in the states which foster the convict lease system, and is brought to bear mainly, against the Negro. The first fifteen years of his freedom he was murdered by masked mobs for trying to vote. Public opinion having made lynching for that cause unpopular, a new reason is given to justify the murders of the past 15 years: The Negro was first charged with attempting to rule white people, and hundreds were murdered on that pretended supposition. He is now charged with assaulting or attempting to assault white women. This charge, as false as it is foul, robs us of the sympathy of the world and is blasting the race's good name. The men who make these charges encourage or lead the mobs which do the lynching. They belong to the race which holds Negro life cheap, which owns the telegraph wires, newspapers, and all other communication with the outside world. They write the reports which justify lynching by painting the Negro as black as possible, and those reports are accepted by the press associations and the world without question or investigation. The mob spirit has increased with alarming frequency and violence. Over a thousand black men, women and children have been thus sacrificed the past ten years. Masks have long since been thrown aside and the lynchings of the present day take place in broad daylight. The sheriffs, police and state officials stand by and see the work well done. The coroner's jury is often formed among those who took part in the lynching and a verdict, "Death at the hands of parties unknown to the jury" is rendered. As the number of lynchings have increased, so has the cruelty and barbarism of the lynchers. Three human beings were burned alive in civilized America during the first six months of this year (1893). Over one hundred have been lynched in this half year. They were hanged, then cut, shot and burned.

The following table published by the *Chicago Tribune* January, 1892, is submitted for thoughtful consideration.

1882, 52 Negroes murdered by mobs
1883, 39 "   "   "   "
1884, 53 "   "   "   "
1885, 77 "   "   "   "
1886, 73 "   "   "   "

1887, 70   "   "   "   "

1888, 72   "   "   "   "

1889, 95   "   "   "   "

1890, 100   "   "   "   "

1891, 169   "   "   "   "

Of this number

269 were charged with rape.

253   "   "   "   murder.

44   "   "   "   robbery.

37   "   "   "   incendiarism.

4   "   "   "   burglary.

27   "   "   "   race prejudice.

13   "   "   "   quarreling with white men.

10   "   "   "   making threats.

7   "   "   "   rioting.

5   "   "   "   miscegenation.

32   "   "   "   no reasons given.

This table shows (1) that only one-third of nearly a thousand murdered black persons have been even charged with the crime of outrage. This crime is only so punished when white women accuse black men, which accusation is never proven. The same crime committed by Negroes against Negroes, or by white men against black women is ignored even in the law courts.

(2) That nearly as many were lynched for murder as for the above crime, which the world believes is the cause of all the lynchings. The world affects to believe that white womanhood and childhood, surrounded by their lawful protectors, are not safe in the neighborhood of the black man, who protected and cared for them during the four years of civil war. The husbands, fathers and brothers of those white women were away for four years, fighting to keep the Negro in slavery, yet not one case of assault has ever been reported!

(3) That "robbery, incendiarism, race prejudice, quarreling with white men, making threats, rioting, miscegenation (marrying a white person), and burglary," are capital offences punishable by death when committed by a black against a white person. Nearly as many blacks were lynched for these charges (and unproven) as for the crime of rape.

(4) That for nearly fifty of these lynchings no reason is given. There is no demand for reasons, or need of concealment for what no one is held responsible. The simple word of any white person against a Negro is sufficient. . . . Under these conditions, white men have only to blacken their

faces, commit crimes against the peace of the community, accuse some Negro, or rest till he is killed by a mob. Will Lewis, an 18 year old Negro youth was lynched at Tullahoma, Tennessee, August 1891, for being "drunk and saucy to white folks."

[Wells says that Black women, too, "have not escaped the fury of the mob," and then tells of the 1892 lynchings that impelled her to begin her anti-lynching crusade. Thomas Moss, Will Stewart, and Calvin McDowell were lynched because their grocery was prospering while "that of a rival white grocer named Barrett had declined." "No effort whatever, says Wells, "was made to punish the murderers" of these men—who were "of splendid reputation for honesty, integrity, and sobriety."]

[Wells goes on to recount or quote lengthy recountings of several lynchings, the last of which, below, describes that of C. J. Miller, at Bardwell, Kentucky, July 7, 1893.]

. . . Two white girls were found murdered near their home on the morning of July 5th; their bodies were horribly mutilated. Although their father had been instrumental in the prosecution and conviction of one of his white neighbors for murder, that was not considered as a motive. A hue and cry was raised that some Negro had committed rape and murder, and a search was immediately begun for a Negro. A bloodhound was put on the trail which he followed to the river and into the boat of a fisherman named Gordon. This fisherman said he had rowed a white man, or a very fair mulatto across the river at six o'clock the evening before. The bloodhound was carried across the river, took up the trail on the Missouri side, and ran about two hundred yards to the cottage of a white farmer, and there lay down refusing to go further.

Meanwhile a strange Negro had been arrested in Sikestown, Missouri, and the authorities telegraphed that fact to Bardwell, Kentucky. The sheriff, without requisition, escorted the prisoner to the Kentucky side and turned him over to the authorities who accompanied the mob. The prisoner was a man with dark brown skin; he said his name was Miller and that he had never been in Kentucky. The fisherman . . . had said the man he rowed over was white. . . .

Failing in any way to connect Miller with the crime, the mob decided to give him the benefit of the doubt and hang, instead of burn him, as was first intended. At 3 o'clock, the hour set for the execution, the mob rushed into the jail, tore off Miller's clothing and tied his shirt around his loins. Some one said the rope was "a white man's death," and a log-chain nearly a hundred feet in length, weighing nearly a hundred pounds was placed about his neck. He was led through the street in that condition and hanged to a telegraph pole. After a photograph of him was taken as he hung, his fingers and toes cut off, and his body otherwise horribly mutilated, it was burned to ashes. This was done within twelve hours after Miller was taken prisoner. Since his death, his assertions regarding his movements have been proven true. But the mob refused the necessary time for investigation.

No more appropriate close for this chapter can be given than an editorial quotation from that most consistent and outspoken journal the *Inter-Ocean*. Commenting on the many barbarous lynchings of these two months (June and July) in its issue of August 5th, 1893, it says:

"So long as it is known that there is one charge against a man which calls for no investigation before taking his life there will be mean men seeking revenge ready to make that charge. Such a condition would soon destroy all law. It would not be tolerated for a day by white men. But the Negroes have been so patient under all their trials that men who no longer feel that they can safely shoot a Negro for attempting to exercise his right as a citizen at the polls are ready to trump up any other charge that will give them the excuse for their crime. It is a singular coincidence that as public sentiment has been hurled against political murders there has been a corresponding increase in lynchings on the charge of attacking white women. The lynchings are conducted in much the same way that they were by the Ku Klux Klans when Negroes were mobbed for attempting to vote. The one great difference is in the cause which the mob assigns for its action . . ."

Robert S. Abbott and the *Chicago Defender*

Robert Sengstacke Abbott (1868–1940) was born on St. Simon's Island, Georgia, and attended Hampton Institute in Virginia and Chicago's Kent College of Law, from which he graduated in 1899. Unable to practice law because of race prejudice, he turned to the newspaper trade, which he had learned at Hampton and from his step-father. Under famous circumstances (already recounted in my introduction), Abbott started a two-cent weekly, which became the most widely circulated Black newspaper in American history. Heralding itself as "The World's Greatest Weekly," the paper made Abbott one of the first self-made Black millionaires. At its height in the 1930s, the paper—bought, passed hand-to-hand, smuggled into the South—is estimated to have had a weekly readership of over 500,000. In 1940, Abbott's nephew John H. Sengstacke took over the paper and continued its championing of full equality. It became the *Chicago Defender Daily* in 1956, and though its circulation has dwindled and the company has experienced recent hard times, its history remains vital. In fact, it is perhaps impossible to exaggerate the influence of the *Chicago Defender* as a champion of Black rights, a source of news about—and a radical, heads-on attack against—the evils of racism, a spur to the great Northern Migration, and—though it practiced its own kind of yellow journalism—an outlet for some of the most influential Black writers and thinkers in America, including Langston Hughes, Gwendolyn Brooks, W. E. B. DuBois, Arna Bontemps, Walter White, and many others. Its success eclipsed the *Broad Ax,* the *Conservator,* and the *Illinois Idea,* though these other important Black Chicago papers deserve mention as well. Below is a small sampling of *Defender* writing.

March 24, 1917
Big Dailies Worried by Recent Migration:
Excitement All Uncalled For—Source from Which It Comes a Surprise
By R. T. Sims, Ex-Secretary, Chicago Office Building Janitor's Union

I have read with interest the various comments by the press upon the recent migration of the Negro to Chicago and I am at loss to understand why all this "teapot tempest" about the Negro. I have noticed train load upon train load of Italians, Hungarians, Irish, Polish, Bohemians, Germans, and in fact, almost every nationality upon the globe migrating to Chicago and through Chicago to other western cities. These people came from a foreign country, unaccustomed to our way of living or to our language, and, in fact, had nothing to recommend them to our midst but their labor power, and when it comes to the undesirable citizenship, I ask, has anyone ever heard of any "blackhand" outrages committed by the Negro, or heard of any Negroes hatching "bomb plots" and blowing up buildings and destroying property?

Notwithstanding the fact that from dirty outrages in the form of lynchings and other unlawful acts that have been perpetrated against the Negro, he would have been far more justified if he had thrown a few bombs to avenge some of the wrongs heaped upon him; however, two wrongs never make one right. The Negro has lived up to that principle and has in thousands of instances proven his sterling worth as a loyal and patriotic citizen. When this country was in its infancy, where in all the world could there be found a man, save the Negro, who was physically equal to the task of going into the tropical regions, clearing the land, tilling the soil and producing a commodity that made America the commercial King of the Globe? FOR FOUR HUNDRED YEARS his head was bowed under the yoke of chattel slavery. FOR THAT FOUR HUNDRED YEARS it was his blood, muscle, bone and sinew that was ground up in the industrial machinery of this country to gain the commercial supremacy that she now enjoys, and now, because he dare to emerge from the "Hell hole of Calcutta" to get an opportunity to breathe a little of God's free air, there must be a great hullabaloo raised about it and especially by some of our WOULD BE Negro leaders, such as Ida B. Wells Barnett, who magnifies it into an outrage. I wonder, did she think it was an outrage when she had to leave Memphis between two ticks of the clock under disguise to save her life? The writer is familiar with her former surroundings in Holly Springs, Miss., and if it was not an outrage for her to come here, why is it an outrage for her brothers and sisters, who are also seeking to get away from tyranny? Every other nationality receives their fellow sufferers who are fleeing from tyranny with open arms and do everything in their power to assist them. Why not the Negro?

BROTHERS AND SISTERS OF MY RACE, FOR GOD'S SAKE, WAKE UP!

[On the same date on the *Defender*'s editorial page is this unsigned item:]

KEEP YOUR MOUTH SHUT, PLEASE!

There is entirely too much loud talking on the street cars among our new comers. Going to and from work the new comers are heard to tell where they were the night before and the kind of good times they had, and talking about their business in public. This should be stopped. Such actions show low breeding. People of Chicago do not engage in such. Preachers should take up a few minutes of Sundays and instruct these new comers on how to act in public places and should take off a day and visit plants, yards and mills and tell them how to act. Their bad deportment on street cars and "L" roads must be stopped. These new comers are wanted here and out west. There is plenty of work for them, but they must not disgrace themselves and our good city. Cut this out, dear reader, and whenever you see one talking loudly hand it to him.

January 14, 1939
The Plight of the Jewish Minority—Can It Happen Here?
By Kelly Miller

The barbarous outrages which the German people are heaping upon their Jewish minority have startled the civilized world to protest and indignation. Vehement denunciation is but a natural reaction against such inhumane atrocities. Condemnation of wrong doing in other affects both moral and intellectual economy. It is easy to magnify the mote in our brother's eye while oblivious of the beam within our own.

It is easier to condemn the wolf for making the "Ewe Bleat for the Lamb" than to psychoanalyze the ferocious nature of the beast of prey.

America leads the chorus condemning Germany's mistreatment of the Jew as if smugly oblivious of her own accusatory record in dealing with her own racial minorities—the Indian and the Negro.

It is now high time for the thoughtful world to seek the deep-seated underlying cause of this sudden outbreak of "Furor Teutonicous" whose arousal according to Tacitus might well cause nations and races to tremble. Sober analysis will not overcome righteous indignation but will furnish a more rational understanding of emotion which it awakens,

May not the nations now casting a reproach in Hitler's teeth be but condemning their own conduct under a change of circumstances and conditioning. The racial intolerance of Nordic nations is a well established fact. The passionate dogma of white supremacy in some parts of this country is but American rendition of the Aryan myth which Hitler has invented to conjure with.

The frequent emergencies of the secret orders in America based on racial and religious intolerance should at least put our country on caution. The suddenness and swiftness with which the Hitler dogma has spread to other nations indicates that the anti-Semitic germ had already infected the soil. It spread like wild-fire throughout Poland, Romania, Hungary, and strange to say Czechoslovakia. Even Italy whose Catholic doctrine is the moral and spiritual unity of mankind instantly approved Hitler's formula which Mussolini put into instant operation by the fiat of his power.

While other nations loudly denounce Germany for making the Jew a vagabond on the face of the earth yet none of them are willing to give the seed of Abraham a home and hospitality. But German's Teutonic racial intolerance is re-enforced by dread of over-population. It is the iron law of self preservation which excludes alien reinforcement "lest there be not enough for you and us." The great nations of the earth have reached the point of saturation with a population which cannot be increased without detriment. For fear of destiny the white nations have stopped non-white re-enforcements from other lands.

Black, brown and yellow peoples are not permitted to enter the United States, Canada, Australia, South Africa, and to all intents and purposes Europe or South America. Non-white contingents already living in these countries are subject to pressure of increasing severity to prevent competition with white masters and overlords in the battle for bread. When the pack of wolves is confronted with a shortage they kill and devour each other. In the last extremity the law of the jungle reasserts itself.

Germany ruthlessly over-riding the moral code seeks to stamp our competition by beginning at the top. Cain killed Abel, because he offered unto the Lord a more acceptable sacrifice. America on the other hand eliminates the Negro from the area of competition because of his alleged inferior capacities. Race prejudice does not look to reason, logic, or religion for its ultimate sanction. This country is now reaching the point where there are more workmen than work to do. Ten thousand unemployed seem to constitute an irreducible army, to whose ranks the Negro contributes a disproportionate number, which condition will not continue indefinitely. The New Deal which President Roosevelt devised in behalf of the forgotten man [is] the Negro's sole hope for industrial and economic survival.

Of all men the Negro must view the lamentable plight of the Jew in Germany with sober if not somber reflection lest it forebode the day when he too will be "battered with the shocks of doom."

February 20 and 27, 1943
The American Negro Press
By W. E. B. DuBois

[The following is a slightly condensed version of the April 1943 *Negro Digest* version of the two-part *Defender* series.]

Journalism among American Negroes is a peculiar and interesting phenomenon which shows how race segregation works in action. White commentators think they have discovered that the Negro press is exciting the mass of Negroes to discontent and even to violence.

As a matter of fact what they are really seeing is the intensity of feeling and resentment which is sweeping over the Negro people. This resentment is echoed in the Negro press much more completely and accurately than similar waves are echoed by the white press.

The critics are mistaking for cause that which is really result.

To a Negro world this comes as a surprise. Is it possible that white America did not know that the Negro had newspapers?

The history of the Negro press goes back a long way. In 1827, Samuel Cornish and the first Negro graduate of an American college, John B. Russworm, published the first Negro newspaper under the name of "Freedmen's Journal."

First of all it may be asked why Negroes should have newspapers? They indicate a sort of voluntary segregation. Negroes are American. They read English. They have access to the great American press. Why should they have a press of their own?

The answer is clear. The American press in the past almost entirely ignored Negroes. Very little of what Negroes wanted to know about themselves, their group action and the relation of public occurrences to their interests were treated by the press. Then came the time when the American press so far as the Negro was concerned was interested in the Negro as a minstrel, a joke, a subject of caricature. He became in time an awful example of democracy gone wrong, of crime and various monstrous acts.

Partly then in defense and partly for information there grew up the little weekly sheet devoted to news of the Negro and interpretation of his situation. This weekly sheet went through all sorts of vicissitudes. It was at first the organ of Negro leaders like Russworm, Frederick Douglass, T. Thomas Fortune and Monroe Trotter. It defended the Negro race, explained facts and exhorted to action.

Then it began to change. It became a newspaper but a kind of personal sheet. It had social notices and mentioned people so that Negroes in Boston could read of their friends in New York and Chicago.

It began to play up the Negro's natural desire for prominence and publicity. One paper especially, the "Indianapolis Freeman," for many years sold its front page, with very little concealment, to persons willing to pay one hundred dollars or more. A large photograph of the distinguished persons was displayed. This, however, proved a little too blatant and the character of the press began to change.

The first World War brought the greatest change. News of Negroes was wanted by their friends and had to be gathered. The Negro press became a news gathering Organization. . . .

Moreover, the editors ceased to emphasize their editorials or to attempt social leadership. They became business men of the American type and following the trend of white newspapers they tried to cater to their public. . . .

The result was a weekly press which reached large circulation and employed considerable numbers of people. The circulation of one paper alone reached some 300,000 copies a week. . . .

In 1940, according to the Bureau of the Census, there were 210 Negro newspapers in the United States, 155 of which had a circulation of 1,250,000. . . .

. . . Doubtlessly by today it reaches at least three million and employs not less than 1,500 persons with a payroll of possibly $100,000 a month. . . .

Today nothing can happen which is of interest to the Negro race which is not publicized, exploited and explained by the Negro newspaper. . . .

From [World War I] on the reading of Negro newspapers by Negroes became habitual. There had been a time even down through Reconstruction when only a Negro here and there read a Negro paper and even then was apologetic about it. Today it is probably true that there is scarcely a Negro in the United States who can read and write who does not read the Negro press. It has become a vital part of his life.

There are certain limitations and peculiarities about the Negro press.

First of all it is more responsive to its readers' demands and attitudes than is the white press. The attitude of the white press is conditioned very largely upon the advertising revenues.

The Negro press on the other hand has comparatively small advertising revenue. . . .

. . . Consequently it depends to a much larger extent upon the demand and good will of its readers and is more sensitive to changes in public opinion.

It could not exist if it insisted on a policy or a line of propaganda which its readers would not support.

On the other hand, needing some revenue from advertising, it has been tempted in the past to questionable advertising policies: giving publicity to fortune tellers, get-rich-quick schemes and projects obviously unfair if not illegal.

In one line of advertising it has had a curious experience and that is in beauty culture. At first there was widespread protest against advertising of hair straighteners and skin bleachers in colored newspapers. . . .

But curiously enough this line of business started by Negroes began to spread to the whites. Today one can buy not simply white skin powder but skin powder of all colors and methods of hair treatment are used by whites quite as much as by Negroes. So that really a new business and source of advertising revenue was developed in the Negro newspapers.

On the whole the Negro press today does not deserve most of the criticism recently made on it.

It is not guilty of stirring up Negroes to revolt. Negro public opinion has stirred the newspapers to voice revolt.

On the whole the Negro press is not guilty of misrepresenting the condition of Negroes. It does play up crime and scandal but not nearly as much as the white press.

It does emphasize, and often exaggerates Negro accomplishment; but even here it has not approached the boastfulness of the national press. . . .

Two things ought to take a place in America: white Americans ought to read regularly and with understanding the best of the Negro newspapers. . . .

The white press ought to report news among Negroes with much more care and regularity than they do, realizing that what is news to Negroes is also news to whites and of interest to both.

It can be taken for granted that already the Negro is familiar with the white newspaper and if in this way an interchange of thought and sympathy could be brought about, there would be a more intelligent comprehension both among whites and blacks of the difficulties of the race problem in America.

April 27, 1946
Simple and the Heads
By Langston Hughes

"I long ago stopped conking my hair down," said Simple. "Also laying it down with grease. That is why I keep it cut short so I do not have to put all that oil and stuff on it."

"I notice you also cut a part in it," I observed.

"Sure, I cut a part in it," said Simple. "That saves me ten minutes in the morning."

"It looks all right," I said.

"But there ought to be a law," said Simple, "against people with greasy heads going around leaning them up against other people's walls and spotting them all up. There also ought to be a law against girls laying all up against a man's new suit when they have just come from the hairdresser's. There really ought to be a law."

"How come you are so hot on that subject this evening?" I asked.

"Man, I just got my spring suit out of the cleaners," yelled Simple, "all nice and light and nice, and I took some new chick I just met to a dance last night. And after she got through leaning all up on me and nestling her head all up under my shoulder—man, the whole side of my suit, lapel and all was just as greasy as it had been eating chitterlings! There ought to be a law against a dame with a greasy head leaning all up on somebody when she is dancing."

"It's not very considerate," I said, "but that is what makes money for the cleaners,"

"I ain't after making no money for no cleaners!" yelled Simple. "Besides, I wanted to wear that suit to Easter Monday dance with Joyce. Do you think it could be worn?"

"I reckon not," I said.

"It could not," said Simple. "I do not see why these hairdressers do not take some of that oil out of women's hair before they turn them loose to damage a man's clothes. I am scared to let a dame rest her head in my lap anymore, lest when I get up it will look like I been to a picnic eating fried chicken without a napkin."

"It's not all that bad," I said.

"Some of these womens is," said Simple, "and mens too. Was you ever in Moe Gale's old office!"

"I know who he is," I said. "You mean the man down on Broadway who books colored bands and theatrical talent?"

"That's who I mean," said Simple. "Well, in Moe Gale's office, before he had it decorated over, there was a bench in the waiting room all around the wall. And about three feet above that bench, there was a black line of hair grease where folks had leaned their heads all up against the wall. Everywhere they had leaned they left their mark. There ought to be law!"

"It's certainly something to think about," I said.

"Moe Gale must have thought about it when he re-done his place," said Simple. "I was down there the other night and a friend of mine who plays in a band, and that new bench is about a foot out from the wall now. There is also a little rail about neck-high, so can't nobody lean back against Mr. Gale's new wall—unless you want to break your neck."

"That little rail is a clever idea," I said.

"I am going to tell it to my Cousin Minnie," said Simple. "She has many gentlemen callers, and she is always yowling about some joker leaning back on her sofa and laying his head up against the wall. She says she spends half her time trying to wash the spots off."

"I expect you lean your head up there too," I said.

"My head is clean," said Simple, "and it do not matter, now, because I am wearing my hair in its natural state. I save money, too."

"To put on the bar," I said.

"Better in my stomach than on my head," said Simple. "When I was young and vain, I was always running to the barber shop getting my hair laid down. But Joyce says she likes me just as well as I is—so I do not bother anymore. Only thing is, if I take some other girl out, and Joyce sees where some strange woman's head has been laying all over my coat, it makes her mad!"

"Naturally," I said.

"That is worse than lipstick," said Simple. "If a little lipstick gets on your shirt collar, you can take the shirt off and send it to the laundry. But you cannot send a suit to the cleaners every time a new head lays on your shoulder."

"You talk like a regular Don Juan," I said.

"Dog-gone is right," said Simple. "I feel like saying more than Dog-gone! There ought to be a law about Womens and their heads!"

"Just women?" I asked.

"Anybody," yelled Simple, "who lays a head full of grease up against anybody else's clothes—or wall. Male or female—anybody! I mean you, too!"

"Not guilty!" I said.

Fenton Johnson (1888–1958)

The only child of a prosperous Chicago family, Fenton Johnson spent most of his time pursuing the arts, and later in editing and journalism. But between 1914 and 1916 he produced three volumes of poetry, *A Little Dreaming, Visions of the Dusk,* and *Songs of the Soil,* which, together with the posthumous *42 WPA Poems,* provide an extraordinary look at the evolution of Black American poetry. Starting out under the inevitable influence of Paul Laurence Dunbar, he then proceeded to "succumb," as Arna Bontemps put it, "to a more rugged influence." Dropping all dialect poems and formal poetry in general, he turned to free verse (perhaps under the influence of Whitman—only without Whitman's optimism) and began expressing profound fatalism and despair. In his poem "The Daily Grind," for example, Johnson conceives of man as caught between Nature and the System. The first may intend "something fine," but the human construct—the System—blighted by racism—intends grinding slavery. All man can do is watch the eternal struggle of the two. "If Nature forgets you, / If the System forgets you, / "God has blest you," Johnson concludes. In introductory comments on Johnson in his ground-breaking anthology *The Book of American Negro Poetry,* James Weldon Johnson says that Fenton Johnson's startling effect on American poetry, "was in some degree due to the fact that it was an idea so foreign to any philosophy of life the Negro in America had ever preached or practiced. Fenton Johnson is the only Negro poet who has ever sounded this precise note." His most famous poems in this manner are "Tired," printed below, "The Banjo Player," and "The Scarlet Woman"—all included in *The Book of American Negro Poetry,* the latter poem ending with the famous line, "Gin is better than all the water in Lethe." But "Prelude," the first poem in *Visions of the Dusk,* already shows a restlessness with traditional verse and issues a veiled critique of what's expected of Black poets. The other two poems below, from the same book but more typical of Black poems of the day, illustrate Johnson's skill at the dialect verse and the world of beautiful dreams he was soon to leave behind.

Tired

I am tired of work; I am tired of building up somebody
    else's civilization.
Let us take a rest, M'Lissy Jane.
I will go down to the Last Chance Saloon, drink a gallon
    or two of gin, shoot a game or two of dice and
    sleep the rest of the night on one of Mike's barrels.
You will let the old shanty go to rot, the white people's
    clothes turn to dust, and the Calvary Baptist Church
    sink to the bottomless pit.

You will spend your days forgetting you married me and
  your nights hunting the warm gin Mike serves the
  ladies in the rear of the Last Chance Saloon.
Throw the children into the river; civilization has given
  us too many. It is better to die than it is to grow up
  and find out that you are colored.
Pluck the stars out of the heavens. The stars mark our
  destiny. The stars marked my destiny.
I am tired of civilization.

Prelude

'Tis twilight dim; the musing dreamer sits
Before his hearth, the sunset on his brow,
And thus he ponders ere the birth of dusk.

Some love the land where grew the laurel tree,
The home of Gods and stern faced warriors,
The altar Nature built and Art preserves;
And long to hear heroic note from Pan.
Such deem their love the freeborn English note,
And others love the freeborn English note,
The music of the songs the lusty sang
In Mermaid Tavern and the Old Boar's Head,
The gift of Shakespeare and the heritage
Of Tennyson, the child romance hath nursed.

And yet some say to me, "O Man of Dusk,
Give us thy songs in broken Afric tongue,—
The music of the peasant in the South—
The native strain alone is poetry.
Be thou as Bums or Dunbar was,
Be thou as Lowell in his adobe home;
The humble peasant is the truest bard."

'Tis not in classic mould or English flame,
Or lilting song from crudest peasant tongue
The soul that seeks the beauty of a truth

FENTON JOHNSON
39

Can gaze upon the ever gleaming light
That flickers on the summit Poesy.
But 'tis in living and the wonder Life
We find the soul of Beauty is a God;
The vision is the thing, and not the word.
Then come with me where Life and Soul hath met;
And hear the mother croon of far-away,
The dying note of Georgia lullaby.

Questions

1.

"Whaih's de twilight, Mammy Lou?"
"'Way beyond de drippin' dew,
Whaih de angels run an' hide
Happy by ol' Jawdon's tide."

2.

Whaih's de moonlight, Mammy Lou?"
"Whaih de day's a-slippin' thoo,
An' de lamp called Lub's tu'ned high—
Nevah kin de moon go dry."

3.

"Whaih's de sunlight, Mammy Lou?"
"Why Ah thought you allus knew
Dat yo' hea't's de wahm sunlight
An' yo' love's de moon o' night."

A Fragment

One sunset when the skies were deepest red,
As if they blushed for all the human sins,
I saw her gather daffodils, and sighed,
For she was sweeter far than those poor flowers
And all the flowers that grace this universe,
And in my dream I saw a crown descend
From out the firmament and drop to earth.

FENTON JOHNSON

It fell beside a brook whose gleaming drops
Shone like the diamonds in the sable night,
And I, the humblest in the realm of men,
Stooped low and placed it on her bonny head.

1927 *Intercollegiate Wonder Book,*
or The Negro in Chicago (1779–1927)

"Realizing the need of an organization to bring together the few colored students attending the college and universities of Chicago in summer and living in various parts of the city, two social workers, Miss Mary McDowell and Mrs. Celia Parker Wooley with Mr. George Arthur, now Executive Secretary of the Wabash Ave. Dept. Y.M.C.A. assisted in establishing the first meeting of its kind about 1909." Thus begins one section of the *Intercollegiate Wonder Book.* The book was compiled and much of it written by the Intercollegiate Club's then-president Frederic H. Robb, who graduated from Hartford Public High School in 1920. His brief biography on page 8 lists such impressive accomplishments as graduating from Howard in three and a quarter years, obtaining a Northwestern J.D., and winning thirteen and tying two of sixteen debates in Chicago. It ends with the words "It can be done" in quotes. Those four words are the real purpose of the *Wonder Book:* to be an ode to, and a goad to, accomplishment. In the middle of the *Wonder Book*'s title page is this description: "Survey of the Negro's Educational, Athletic, Civic and Commercial Life from 1779 to 1927. History, Who's Who in Chicago, Directory, Facts and Figures About the Negro for 8000 years." In its own way, it just about delivers all this, providing a remarkable window into a rising segment of Chicago Black life in the late 1920s, and testifying to Robb's and others' efforts to draw Black students into a powerful, organized community. Between inspirational and historical essays and pages of facts and figures are lists upon lists: of Chicago civic leaders; of Chicago musicians; even of suggested events the Intercollegiate Club could plan for the future to entertain its members, to urge them to travel, to highlight avenues to community involvement, and to "Encourage Students to Take Part in Extra Curricular Activities." Below are three short pieces and a remarkable cartoon related to the third piece. Frederick Robb might have written the first and third pieces; the second bears the name J. M. Davis. The second and third selections appear on a page with the headline "Be An Intercollegiate Booster." Bill Moore's cartoon is said to have been "inspired by Horace Bond's Address at the Intercollegiate's Grace Lyceum Program."

From "Organized Students Are Powerful"

[After describing many club activities, including how Horace Bond and Frederic Robb "invaded Indianapolis and defeated another set of debaters for the second time this season in a debate on Birth Control," this essay ends with the following:]

Since March, our greatest energy has been centered on the surveys and work relative to the publishing of the year book. The "Y" has assisted greatly in ensuring the success of this publication by furnishing office, space, desk and telephone service.

In completing this task, the club feels that we are presenting to Chicago and to the nation at large, the most complete survey of the constructive progress of the Negro in Chicago that has been affected. The educational Day Exercises in June manifested to the citizens of Chicago our sincere interest in the highest education. The two scholarships awarded to the Wendell Phillips High School students are just small symbols of what the organization hopes to do in the future. The beach party at Pine Beach, the picnic to Sunset Hills and Monster Dance celebrating the coming of the Intercollegiate are only a few of the important events. The Founder Day Program was indeed unique.

At each meeting prominent speakers and musicians have entertained those present. As the present Mr. Robb was among those graduating in June and plans to leave next season for study abroad, another one must take up the work. May the successor have imbibed so much of the dauntless spirit of the present leader, that Intercollegiate history will remain brilliant.

Entering Chicago

Santa Fe from the West crawls noisily into Chicago guided by two shining ribbons of steel—Southside factories look disinterestedly down on moving cars from dirty windows—Dearborn Station with its many sky-lights houses the Santa Fe in from its long trip eastward.

Moving yellow and red surface cars against the drabness of brown and gray State Street Stores—filthy snow poled high on paved Chicago streets—28th Street and one block eastward four stories of red brick house—"The Wabash Y."

Two gypsy women in roomy dresses of many hues spill a jargon of foreign words from painted lips to a stocky man who walks with them—a blind man sings of Christ as he strokes the strings of a battered guitar—a dapper young Jew will wager that he knows what card is next in his deck—a brown girl of eight runs lithely down South State shouting in abandon—a cosmopolitan aggregation of persons people Chicago flats and no two alike.—J. M. Davis

The New Negro

By the New Negro is not meant his chronological age, but a Negro whose type is new compared to the type of Negro common today. Not new in physical perfection or imperfection, not a biological mutation but a Negro whose habits and ideas are entirely different from the Negro of fifty years ago.

'Tis true the Negro, he is new, he is old as the forests primeval, but the new Negro is a new type of "Homo-Sapiens" psychologically. He believes in preparation, he believes in himself, he believes in fighting but not merely by petitions, orating, and delegations, but believes in using the courts to insist on his civil rights, the effective intelligent use of the ballot to oust those who would disgrace the race. He favors better schools, more teachers with higher salaries, numerous parks and playgrounds, sanitary alleys, paved streets, more qualified court officials; rather than mere vice privileges, mediocre "political plums" and money. He thinks in terms of the future welfare of his children. He has no narrow religious creed, he supports human principles instead of race prejudices, he ignores the unfounded flatteries heaped upon the Negro, he does not boast, but achieves, he has a scientific mind. He is opposed to superstitions, he is opposed to that loyalty and patriotism which supports a government with its all in war to be satisfied to be Jim Crowed, segregated, lynched, moved, kept from many schools, West Point, Annapolis and Air Service in time of peace. The New Negro has no respect for age for age's sake but has respect because of their storehouse of wisdom and accomplishments. He is broad minded, opposer of war, lover of world brotherhood, welcomes criticism as a stepping stone to progress, is not conceited, but glories in the colored man's contribution to civilization. He does not seek philanthropy but opportunity. The New Negro, that creation of the twentieth century, is because he is a fusion of all the races of the world.

The Intercollegiate's New Negro

Rev. John L. Tilley (1898–1971)

Because he had to work to help support his family and could not attend school regularly, John Tilley did not graduate high school until he was twenty-three. He went to Shaw University for a B.A., and then—as important as land was to newly freed Blacks—John Tilley's parents mortgaged their tobacco farm so their son could come to study at the University of Chicago. He earned a masters degree and completed Ph.D. course work, but before he could complete his dissertation, Shaw persuaded him to return. It awarded him the Doctor of Divinity, and he stayed from 1927 to 1944, becoming its acting president during the Depression and the first dean of its School of Religion. From 1944 to 1949, he served as president of Florida Normal and Industrial College, and then went to Baltimore as dean of the Maryland Baptist Center and School of Religion, as well as becoming pastor of the Metropolitan Baptist Church. In 1957, he became director for the NAACP's Register and Vote campaign in Baltimore, adding thirty-five thousand voters in one year. This led Martin Luther King Jr. to call him to be the national executive secretary of the Southern Christian Leadership Conference. While a student in Chicago, he was an active member of the Washington Intercollegiate Club, and one of his two books—*A Brief History of the Negro in Chicago, 1779–1933*—updated sections of the *Intercollegiate Wonder Book*. In 1927, just before leaving Chicago, Tilley sat at the base of Lorado Taft's monumental sculpture "Fountain of Time" at the entrance to the Midway and penned the following poem. Prescient about the life of hardship and accomplishment ahead, it is imbued with themes and an articulate melancholy not uncommon in the Black poetry of the time. It represents a midpoint between the optimism of the Intercollegiate crowd and the pessimism of a Fenton Johnson. His daughter, Glennette Tilley Turner, still lives in the Chicago area and has written extensively on the Underground Railroad.

When Day Is Done

When shadows fall at length across the earth,
The sky's bedecked with myriad hues of light,
Birds have ceased their daily songs of myrth,
The day is gone and all that's gay and bright;

I think of life and all it means today
Bright hopes and all that seems to be worthwhile
The rose so fresh that soon must fade away,
Faces bright that ever wear a smile.

Yes, pleasures come but never come to stay.
They thrill us through but pass forever on,

And as they pass to us they seem to say,
"To thrill and pain and leave as why we were born."

When life is over and all my work is done,
When last I've laughed and sung and cried
May I but have the joy that I have won
For some sad hearts real joys that will abide.

Frank Marshall Davis (1905–1987)

For most of his life, Frank Marshall Davis worked as a journalist for papers such as the *Gary American,* the *Atlanta World,* and the *Chicago Star,* a labor weekly he cofounded and served as executive editor. Moving to Hawaii, he worked for the *Honolulu Record* and made the acquaintance of the young Barack Obama, who is included later in this anthology. He also wrote fiction and published a classic essay in the "My Most Humiliating Jim Crow Experience" series in *Negro Digest* in 1944. Because of his antiracist stands and his association with labor and the Communist Party, the FBI maintained a file on him from the mid-1940s to the mid-1960s, and he was pressured by the House on Un-American Activities Committee. Through all this, Davis also managed to produce a significant body of poetry. "Rarely in African American literary history," writes John Edgar Tidwell, "has one poet been made to serve the interests of two movements"—meaning that Marshall's career held major significance for the so-called "Negro Renaissance" in the late 1920s and early 1930s, as well as for the Black Arts Movement of the 1960s. In addition to many uncollected poems, his poetry books include *Black Man's Verse* (1935), *I Am the American Negro* (1937), *47th Street* (1948), *Jazz Interludes* (1976), and *Awakening and Other Poems* (1978). *Black Man's Verse* begins with the classic lines: "Chicago is an overgrown woman / wearing her skyscrapers / like a necklace . . ." In his foreword to *47th Street,* he writes:

> I am a Negro writer.
>
> A Negro is an individual who has been shunted aside for discriminatory treatment as an inferior because an ancestor is known to have been a dark African native. That is the only possible definition of Negro on the basis of science and actuality.
>
> You see, Negroes do not belong to a distinct race because there is no such thing as a Negro or black race, just as there is no Caucasian or white race, and no Mongolian or yellow race. The so-called black race has blue eyed blonds who are lighter than the swarthy brunettes classed as members of the alleged white race. To call a blue eyed blonde a member of the black race is a monstrous absurdity to be expected only of the United States which boasts it has bigger and better everything, which automatically includes absurdities. . . .
>
> American will have Negro writers until the whole concept of race is erased.

Davis's poetry is notable not only for its social engagement, especially in the fight against racism, but also for its fluent language and stunning imagery, and, though he produced many short lyrics, for its dedication to long-form poetry, often arranged as mini-dramas. Space and high permission fees prohibited excerpts from a monumental poem like "Washington Park," for example, which begins famously with, "The heat roars / Like a tidal wave / Over Chicago's Congo . . ." and includes sketches of the park's inhabitants, from a homeless man to a Communist organizer. We content ourselves, then, with two contrasting works: a short, gorgeous lyric, and Davis' postmortem on himself, the latter coming from the series "Ebony Under Granite," which gave imagined, poetic postmortems on a variety of Black people.

Four Glimpses of Night

I.

> Eagerly
> Like a woman hurrying to her lover
> Night comes to the room of the world
> And lies, yielding and content
> Against the cool round face
> Of the moon.

II.

> Night is a curious child, wandering
> Between earth and sky, creeping
> In windows and doors, daubing
> The entire neighborhood
> With purple paint.
> Day
> Is an apologetic mother
> Cloth in hand
> Following after.

III.

> Peddling
> From door to door
> Night sells
> Black bags of peppermint stars
> Heaping cones of vanilla moon
> Until
> His wares are gone
> Then shuffles homeward
> Jingling the gray coins
> Of daybreak.

IV.

> Night's brittle song, sliver-thin,
> Shatters into a billion fragments

FRANK MARSHALL DAVIS

Of quiet shadows
At the blaring jazz
Of a morning sun.

Frank Marshall Davis: Writer

"He is bitter
A bitter bitter
Cynic"
They said
"And his wine
He brews from wormwood"

I was black and black I always was

From the ebony house of me I watched days swing into weeks to
    months to years

I hunted golden orchids where "All Men are Created Free and
    Equal"—and my skin lay raw and sore from the poison ivy of
    discrimination and the hidden brambles of Jim Crow

I say no sensitive Negro can spend his life in America without
    finding his cup holds vinegar and his meat is seasoned with
    gall

A Mississippi manpack, mobbing bent, beat a tinpan bedlam
    when I would pluck sweet airs from a Muse's harp

I aimed my eyes at the holy doors of a white man's church and I
    heard God's Servant say "Niggers must be saved elsewhere"

While thousands cheered as the Governor of Georgia thundered
    "Stand pat on the Constitution" I saw the hungry mouths of
    six-guns daring his black folk to come to the polls and vote

I turned to what was called my own race . . . and I looked at a
    white man's drama acted by inky performers

I was a weaver of jagged words
A warbler of garbled tunes
A singer of savage songs
I was bitter
Yes
Bitter and sorely sad
For when I wrote
I dipped my pen
In the crazy heart
Of mad America

Wormwood wine?
Vinegar?
Gall?
A daily diet—
But
I did not die
Of diabetes.

FRANK MARSHALL DAVIS

Leonidas M. Berry (1902–1995)

Leonidas Berry wrote *I Wouldn't Take Nothin' for My Journey: Two Centuries of an Afro-American Minister* in 1981 after a successful career as an M.D. specializing in gastroenterology. He was senior author and editor of the textbook *Gastroentestinal Panendoscopy* (1974) and worked at Provident Hospital from 1936 to 1970, founding and chairing the division of gastroenterology. He taught at the University of Illinois medical school and the Cook County Graduate School of Medicine and traveled for the State Department as a foreign cultural exchange lecturer to Africa, Asia, and the Philippines. He organized clinics for medical counseling, a council on medical careers, and the Flying Black Medics group in Chicago and Cairo, Illinois. His daughter, Judith Berry Griffin, directs the organization Pathways to College.

From *I Wouldn't Take Nothin' for My Journey*

AUTHOR'S PREFACE

I wouldn't take nothin' for my journey is part of an expressive stanza in a Negro spiritual. It says that life on this earth is only a journey. It can be an experience of success and joy in spite of overwhelming hardships. . . .

The narrative which follows is a true story of an Afro-American minister and his family. . . . The story unfolds the identification and achievements of individuals who make up a continuous multi-nuclear family unit, across the generations, for two centuries on American soil. It emphasizes cultural progress against formidable odds. It points out the discovery and recognition of the ingredients of continuous family adhesiveness and love that held together blood related but separate nuclear families across the decades. These ingredients were developed before the Civil War despite the divisiveness of slavery, when family adhesiveness and love were essential to physical and spiritual survival.

. . . Since the Civil War the families of the Jenifer-Berry-Harris-Jordan family clan have been of the nuclear variety. That's to say they have had the presence and support of father as well as mother during formative and other years in each family unit. The African Methodist Episcopal Church has had a most important influence in maintaining family stability, through its unique spirituality and its preachments for education since the pre-organized founding of the church under Richard Allen in 1787. In its establishment of Wilberforce University of Ohio in 1856, the first Negro College, the church has promoted the cultural progress and achievements observed in this family clan.

The author has been prompted to tell this story because . . . he has felt for many years that it is time to tell more stories of single related Black families who have developed and achieved on their own individual economic resources. There has been far too much of a continuous, "mass"-analysis and "statistical" treatment, more often depreciatory, of the "total family" and special "racial" categories of Black American families. . . . The first dramatic episode begins with the escape of "Doc" Henry Jenifer from St. Mary's County, Maryland, to Canada by way of the Underground Railroad in 1848. The second dramatic episode involves the escape of Nace Jenifer's son Sam Jenifer and John Berry who joined the Union Army in 1864. . . .

There is no claim of family exclusiveness. Tens of thousands of Black families have climbed the same mountains to achieve middle-class status and bi-parental relationships. To get there, they have fought the same battles against racial prejudice, unequal opportunities and poverty. The present youngest generation of the Jenifer-Berry-Harris-Jordan family shows striking evidence of accelerated cultural growth and exciting prospects for the future of individuals and Black American families. . . .

From "Slavery in Old St. Mary's of Maryland"

The "Ark and the Dove" had nothing to do with the Bible story of Noah. It indeed was a ship of sorts—vintage 1634. . . . It was swept by wind and sail across the turbulent Atlantic and anchored near the shores of Maryland; the first English vessel to make it. The success of the voyage was influenced by the religious faith of Jesuit Father Andrew White. . . . His goals were religious freedom, acquisition of land and survival. To wit, his ship log recorded sixty men and women passengers including two "mulattos", indentured servants, Matthias Sousa and Francisco. Leonard Calvert, the proprietary Lord Baltimore, bargained with a certain ship master for the delivery of thirteen 'niggar' slaves at St. Mary's in 1621. Thus, began the nefarious traffic in human cargo and slavery at St. Mary's. From then until now, Maryland, her sister colonies and states have never been free of the burden nor the attributes of the forced immigrants from Black Africa.

It is not known whether Matthias and Francisco were religiously sprinkled with sea water enroute to Maryland. It is known that as the Catholic Jesuits claimed thousands of acres and acquired hundreds of slaves, religious conflicts between the laws of St. Mary's and the English and Roman Catholic church became greater and greater through the years. "To baptise or not to baptise" the slaves and purge them of their heathenism, "that was the question." But once they were purged of their congenital sins, raising the missionary stature and mercifulness of the church wasn't it a "sin-before-God" to keep them enslaved. The very Reverend Thomas Story reprimanded one of his clergymen at West River in 1699, for baptizing his slaves without conferring their freedom. . . . Politicians both secular and sacred always come to the rescue where there is a religious dilemma. With the pressure from the tobacco barons, laws were passed denying that Christianizing slaves should make them free. The powerful church of England and their American counterparts fought these colonial laws and the tug of war between business profits and religion went on and on.

Meanwhile, the growth of slavery in this fertile tobacco raising coast line was a gradual but every increasing way of life. Like an octopus, its tentacles stretched, eventually engulfing every activity of the colony. Europe had virtually "gone mad" for the new world tobacco leaf and Indian rum. The barons of Maryland with land confiscated from the Indians and ceded to them by the British crown, were literally "wallowing" in rich flat tobacco land. . . . With thousands of acres out of proportion to manpower, all that was needed for the "bed-rock" of the future American economy were slaves and more slaves.

The flood of manpower from Africa by way of England often included poor whites as indentured servants bonded for seven to ten years. As the exploitation of the slave system continued, Black and white victims found themselves banded together by common interests. For many years political, economic and social status was more important than race. There was free intermarriage between Black and white without regard to free or indentured status. Vigorous proselytizing and evangelizing was continuous by the Catholic Jesuits who came to St. Mary's in the first place to establish a religious sanctuary from the British monarchy. They had no hesitancy in bestowing the blessing of marriage or intermarriage upon Black and white. . . .

Early in the 18th century intermarriage between Black and white, slaves, indentures, and the free and poor posed a serious problem for the ruling class.

So back to the legislature they went with revision of the slave codes. One such revision read, "Divers free born English women forgetful of their condition and to the disgrace of their Nation are intermarrying with Negroes. Such women so marrying must remain slaves; and their children shall serve as endentures for 30 years." [However,] free born English women continued to be forgetful of their condition and to "disgrace their Nation."

LEONIDAS M. BERRY

Some of the most brilliant men of Maryland's history like Daniel Coker, and Benjamin Benneker were mulattos with Caucasian mothers and Negro fathers—slave and free. . . .

From "Where Ya Goin' Boy?"

"Where ya goin' boy?" This was an expression as common as "good morning" in the white man's slave parlance of southern Maryland in 1864. "Yes suh! I goin' after a horse for Massa," was the answer. It was a fact that the white man did not know that "the boy" (getting to be a man) was 10 miles away from the plantation of Tom Gardner where he belonged.

It was near noon on this chilly January morning and there was a bright sun, shining directly overhead. The inquirer was astride a prancing blazed-faced horse with white hoofs; a bag was hanging from each side of his saddle. Protruding from one of them was a bullwhip and from the other a set of leg irons. A pistol protruded from a holster over the rider's left hip and a crude cowboy type lasso was curled around the right front post of the saddle. The rider was unmistakably a roving "slave catcher" on his morning prowl.

However, the twenty-year-old slave "boy" had an effective decoy, that turned the hated hunter of Black humanity, unsuspectingly galloping away. The "boy," not nearly as dumb as the slave hunter thought him to be, had an easily visible horse bridle thrown over his right shoulder. Nor had the white hunter noted the bulging pockets under the ragged overcoat and patched overalls caused by his survival rations. "Praise God, from whom all blessing flow," cried John Berry, for he had just made another hurdle in his plan to break the chains of slavery, escape, find and hopefully join "Massa Linkuns" army, which the Black grapevine had placed several more miles in the woods near Point Lookout, Maryland.

Years later, John Berry told this story many times to his inquisitive young son, Llewellyn, as he relived the dramatic and courageous experience of his escape from slavery; the beginning of his life as John Berry, free man; and the end of his life as Johnny Miles, slave.

From "Back to Ole Virginny to Study War No More"

[This chapter begins after Berry's grandfather, John, starts farming on the land of "a rebel plantation owner" which had been provided to Black Civil War veterans. Among those veterans who join John Berry is his buddy Sam Jenifer, who comes to Taylor's Farm with his sister Nancy. "On September 26, 1867, Rev. Richard Parker united John Berry and Nancy Jenifer in marriage at the St. John's church."]

LEONIDAS M. BERRY

By a system of underground communication and word-of-mouth, many Marylanders from Old St. Mary's County drifted into the Norfolk area and John Berry was reunited with some members of his family. Between 1866 and '69, Daniel and William Miles, half-brothers of John Berry, also staked out small farms on the old Taylor's Plantation.

For two or three years, things went rather well with these veterans. . . . But rumors began to spread that President Andrew Johnson . . . would return the confiscated land to their original owners. In due time it happened by Executive Order of the President. The sheriffs of Norfolk County and other counties throughout the South ordered the Blacks off the land. John Berry and the other veterans had improved their cabins, cultivated the land and were growing crops, raising chickens and hogs to supply food for their families. They decided to resist the take over. Many of the veterans had guns and ammunition which they had managed to hide away in gunny sacks upon being mustered out of the service. There had been no bloodshed when the sheriff finally gave them forty-eight hours to get off the land or be taken prisoners by Federal Troops. There was a feeling of hopelessness among this band of refugees and veterans. The sheriff's men showed they meant business by breaking down all unoccupied shacks and sheds. But the Blacks held them off their homes for two weeks with their firepower.

Finally, they called a special meeting in large barn which had been used as a gathering place usually for religious worship. Nearly all night they sang their songs of bondage which they knew so well. They had volunteered to fight the confederacy at the Call of Lincoln; they had tipped the balance of victory in war for the Union and now they faced the stark reality that the Rebels, their former masters were winning the peace. . . .

However, two years before the showdown at Taylor's Farm Gen. Benjamin Butler had acquired 115 acres of land a few miles north of Hampton to be broken up into seven-acre plots and made available for purchase by Freedmen. Some of the people on the Taylor's Plantation had heard about the Butler's Farm but they had no previous need to consider its availability to them.

Late one evening while praying and singing could be heard inside the assembly barn a heated argument was going on outside. There was serious talk of hiding out in the woods and taking on a last ditch skirmish with the law.

At this point up came a squarely built young veteran who stood 5'9" and weighed 175 lbs. with broad shoulders and muscular arms. This was John

Berry, age 25, who had grown long sideburns reaching a heavy mustache. With an air of quiet sagacity for his young years he spoke to the group in a firm voice, "Just a minute fellows, these angry speeches won't get us anywhere. I got an idea that I think will work. I was in General Butler's Army and I hear that he has a farm for veterans back of Hampton. They are selling a few acres on easy terms for each family. Now I know that country from the war days; it is near Back River, which flows into Hampton Roads a few miles above Old Point Comfort. How come we can't go down to the river, build two or three rafts, then pull down our houses, load up the lumber and all our belongings, row cross Hampton Roads towing some of the lumber and come into Back River right next to the new Butler Plantation. We built the pontoons and took an army across the James and across the Rappahannock and we forded the Chickahominy River and, by God, if we pull together, we can cross Hampton Roads to the Butler's Farm. . . ."

FROM "CROSSING HAMPTON ROADS"

When the big meeting closed that night the men went to their cabins lit their kerosene lamps, turned them down low and spent most of the night discussing with their wives what they had to do. These farm women were as rugged as the men. They knew how to roll logs with canhooks and chop down small trees. Early the next morning the men and some of the women met at the waterfront. John said, "How many men and families can we depend on." John Pie said, "There are seven of us here." Dick Miles spoke up—"What you think we're here fo." They all chimed in, "We got muscle, we got de nerve, we ain't 'fraid of de water and, by God, we can fight if anybody mess with us on land or sea . . ."

. . . They knew it would be necessary for some of them to go to Hampton and see the Butler's Farm that they had heard about. . . . The party of three, Berry, Miles and Carr, caught the early morning ferry the next day from Willoughby Spit cross Hampton Roads to Old Point Comfort, about a 45 minute ride. . . .

Arriving at Soldiers Home they were ushered in to see Colonel Raymond. "Howdy do men. I'm glad to see you. I had hoped you'd come." "Yes sir, Colonel," spoke John Berry, "we saved some money from the war and the Freedmen's Bureau helped us with rations. We think we can buy the land and we have a plan to tear down our houses, bring the logs and lumber 'cross Hampton Roads to the farms." "What!" said Colonel Raymond, "that sounds impossible." Miles and Berry responded, "We worked around Potomac and

Patuxent Rivers all our lives and the Chesapeake Bay too." Carr said, "We build rafts and floating bridges in the war and dey drivin' us off the Taylor Farm: we got to do sumpnn." "If you think you can do it," said Colonel, "I'll give all the help I can, and General Butler wants to help his boys. Rev. L. L. Lively will show you all the available land out there." "It's already surveyed into seven-acre plots. Some families have built already, there are 110 acres in all and part of it borders near Back River." "Yes," said Berry, "and that river connects with Hampton Roads." The men asked the Colonel if they could talk with him after they saw the land. "Yes," he replied, "I want to, this sounds like a very risky project. But I am willing to listen."

Meanwhile, old man Taylor, the former rebel plantation owner, had returned to his old mansion following President Johnson's Executive Order. He found it partly in shambles and was trying to rebuild and take over his former property. He approached the Black vets packing to leave. "What you boys doin'," said Taylor. "We leaving this land 'cause you called the sheriff and we ti'ed 'er fightin'. It really don't b'long to you. You run when the Yankees come. We fought for it, some give up their lives, we won't. We built these houses, cut these logs, raised these crops, they belong to us. Since yo' folks 'sassinate President Lincun, the Army forced us to leave but we taking all our belongings." Taylor said, "I am not goin' to try to stop you. Remember, I suffered, too; all this land was mine, but I am nearly broke. . . . Some of you folks want to work for me on shares it will be good for both of us." "We wouldn't work for you 'cause we don't believe you would treat us man-to-man."

After about a month the seven families had pulled down their houses, dragged and hauled the lumber and much of their belongings, crates of chickens and pigs, they were ready to sail with the tide and sunrise to the shores of Hampton Roads. They built a substantial raft of logs, slabs, lumber tied together with Navy rope, wooden pegs, rail spikes, and a large canvas movable sail to take advantage of tail winds. They took lanterns in case of darkness or heavy fog; took signal flags which they learned to use in the war. They figured to make the 15 mile trip between sun up and sun down.

So on an appointed day at sunrise, they said a prayer with joined hands, and sailed with the morning tide. The trips were made one week apart. They built three rafts one at a time out of the lumber from their cabins, dismantling each raft on the banks of Back River on Butler's Farm. They returned by ferry between each trip. The families doubled up in the remaining cabins and finally lived in tents made of quilts and old canvas and young tree stoves. The backbreaking trip across Hampton Roads was a rough experi-ence as everybody knew it would be. On the first crossing they had to find the bell buoys to avoid the lanes of the big Old Dominion and Merchant Miners ships, Philadelphia, New York and Boston. They were sighted by a commercial tug boat which steamed over out of curiosity, and asked if they were in trouble. Nearing Old Point Comfort, another boat blew a distress whistle to see if they were what was left of a sunken ship. Finally these water vagabonds pulled into Back River where there was no traffic. . . . On the last crossing they were caught in a squall, and high waves from an Old Dominion Passenger liner enroute to Norfolk, swept the raft off course. . . .

While their cabins were being rebuilt, mattresses were made of straw stuffed in bags, flattened and spread on the ground. When the last raft with house furnishings and farm utensils were landed, cabins were already being rebuilt.

By the first frost in the fall of 1870, the Berry, Jenifer, Miles and Garner families had completed their crude cabins, launched out on their undevel-oped but independent farm life to rear their children and serve their God.

Era Bell Thompson (1907–1986)

Leaving her native North Dakota in 1931, Era Bell Thompson came to settle in Chicago in 1933. In 1945, she received a Fellowship in Midwestern Studies from the Newberry Library to write her classic autobiography *American Daughter*. ("Usually an autobiography is written near the end of a long and distinguished career," she said, "but not taking any chances, I wrote mine first.") *American Daughter* was published with great success the following year. Soon afterwards, John H. Johnson hired her to work at his publishing firm and by 1951 she was co–managing editor of *Ebony*, a job she held until 1964 when she became the magazine's international editor, a post that nourished her ever-present need to wander and resulted in her 1954 book *Africa: Land of My Fathers*. In 1963, she edited the interesting *White on Black: Views of Twenty-two White Americans on the Negro*. The University of North Dakota awarded her an honorary doctorate in 1969, and in 1976, she received the state's highest award, the Teddy Roosevelt Rough Rider Award. The excerpt below from near the end of *American Daughter* begins with a near-mythic meeting between Thompson, representing another era of Black aspiration, and Robert S. Abbott, a now old and—at least as Thompson sees him—"bitter" symbol of the old guard for whom race was an ever-present obstacle. Though obviously greatly plagued by race herself, Thompson is more willing to take to heart the words of the elderly guide she meets on her first visit to the Chicago Board of Trade. Beaming when she tells him she is going to school and holding up to her the example of someone who has "made it," he says: "No matter what you do, do it well, be the best there is, and remember, here in America all things are possible, everyone has the opportunity to become great."

From *American Daughter*

FROM CHAPTER 15: "CHICAGO, HERE I COME!"

Hordes of people poured into Chicago in 1933 to see the World's Fair, but I came seeking work and a home among my people. This time the big city held neither glitter nor glamour for me. No longer was I awed by the girls at the Y, where again I found lodging, for all my thoughts and energies went into the finding of a job.

The first week I exhausted the list of names Dr. Riley had given me and made the rounds of the various social agencies without results, for I had neither Chicago training, field case-work experience, nor political affiliation. . . .

At the University's Settlement House I met Mary McDowell, ill and almost inactive. She took me upstairs to her rooms and, though she had no place for me on her staff, gave me something bigger than a job. She restored my self-confidence, confirmed my ideals, told me no obstacle was too great, nothing came too easily.

The second week, I made the rounds of the colored business houses and newspaper offices, beginning with the *Chicago Defender*. Representing myself as more of a former contributor than I had been, I managed to get an appointment with Robert S. Abbott himself. When I arrived at the sumptuous Abbott home, I was shown into a beautiful room, richly and lavishly appointed. A short, dark man, clad in a silk bathrobe, came slowly down the stairs and into the room. He glanced at the gold clock on the mantel.

"You're on time," he said, breathing heavily. "Had you been a minute late, I would not have seen you."

Thus began my conversation with the man who was founder and publisher of the largest Negro newspaper in the world, a man who was known on two continents, who fought the prejudices and hates of the white man, glorified the heritage and color of the black man, yet married two women so fair that even Negroes questioned their racial origin.

Mr. Abbott, old and ill, was no longer able to leave his home. With bitterness he told me how his trust in others had been betrayed, of the need for loyal, intelligent young men and women to carry on in his place, yet he knew the note he was giving me to take to his office would do no good, that his recommendation no longer carried weight.

The three weeks were up, and I was still looking, searching, walking the streets, but I refused to give up and go home. Sometimes I paired off with one of the girls at the Y, and together we answered ads, waited hopefully in employment offices for jobs to come in: factory, housework, any kind of job now. There were growing hordes of us seeking employment. Those who had jobs were tight-lipped, mysterious, refusing to talk about their jobs, and when they did talk they lied, saying they worked where they could not, making wages they did not.

Finally I inserted an ad for domestic work in a daily paper. Two of the three inquirers lost interest when they learned I was colored. The third, a West Side woman desperately in need of help, hired me. I lasted only a week. Besides cleaning, ironing, personal laundry, washing windows, and scrubbing floors, there was the curling of an ungrateful little girl's very straight hair, and lugging two-ton Junior to the bathroom all through the night to keep him from drowning in bed. As soon as the house was all clean and shining, my employer paid me off and said she was sorry, I wouldn't do.

Followed more hunting and searching for a job. I paid precious money to the numerous little employment agencies that dotted the streets and was sent to places I was afraid to enter, places where jobs never existed. Now and then, I got odd jobs—a little typing, bussing dishes at the Loop Y. By scrimping, by walking until the soles of my pumps were thin and the heels worn down to nubs, I managed to live. Every letter from Susan was a plea to come home, but always there was another job in sight, another promise or hope for the morrow. We weren't allowed to cook in the Y, so many of us, whose resources were too low to afford even the nominal Y meals, sneaked crackers and cheese, even milk, into our rooms or pooled our food and cooked it on the laundry stove in the basement. For some of us, that was the only hot food we had, unless we were lucky enough to get work in a restaurant or private home.

From Chapter 16: "My America, Too"

Again long days of job seeking, of walking in the rain and snow, of answering ads, inquiring at offices, filing applications. The Chicago Relief Administration gave me first hope, then assurance, of a clerical job at a hundred dollars a month. I waited two weeks, then went back and was told I would be called in a few more days; but days passed, then another week, and still no word, so again I returned.

"Oh," said the lady who had hired me, "didn't we notify you? The funds were withdrawn. We can't possibly use you."

[Unwilling to go on relief, Thompson continues her unsuccessful search for stable work. Going to interview for a designer's job at a furniture company, she hears the receptionist "tipping off" the boss by whispering, "A colored girl . . . A N-e-g-r-o to see you." Of course, the job suddenly disappears. She buys a portable typewriter and enrolls in night school at Northwestern, hoping to study journalism. She is the only Black in class. "There was also a certain amount of pride placed upon the doubtful distinction of being an 'only Negro,' the thing I came to Chicago to escape. The world was becoming very small indeed. The white students, also conscious of racial patterns, made few overtures, so my little experiment of going to college with money and clothes and a job proved to be the loneliest school days of my life." But her studies take her to the above-mentioned Chicago Board of Trade visit where she finally winds up paying $30.00 to have an Irish guide teach her "more in half an hour than the learned professor did in a semester." She lands a filing job at the Mart where, as a diversion, she writes a one-page newspaper "poking fun at the higher ups and flattering my best friends." It's a success, even with the "Big Supe." It becomes the *Giggle Sheet*, and, her talent now acknowledged, it grows bigger and launches her writing career.]

By vacation time, I had saved a travel fund of fifty dollars—enough to go East, for I had to see more of America; rural urban Midwest was not enough. Traveling by bus, I was able to make the trip East on forty-five dollars, and didn't miss a thing, not even an automat. I stopped in Detroit to see Harry. It was like getting acquainted all over again, and I think Harry suddenly finding a strange sister on his hands, was quite relieved when my stay was over.

As I boarded the bus for Canada, an irascible old woman was having an argument with the driver about her suitcase. Exasperated, the middle-aged man accompanying her moved over to the seat next to me.

"My aunt can make me so angry," he exclaimed. "But I fixed her; I told her I'd sit with you!"

I looked at him.

"She doesn't like colored people," he explained. "She doesn't like anybody but herself."

I raised the window. It was getting stuffy.

"Good!" he said happily. "I like plenty of air. I was afraid you wouldn't want the window up."

I buried myself in a magazine. When the bus picked up speed, the early September breeze whistled through the window. "Now, if that wind is too much for you," he began.

"Oh, no," I said, trying to keep my teeth from chattering. "It's quite all right."

He was silent for a while. The wind blew harder, blew through his thin, grayish hair, until he pulled his coat collar up around his neck. "I'm afraid you'll catch cold in that draft," he said, reaching for the window. It came crashing down on his little finger. Wringing his hand, he jumped up and down in the aisle, threatening to sue the bus company. "Just look at my finger!" he cried, thrusting it under my eyes. "Don't you think it's broken? Can't you see it swelling?"

I couldn't.

Eventually he calmed down, but he never stopped talking until we parted that evening at Niagara Falls. After the inevitable race question was disposed of, he told me about his student days at college and showed me points of interest all along the highway, an old route to him. As we passed a Heinz plant he described seven of their fifty-seven varieties; he knew the exact place where beautiful Lake Superior came into view, and he pointed out tobacco plants, the first I had ever seen. When we I stopped for lunch, my friend joined his pouting aunt, who I strongly suspect, held the family purse strings. After lunch, I stood by a post near the bus reading a Canadian news-paper. I saw my friend come out of the lunchroom and disappear behind the buses, then run back to the lunchroom, look inside, and run toward the ladies' rest room and I wondered what he'd lost in there.

"You can't go off and leave her," he told the driver excitedly, as he came back to search the bus. "I know she's around here somewhere!"

"Can't wait much longer," said the driver. "We're late now."

I looked up at the bus in front of me. It said "Indianapolis." They were looking for me.

[After recounting her trips across the United States, Thompson brings the book to a close by telling us about her finally getting a stable job with the civil service at the Merchandise Mart as an employment service interviewer. In "Chicago, the crossroads of America," she meets a wide variety of people looking for work, a cross-section of America. "Sometimes they are a little reluctant to talk to me," she writes," because I am a government employee and some people just don't like government employees; because I am a woman, and what does a woman know about an annealer in a foundry? Because I am a Negro." After sharing several anecdotes, some about grumbling ap-plicants, she writes:]

Most of the applicants are good-natured, friendly people, eager to see the sunny side. They exhibit pictures of sweethearts and children, bring in poems they have written, letters they have received. A miner from Nevada returned to show me a beautiful diamond ring he bought for his fiancée; a policeman, after his interview, said the only difference between talking to me and going to the priest was absolution; and a woman admitted she had had a little trouble with her last job, but everything was all right now. Her employer was dead. She should know; she killed him.

Cranks, philanthropists, or plain, everyday Americans, I like them all. For every bad one, there are twenty good ones. We can't always find jobs for them, we aren't always successful in getting them to take the jobs we find, but we can give them a kind and sympathetic audience. It is surprising to know how many people in the world are hungry for kindness, to have someone believe in them. And I do believe in them.

When a forelady in a box factory asks, "Isn't it wonderful to live in a country where you can sit down and tell your troubles to someone and have them listen?"

When an old man, a retired engineer, comes up to your desk, saying, "Last night I heard the President's voice. He said he needed me. I don't want pay; I want to help my country."

ERA BELL THOMPSON

When those things are said, I know there is still good in the world, that way down underneath, most Americans are fair; that my people and your people can work together and live in peace and happiness, if they but have the opportunity to know and understand each other.

The chasm is growing narrower. When it closes, my feet will rest on a united America.

Alice Browning (1907–1985)

A writer of stories, poems, plays, and essays, Alice Browning made perhaps her greatest contributions as an editor and literary organizer. Among the magazines she edited were *Black Writers News*, *Travel News*, and *Childplay*, a children's literary magazine. She also published an autobiography and two books of cartoons and edited *The Lionel Hampton Swing Book*. Most of all, from 1944 to 1946 she edited, with Fern Gayden, the short-lived but highly influential *Negro Story* magazine. In 1970, she also founded the International Black Writers Conference, directing it until 1984. *Negro Story*'s importance lies not only in its nourishing of the careers of such writers as Chester Himes, Ralph Ellison, and Richard Wright, but also for manifesting the tensions between radical Blackness and growing, less radical, middle-class Black values. Subtitled "Short Stories By or About Negroes for All Americans," the magazine also printed white writers (each identified as such) and encouraged a bi-racial vision of America while at the same time continuing to rail against racism and its injustices. Seen at times as a voracious publicity seeker—the radicalism generally seen as coming from Gayden and her replacement, Earl Conrad—Browning was also a good writer. She once characterized a story in *Negro Story* as being "another terrific story from Richard Bentley"—Bentley being the pseudonym under which she published her stories in the magazine. Indeed, the following is one of her best works. It appeared in the May–June 1945 issue.

Old Mis' Cane

"Old white bitch—she make me sick."

"Sho do—all time hollerin' an' raisin' cain."

"An' chasin' children off her lawn."

"White folks always like that."

"Think they own the world."

"She got her nerve—livin' roun' here and married to a colored man too."

The two black women, Mrs. Fletcher and Mrs. Young cast baleful glances at the short, squat white woman across the street sweeping off her porch.

"Mis' Cane is a good name for her."

"Suits her fine."

The white woman was shaking her fist at two little Negro boys.

"If you imps don't stay off my lawn."

But the two brown boys with the clean-shaven heads stuck out their tongues and danced away putting their thumbs to their noses and wriggling their fingers.

"Old Miss Cane is so mean

Worst old thing we've ever seen."

They darted into the huge flat building on the corner. This building was six stories tall, and it had once been red but the brick was so grimy with smoke and dirt you could hardly know what color it was. At its many windows were soiled ragged curtains for the most part, although sometimes spotless dainty ones showed the greater industry of the people in a particular apartment. The windows in the basement were boarded up, and people passing the place were sickened by the damp musty odor which came from it. Occasionally, bricks fell from its roof endangering the lives of the passers-by.

"Isn't it awful," they would say. "Something should be done about it."

The more prosperous property owners detested this eyesore. Out in front near the street, the water ran continually from the fire plug flooding the street with dirty water. It was a breeding place for mosquito larvae in the spring. Ragged little dark children loved to sail pieces of paper and wood in this muddy lake. To them it was great sport. But Ann Blair who owned the three-story grey stone house down the street was even now circulating a petition to have the building condemned and razed. Here the most disreputable bunch of cut throats in the city congregated because there were no rents to pay with an absentee landlord. There was no fire escape, and the people living there said that there was only one community bathroom to each floor. But many poor people found this a haven. In the alley, their garbage was piled in a huge mountain as there were no garbage cans. Ann Blair was using this as one of the ways to condemn the building for a public health menace.

Old Mis' Cane waddled across the street on her way to the store; her fat round legs trudged along beneath her old fashioned brown coat. She had a sallow complexion, and her stringy grey hair was brushed down tightly in a small bun on her broad neck.

"Hello there," she waved in a friendly fashion to the women who had been talking about her a few minutes before.

"Did you ever see such bad children in all your day?"

"No, Mis' Cane, ain't they terrible," they chorused showing their teeth as they giggled and flung themselves around.

"How yuh do today Mis' Cane?"

"Oh, I'm just fine—on my way to the store."

As she moved away, Mrs. Fletcher said to Mrs. Young in a low voice.

"There she go—looking like a sack of potatoes with a string tied around the middle—ol' she devil."

ALICE BROWNING

"She sho' is crazy about that old crippled husband of hern." "Sho is."

One woman lowered her voice, "I heard she took him away from his colored wife in Cincinnati where they come from."

"You know how these white women is—is she really white?"

"Can't you tell 'em—can always tell 'em no matter how white a Negro is and vice versey."

"Well she look white, but she so dark, she could pass for colored—she look colored to me, Miss Young."

"Uh huh—you know I bet that husband of hern was a good looking man when he was young."

"He white as she is."

"Whiter, you mean."

"He fine-looking now, as old as he is."

"I bet she'd die ef anything happen to him—she comes to the door with him every morning, an' waves all up and down the street."

"I heard he lost his leg at the place he worked, and the company gave him fifty thousand dollars."

"They don't seem to have many friends—"

"Naw she ain' got nobody but him."

"That's why she so crazy about him."

"You know he got that wooden leg."

"That don't hurt nothing—don' keep him from . . ."

"Oh, you know they too old for all that foolishness."

"What you talking about—don' never get too old for that."

"Not even in the change."

"I hear sometimes you worse then."

"I hope so."

Mrs. Young giggled. "I does too—ain't nothing better, is there?"

"I ain't found nothing."

Old Mis, Cain had gone home from the store. She trudged painfully up her new cement steps, breathing heavily when she got to the top. As she crossed over the threshold with her arms full of packages, the screen door slammed behind her almost catching her fat heels.

"Heavens I'm tired," she gasped as she let the large bags drop on the table. A couple of potatoes fell and rolled to the floor. She grunted as she tried to get them. The stays in her corset prevented her reaching them, and she had to pull a chair over, sit down and lean on the side of it before scooping up the potatoes into her hand.

She sighed and sat there looking about her electric kitchen. The kitchen had been recently remodeled. Mrs. Cane glanced around her and the shiny whiteness of her new Westinghouse refrigerator, her electric dishwasher, her metal cabinets and the new electric stove overwhelmed her. She beamed. Everything was white and perfect—set off by the bright red checked curtains and the red leather chrome-legged chairs. The beauty of her kitchen gave her a sense of peace.

"I must get dinner ready for Phil," she thought, but she could hardly move.

She was a good cook and a good housekeeper, and Phil's delicious dinner was always ready when he returned from work.

But recently her breath was short, and she couldn't work as much as usual. She felt a little lonely and depressed. She would have to get a girl to help her, and she hated having anyone in the house. Sometimes she realized that she had no friends. After all, she was white living in a colored neighborhood. Sometimes an old childhood friend of hers looked her up and came over.

Usually, ideas for improving her home filled her thoughts daily. This was her recreation. It was about all she lived for—her home and Phil. She sunk deeply into one of the down-filled chairs; its softness gave beneath her monstrous hips. She sighed again. A sense of depression, of loneliness, that had been following her all day weighed down upon her heavily.

"I must get dinner ready for Phil," she thought. But she could not move. The heavy feeling chained her to the chair. She loved her home and kept it spotless. All day she worked to preserve her house and belongings, dusting the furniture, vacuuming the rugs, waxing the kitchen, scrubbing the tile, all of the minute details that make a house neat and homelike. This kept her busy. She was a good cook too . . .

But sometimes and certainly more often recently, since her breath was short and she couldn't work as much as usual, she had begun to feel lonely and depressed. It wasn't that she didn't appreciate her home and her husband—he was a good husband—but sometimes she realized that she had no friends. Upon moving to this city from Cincinnati, she had not tried to make friends. After all, she was white, and they were colored. She spoke pleasantly enough to the neighbors, but she knew they were her inferiors. They disliked her, and that hurt. She desired no close contact with them, but wanted them to look up to her. Didn't they realize that she was white? That was another thing. Some of them didn't seem to realize she was white. Her complexion was sallow, more sallow now that she was older, making her almost as dark as her neighbors. When she was young her swarthy complexion and black hair, with her red lips had been attractive. Sometimes, she had an impulse to let the neighbors know she was white, especially the newcomers. But after all, she knew the older neighbors would tell them in time. She did not want to be mistaken for one of them even if she was married to a Negro.

She yelled at the children to stay off her lawn; she shook her fist at the peddlers when they drove by the front instead of going down the alley.

"Ignorant things," she said. As she sat there thinking, the door bell rang. It was Ann Blair and some of the homeowners of the block who had come to visit her. Ann Blair was a social worker, and all of the others were professional men and women.

"We'd like for you to join our league—our home improvement league," Ann said.

"Yes, Mis' Cane, your house is so beautiful," said Mrs. Prince, a thin, aristocratic grey haired school teacher wearing glasses on a black ribbon, looking around in great awe.

She looked at them. She tried to be pleasant. If she had wanted friends, associates, here they were for her. But she disliked these Negroes even more than the others. They were always trying to act like white people. Their homes were as good as hers; better, in some instances. They had cars, servants. She didn't like feeling inferior to them. She had less education than most of them, only having completed high school and some of them, like Ann, reminded her of her youth, her lost beauty. She would be happier alone than among this group of people.

"I am so sorry," she tried to smile. "But I simply can't join—I've too much to do."

"But Mis' Cane, you wouldn't have to come to all of the meetings—we'd just like to have your support."

"Oh come on Mrs. Cane," said Mrs. Prince, "We need you."

She would like to tell Mrs. Prince what she thought of her—dried up old brown fool.

"We're counting on you."

"Please Mrs. Cane; you're a homeowner."

"No, no, I can't, I just can't—"

After several attempts to persuade her Ann spoke, "Well Mrs. Cane we will not press you further; think it over and maybe you'll decide later."

"But," Ann continued unfolding a long crackling sheet of paper, "I wonder if you would just sign this petition."

"What petition?"

"It's a petition against Jack Moore. He is planning to open a tavern down the street from you—you don't want that do you?"

No, Mrs. Cain didn't want that. She hated the thought of a tavern. For a moment she hesitated. But she disliked these people more than she hated the tavern. Jack Moore treated her with courtesy.

She exploded suddenly.

"No, I should say not—I'll not sign a petition against Jack Moore—Jack Moore, why he's the main friend I have. He keeps the children from bothering me. He tips his hat politely to me whenever I see him. He protects me. He's respectful; courteous—He's a fine man. He's—"

She wanted to say he's the only one who treats me as if I am white, but she stopped herself.

"No, Mrs. Blair—I absolutely will have no part of it—that is final."

It was a dismissal, and they sat there stunned—completely beaten—amazed. They had counted on her.

Then Ann spoke in a fiery manner. "Very well, Mrs. Cane; you'll be sorry later if Mr. Moore's tavern gets in and the racket interferes with your sleep at nights—but let me tell you one thing, if you so much as breathe to Jack Moore one word of our plans, I cannot vouch for what might happen to you or your home. Good day, Mrs. Cane."

They trouped out like a pack of dogs. She slammed the door viciously behind them. All day she had felt distressed. Now she was furious.

It was two o'clock. She must hurry with dinner. She went out to the kitchen and later when she heard Phil's key click at the door, dinner was all ready and the table beautifully set.

Phil came in, his wooden leg sounding against the hard wood floor. He was big and his shock of white hair lighted up his countenance. She never thought of Phil as belonging to these people. Her face beamed. He took her in his arms and kissed her. "Hello darling," he said, "How did the day go with you?"

"Fine Phil—just fine. Come on and get your dinner."

After dinner, they washed and dried the dishes laughing gaily, and reminiscing. "You're a good wife Eva", he said—"a good wife—enjoyed the dinner."

He put his arm around her and they went into the parlor and turned on the *Hallie Q* program. She picked up her crochet and talked to Phil while he read his newspapers. Suddenly, she realized that he wasn't answering her. Getting up she saw that he was sound asleep, his newspaper held before him, as if he were reading.

Smiling to herself, she sat back down and crocheted, her pleasant thoughts wrapping her like a warm robe. The radio droned on. Its music was making her drowsy. She was getting sleepier and sleepier and sleepier. Tomorrow she would tell Jack Moore about the petition. But how she loved these quiet evenings with Phil. As long as she had Phil nothing else mattered. She was rich indeed. Life was worthwhile. There was something about Phil that filled her life—his kindness, his gentleness, his tenderness. As she mused, her mind went over her whole life. She felt soothed, relaxed, happy.

Then suddenly she realized it was time for Phil to set the furnace for the night. "Phil," she said, "Phil, honey."

He did not answer.

"Phil—wake up—the furnace honey—It's time for the furnace."

Still no answer.

Painfully she pulled herself up and waddled over to his chair.

"Phil," she placed her head on his warm forehead.

Then she stared at him. He was quiet. His eyes looked queer. She pushed his eyes open. He did not move. She put her hand to his heart. It was beating faintly, and as she spoke she heard a gasp. He was trying hard to breathe. She kissed him and called to him. She began to pray.

"Oh God, let him live—please—he's all I have."

She ran to the phone and frantically dialed for Dr. Webster. It seemed an interminable period before he came. Phil's breath was coming in gasps. He was regaining consciousness.

He kept repeating, "Where am I—what happened?"

"Keep quiet honey—you've been ill—you will be all right."

When the doctor came, he listened to Phil's heart with his stethoscope and said nothing.

She hovered anxiously about him, trying to tell from the expression on his face what he was thinking and trying to pray.

"Help me get him to bed."

Together they got him on the day bed in the dining room and undressed him. He turned over painfully to sleep. They tiptoed out.

ALICE BROWNING

"Doctor," Mrs. Cane said wearily and fright was gripping her body until her underarms were wet and her stomach was drawn tight. It seemed that there was a hot ball of fire under her breastbone. The doctor hesitated.

"He had a cerebral hemorrhage." This was serious she knew.

"Hardening of the arteries."

"Is there any hope?"

"Oh yes, he may live for ten years yet with good care—light meat diet—rest—"

"Yes, doctor."

"He should stop work."

Of course he could—they had saved enough money to last for the rest of their lives.

"Give him these when he awakens—make him drink liquids—he should rest three weeks."

Three weeks at home. And she could care for him. There was hope. That was all that mattered. He could live. She had Phil. They could go away when he got better—to California—for a vacation. She got painfully down on her knees to thank God and tears were running down her cheeks. Nothing mattered except this. They were nearing the end of life together, and they had peace. It didn't matter that she had no friends, that she was married to a Negro. It only mattered that she loved Phil, that their lives had been good together and that they would spend the rest of their lives quietly together—she with her good husband—alone and happy.

Richard Wright (1908–1960)

Constantly controversial for both the blunt power of his literary style, as well as the directness with which he confronted racism, injustice, and all that would curtail social and personal freedom, Richard Wright was a towering figure of American letters. His early writings appeared in small, mostly left-wing publications like the magazine *New Masses*, but after 1938, most of his major work acquired landmark status, including *Uncle Tom's Children* (1938), *Native Son* (1940), *12 Million Black Voices: A Folk History of the Negro in the United States* (1941), *Black Boy* (1944), and *The Outsider* (1953). *12 Million Black Voices* caused the FBI to monitor him for the rest of his life.

Mississippi-born, Wright moved to Chicago in the 1920s, and much of his work is set against the city's backdrop. In 1944, the Book-of-the-Month Club, which had helped make *Native Son* a national sensation (it sold over 200,000 copies in less than three weeks), said it would accept only the first part of Wright's massive autobiography *American Hunger*. Wright renamed that first part *Black Boy*. The second part, retaining the name *American Hunger,* would not be published until 1977. However, in 1944 the *Atlantic Monthly* published an excerpt of *American Hunger* in two parts (in August and September). A shortened version of this original *Atlantic* piece with my summaries of the omitted parts appears below. It chronicles a crucial period in Wright's life, 1933 to 1937, where he is publishing his first work and laying the foundations for nearly all his major work to come. Among the works mentioned or alluded to are the "crude" revolutionary poem "I Have Seen Black Hands"; his first piece of journalism, "Joe Louis Uncovers Dynamite" (about Black Chicago's reaction to the Louis-Baer fight); and "Big Boy Leaves Home," which would become one of the four stories in *Uncle Tom's Children*. The subject that dominates the narrative, however, is his relationship with the Communist Party. The relationship was strained nearly from the beginning because Wright saw the party as handing down "decisions" regardless of what its local members felt, and because it attempted to control personal freedoms, especially the freedom of artists and writers. This piece represented Wright's public break with the party, a break that had been made nearly seven years earlier. When the piece appeared, *New Masses*, the site of so many of his early works, denounced him.

From "I Tried to Be a Communist"

One Thursday night I received an invitation from a group of white boys I had known when I was working in the post office to meet in one of Chicago's South Side hotels and argue the state of the world. About ten of us gathered, and ate salami sandwiches, drank beer, and talked. I was amazed to discover that many of them had joined the Communist Party. I challenged them by reciting the antics of the Negro Communists I had seen in the parks, and I was told that those antics were "tactics" and were all right. I was dubious.

Then one Thursday night Sol, a Jewish chap, startled us by announcing that he had had a short story accepted by a little magazine called the *Anvil*, edited by Jack Conroy, and that he had joined a revolutionary artist organization, the John Reed Club. Sol repeatedly begged me to attend the meetings of the club.

"You'd like them," Sol said.

"I don't want to be organized," I said.

"They can help you to write," he said.

"Nobody can tell me how or what to write," I said. . .

I felt that Communists could not possibly have a sincere interest in Negroes. I was cynical and I would rather have heard a white man say that he hated Negroes, which I could have readily believed. . .

One Saturday night, bored with reading, I decided to appear at the John Reed Club in the capacity of an amused spectator. I rode to the Loop and found the number. . . . I mounted the stairs to a door that was lettered: THE CHICAGO JOHN REED CLUB.

I opened it and stepped into the strangest room I had ever seen. Paper and cigarette butts lay on the floor. A few benches ran along the walls, above which were vivid colors depicting colossal figures of workers carrying streaming banners. The mouths of the workers gaped in wild cries; their legs were sprawled over cities.

"Hello."

I turned and saw a white man smiling at me.

"You're welcome here," the white man said. . . . "Do you paint?". . .

"No," I said, "I try to write."

"Then sit in on the editorial meeting of our magazine, *Left Front,*" he suggested.

"I know nothing of editing," I said. "You can learn," he said. I stared at him, doubting. . . .

"My name's Grimm," he said.

I told him my name and we shook hands. He went to a closet and returned with an armful of magazines.

"Here are some back issues of the *Masses,*" he said. "Have you ever read it?"

"No," I said.

"Some of the best writers in America publish in it," he explained. He also gave me copies of a magazine called *International Literature.* "There's stuff here from Gide, Gorky—"

I assured him that I would read them. He took me to an office and introduced me to a Jewish boy who was to become one of the nation's leading painters, to a chap who was to become one of the eminent composers of his day, to a writer who was to create some of the best novels of his generation, to a young Jewish boy who was destined to film the Nazi occupation of Czechoslovakia. I was meeting men and women whom I should know for decades to come, who were to form the first sustained relationships in my life.

I sat in a corner and listened while they discussed their magazine, *Left Front*. Were they treating me courteously because I was a Negro? I must let cold reason guide me with these people, I told myself.... After the meeting I met an Irish girl who worked for an advertising agency, a girl who did social work, a schoolteacher, and the wife of a prominent university professor. I had once worked as a servant for people like these and I was skeptical. I tried to fathom their motives, but I could detect no condescension in them.

[Wright goes home with the magazines Grimm has given him, reads them, and is amazed that "there did exist in the world an organized search for the truth of the lives of the oppressed." But while he's reading them, his mother picks up a copy of the *Masses*. She is horrified by the cover, which depicts a man in "a lurid May Day cartoon." "What do communists think people are?" she asks, and this gives Wright his first sense of a mission he can fulfill if he is to join these people.]

Here, then, was something that I could do, reveal, say. The Communists, I felt, had oversimplified the experience of those whom they sought to lead. In their efforts to recruit masses, they had missed the meaning of the lives of the masses, had conceived of people in too abstract a manner. I would try to put some of that meaning back. I would tell Communists how common people felt, and I would tell common people of the self-sacrifice of Communists who strove for unity among them.

The editor of *Left Front* accepted two of my crude poems for publication, sent two of them to Jack Conroy's *Anvil*, and sent another to the *New Masses*, the successor of the *Masses*. Doubts still lingered in my mind.

"Don't send them if you think they aren't good enough," I said to him.

"They're good enough," he said.

"Are you doing this to get me to join up?" I asked.

"No," he said. "Your poems are crude, but good for us. You see, we're all new in this. We write articles about Negroes, but we never see any Negroes. We need your stuff."

RICHARD WRIGHT

I sat through several meetings of the club and was impressed by the scope and seriousness of its activities. . . . The members were fervent, democratic, restless, eager, self-sacrificing. I was convinced, and my response was to set myself the task of making Negroes know what Communists were. I got the notion of writing a series of biographical sketches of Negro Communists. I told no one of my intentions, and I did not know how fantastically naive my ambition was.

[Wright joins the John Reed Club but soon realizes a "bitter factional fight was in progress between two groups of members of the club," the painters and the writers. The writers, wanting to protect the publication of the *Left Front* magazine, take over the club, and Wright is elected the club's new executive secretary. Later he learns that "the writers of the club had decided to oust the painters, who were [Communist] party members. . . . Without my knowledge and consent, they confronted the members of the party with a Negro, knowing that it would be difficult for Communists to refuse to vote for a man representing the largest single racial minority in the nation, inasmuch as Negro equality was one of the main tenets of Communism." But the Communist Party sends word through its "fraction" that the *Left Front* is to be dissolved anyway, and Wright is told he must join the party if he wants to remain the executive secretary. Because he is somewhat successful in arguing for a more liberal attitude, he signs the membership card. But the club's trials are hardly over. Wright tells of an escaped mental patient who rises to a leadership position only to cause turmoil by bringing false charges against another member. "What kind of a club did we run," asks Wright, "that a lunatic could step into it and help run it? Were we all so mad that we could not detect a madman when we saw one?" This sense of "madness" at many levels and guises grows in Wright. Nevertheless, he accepts assignment "to full duty in the work of the club" and tells next about a report he is instructed to give at a "unit meeting" of the party on all his activities.]

About twenty Negroes were gathered. The time came for me to make my report and I took out my notes and told them how I had come to join the party, what few stray items I had published, what my duties were in the John Reed Club. I finished and waited for comment. There was silence. I looked about. Most of the comrades sat with bowed heads. Then I was surprised to catch a twitching smile on the lips of a Negro woman. Minutes passed. The Negro woman lifted her head and looked at the organizer. The organizer smothered a smile. Then the woman broke into unrestrained laughter, bending forward and burying her face in her hands. I stared. Had I said something funny?

"What's the matter?" I asked. The giggling became general. The unit organizer, who had been dallying with his pencil, looked up.

"It's all right, comrade," he said. "We're glad to have a writer in the party."

There was more smothered laughter. What kind of people were these? I had made a serious report and now I heard giggles.

"I did the best I could," I said uneasily. "I realize that writing is not basic or important. But, given time, I think I can make a contribution."

"We know you can, comrade," the black organizer said.

His tone was more patronizing than that of a Southern white man. I grew angry. I thought I knew these people, but evidently I did not. I wanted to take issue with their attitude, but caution urged me to talk it over with others first.

During the following days I learned through discreet questioning that I had seemed a fantastic element to the black Communists. I was shocked to hear that I, who had been only to grammar school, had been classified as an intellectual. What was an intellectual? I had never heard the word used in the sense in which it was applied to me. I had thought that they might refuse me on the ground that I was not politically advanced; I had thought they might say I would have to be investigated. But they had simply laughed.

I learned, to my dismay, that the black Communists in my unit had commented upon my shined shoes, my clean shirt, and the tie I had worn. Above all, my manner of speech had seemed an alien thing to them.

"He talks like a book," one of the Negro comrades had said. And that was enough to condemn me forever as bourgeois.

[Still possessed by the idea of writing biographical sketches, Wright begins to interview Ross, a "Negro Communist" who is "under indictment for 'inciting to riot.'" Wright says Ross typified the effective street agitator. A migrant from the South, "his life reflected the crude hopes and frustrations of the peasant in the city. Distrustful but aggressive, he was a bundle of weaknesses and virtues of a man struggling blindly between two societies, of a man living on the margin of a culture." The Communists themselves are suspicious of Ross. A "quiet black Communist" visits Wright, talks about Trotsky's betrayal of the party, and tells him that "Intellectuals don't fit well into the party": "The Soviet Union has had to shoot a lot of intellectuals." "Good God!" Wright exclaims, "You're not in Russia. You're standing on a sidewalk in Chicago. You talk like a man lost in fantasy," but more warnings, more trouble ensue over his involvement with Ross.]

I sat one morning in Ross's home with his wife and child. I was scribbling furiously upon my yellow sheets of paper. The doorbell rang and Ross's wife admitted a black Communist, one Ed Green. He was tall, taciturn, soldierly, square-shouldered. I was introduced to him and he nodded stiffly.

"What's happening here?" he asked bluntly.

Ross explained my project to him, and as Ross talked I could see Ed Green's face darken. He had not sat down and when Ross's wife offered him a chair he did not hear her.

"What're you going to do with these notes?" he asked me.

There was no answer.

"You lost people!" I cried, and banged my fist on the table.

Ross was shaken and ashamed. "Aw, Ed Green's just supercautious," he mumbled.

"Ross," I asked, "do you trust me?"

"Oh, yes," he said uneasily.

We two black men sat in the same room looking at each other in fear. Both of us were hungry. Both of us depended upon public charity to eat and for a place to sleep. Yet we had more doubt in our hearts of each other than of the men who had cast the mold of our lives.

I continued to take notes on Ross's life, but each successive morning found him more reticent . . .

In spite of their fears, I became drenched in the details of their lives. I gave up the idea of the biographical sketches and settled finally upon writing a series of short stories, using the material I had got from Ross and his friends, building upon it, inventing. I wove a tale of a group of black boys trespassing upon the property of a white man and the lynching that followed. The story was published in an anthology under the title of "Big Boy Leaves Home," but its appearance came too late to influence the Communists who were questioning the use to which I was putting their lives.

My fitful work assignments from the relief officials ceased and I looked for work that did not exist. I borrowed money to ride to and fro on the club's business. I found a cramped attic for my mother and aunt and brother behind some railroad tracks. At last the relief authorities placed me in the South Side Boys' Club and my wages were just enough to provide a bare living for my family.

Then political problems rose to plague me. Ross, whose life I had tried to write, was charged by the Communist Party with "anti-leadership tendencies," "class collaborationist attitudes," and "ideological factionalism"— phrases so fanciful that I gaped when I heard them. And it was rumored that I, too, would face similar charges. . . .

One night a group of black comrades came to my house and ordered me to stay away from Ross.

"But why?" I demanded.

"He's an unhealthy element," they said. "Can't you accept a decision?"

"Is this a decision of the Communist Party?"

"Yes," they said.

If I were guilty of something, I'd feel bound to keep your decision," I said. "But I've done nothing."

"Comrade, you don't understand," they said. "Members of the party do not violate the party's decisions."

"But your decision does not apply to me," I said. "I'll be damned if I'll act as if it does."

"Your attitude does not merit our trust," they said.

I was angry.

"Look," I exploded, rising and sweeping my arms at the bleak attic in which I lived. "What is it here that frightens you? You know where I work. You know what I earn. You know my friends. Now, what in God's name is wrong?"

They left with mirthless smiles which implied that I would soon know what was wrong.

But there was relief from these shadowy political bouts. I found my work in the South Side Boys' Club deeply engrossing. Each day black boys between the ages of eight and twenty-five came to swim, draw, and read. They were a wild and homeless lot, culturally lost, spiritually disinherited, candidates for the clinics, morgues, prisons, reformatories, and the electric chair of the state's death house. For hours I listened to their talk of planes, women, guns, politics, and crime. Their figures of speech were as forceful and colorful as any ever used by English-speaking people. I kept pencil and paper in my pocket to jot down their word-rhythms and reactions. These boys did not fear people to the extent that every man looked like a spy. The Communists who doubted my motives did not know these boys, their twisted dreams, their all too clear destinies; and I doubted if I should ever be able to convey to them the tragedy I saw here.

[Trying to control writers and other "intellectuals," the party dissolves the John Reed clubs, and Wright dwells in particular on a couple of writers' congresses in 1934 and 1935 where the survival of the clubs is fought over. Describing the 1935 congress held in New York, Wright tells the all-too-familiar tale of being unable to find a hotel room—even in the middle of Harlem. On the night before the John Reed clubs are formally dissolved, he sleeps in "the Negro Young Men's Christian Association, that bulwark of Jim Crowism for young black men." During this period, his gloominess is condemned as "defeatism," and the party, he feels, now suspects him of being a dangerous enemy. "I had learned," he says, "that denial of accusations was useless." The party announces plans for a larger, more powerful writing organization, but Wright knows his writing will probably not fit the new official mode. "My writing, he says, "was my way of seeing," and who could change his sight, his sense of direction, his senses?]

With the John Reed clubs now dissolved, I was free of all party relations. I avoided unit meetings for fear of being subjected to discipline. Occasionally a Negro Communist—defying the code that enjoined him to shun suspect elements—came to my home and informed me of the current charges that Communists were bringing against one another. To my astonishment I heard that Buddy Nealson had branded me a "smuggler of reaction."

Buddy Nealson was the Negro who had formulated the Communist position for the American Negro; he had made speeches in the Kremlin; he had spoken before Stalin himself.

"Why does Nealson call me that?" I asked.

"He says that you are a petty bourgeois degenerate," I was told.

"What does that mean?"

"He says that you are corrupting the party with your ideas."

"How?"

There was no answer. I decided that my relationship with the party was about over; I should have to leave it. The attacks were growing worse, and my refusal to react incited Nealson into coining more absurd phrases. I was termed a "bastard intellectual," an "incipient Trotskyite"; it was claimed that I possessed an "anti-leadership attitude" and that I was manifesting "seraphim tendencies"—a phrase meaning that one has withdrawn from the struggle of life and considers oneself infallible.

Working all day and writing half the night brought me down with a severe chest ailment. . . .

. . . When my chest healed, I sought an appointment with Buddy Nealson. He was a short, black man with an ever ready smile, thick lips, a furtive manner, and a greasy, sweaty look. His bearing was nervous, self-conscious; he seemed always to be hiding some deep irritation. He spoke in short, jerky sentences, hopping nimbly from thought to thought, as though his mind worked in a free, associational manner. He suffered from asthma and would snort at unexpected intervals. Now and then he would punctuate his flow of words by taking a nip from a bottle of whiskey. He had traveled half around the world and his talk was pitted with vague allusions to European cities. I met him in his apartment, listened to him intently, observed him minutely, for I knew that I was facing one of the leaders of World Communism.

"Hello, Wright," he snorted. "I've heard about you."

As we shook hands he burst into a loud, seemingly causeless laugh; and as he guffawed I could not tell whether his mirth was directed at me or was meant to hide his uneasiness.

"I hope what you've heard about me is good," I parried.

"Sit down," he laughed again, waving me to a chair. "Yes, they tell me you write."

"I try to," I said.

"You can write," he snorted. "I read that article you wrote for the *New Masses* about Joe Louis. Good stuff. First political treatment of sports we've yet had. Ha-ha."

I waited. I had thought that I should encounter a man of ideas, but he was not that. Then perhaps he was a man of action? But that was not indicated either.

"They tell me that you are a friend of Ross," he shot at me.

I paused before answering. He had not asked me directly, but had hinted in a neutral, teasing way. Ross, I had been told, was slated for expulsion from the party on the ground that he was "anti-leadership"; and if a member of the Communist International was asking me if I was a friend of a man about to be expelled, he was indirectly asking me if I was loyal or not.

"Ross is not particularly a friend of mine," I said frankly. "But I know him well; in fact, quite well."

"If he isn't your friend, how do you happen to know him so well?" he asked, laughing to soften the hard threat of his question.

"I was writing an account of his life and I know him as well, perhaps, as anybody," I told him.

"I heard about that," he said. "Wright. Ha-ha. Say, let me call you Dick, hunh?"

"Go ahead," I said.

"Dick," he said, "Ross is a nationalist." He paused to let the weight of his accusation sink in. He meant that Ross's militancy was extreme. "We Communists don't dramatize Negro nationalism," he said in a voice that laughed, accused, and drawled.

"What do you mean?" I asked.

"We're not advertising Ross." He spoke directly now.

"We're talking about two different things," I said. "You seem worried about my making Ross popular because he is your political opponent. But I'm not concerned about Ross's politics at all. The man struck me as one who typified certain traits of the Negro migrant. I've already sold a story based upon an incident in his life."

Nealson became excited.

"What was the incident?" he asked.

"Some trouble he got into when he was thirteen years old," I said.

"Oh, I thought it was political," he said, shrugging.

"But I'm telling you that you are wrong about that," I explained. "I'm not trying to fight you with my writing. . . . I'm trying to depict Negro life."

"Have you finished writing about Ross?"

"No," I said. "I dropped the idea. Our party members were suspicious of me and were afraid to talk." He laughed.

"Dick," he began, "we're short of forces. We're facing a grave crisis."

"The party's always facing a crisis," I said. His smile left and he stared at me.

"You're not cynical, are you, Dick?" he asked.

"No," I said. "But it's the truth. Each week, each month there's a crisis."

"You're a funny guy," he said, laughing, snorting again. "But we've got a job to do. We're altering our work. Fascism's the danger, the danger now to all people."

"I understand," I said.

"We've got to defeat the Fascists," he said, snorting from asthma. "We've discussed you and know your abilities. We want you to work with us. We've got to crash out of our narrow way of working and get our message to the church people, students, club people, professionals, middle class."

"I've been called names," I said softly. "Is that crashing out of the narrow way?"

"Forget that," he said.

He had not denied the name-calling. That meant that, if I did not obey him, the name-calling would begin again.

"I don't know if I fit into things," I said openly.

"We want to trust you with an important assignment," he said.

"What do you want me to do?"

"We want you to organize a committee against the high cost of living?"

"The high cost of living," I exclaimed. "What do I know about such things?"

"It's easy. You can learn," he said. I was in the midst of writing a novel and he was calling me from it to tabulate the price of groceries. "He doesn't think much of what I'm trying to do," I thought.

"Comrade Nealson," I said, "a writer who hasn't written anything worth while is a most doubtful person. Now, I'm in that category. . . . I'm in the midst of a book which I hope to complete in six months or so. Let me convince myself that I'm wrong about my hankering to write and then I'll be with you all the way."

"Dick," he said, turning in his chair and waving his hand as though to brush away an insect that was annoying him, "you've got to get to the masses of people."

"You've seen some of my work," I said. "Isn't it just barely good enough?"

"The party can't deal with your feelings," he said.

"Maybe I don't belong in the party," I stated it in full.

"Oh, no! Don't say that," he said, snorting. He looked at me. "You're blunt."

"I put things the way I feel them," I said. "I want to start in right with you. I've had too damn much crazy trouble in the party." He laughed and lit a cigarette.

"Dick," he said, shaking his head, "the trouble with you is that you've been around with those white artists on the North Side too much. You even talk like 'em. You've got to know your own people."

"I think I know them," I said, realizing that I could never really talk with him. "I've been inside of three fourths of the Negroes' homes on the South Side."

"But you've got to work with 'em," he said.

"I was working with Ross until I was suspected of being a spy," I said.

"Dick," he spoke seriously now, "the party has decided that you are to accept this task."

I was silent. I knew the meaning of what he had said. A decision was the highest injunction that a Communist could receive from his party. . . . In principle I heartily agreed with this, for I knew that it was impossible for working people to forge instruments of political power until they had achieved unity of action. Oppressed for centuries; divided, hopeless, corrupted, misled, they were cynical—as I had once been—and the Communist method of unity had been found historically to be the only means of achieving discipline . . . I wanted to shape people's feelings, awaken their hearts. But I could not tell Nealson that; he would only have snorted.

RICHARD WRIGHT

"I'll organize the committee and turn it over to someone else," I suggested.

"You don't want to do this, do you?" he asked.

"No," I said firmly. "What would you like to do on the South Side, then?"

"I'd like to organize Negro artists," I said.

"But the party doesn't need that now," he said. I rose, knowing that he had no intention of letting me go after I had organized the committee. I wanted to tell him that I was through, but I was not ready to bring matters to a head. I went out, angry with myself, angry with him, angry with the party. Well, I had not broken the decision, but neither had I accepted it wholly. I had dodged, trying to save time for writing, time to think.

[Despite his dodge, Wright begins attending meetings on the South Side. But believing that an "offer" to go to Switzerland as a youth delegate is another ploy to control and get rid of him, he begins making decisive breaks with the party. He is accused of being a Trotskyite. Two "Negro Communists" tell him that, "No one can resign from the Communist Party," and suddenly he is transferred from the South Side Boys' Club to the Federal Negro Theater.]

The Federal Negro Theater, for which I was doing publicity, had run a series of ordinary plays, all of which had been revamped to "Negro style," with jungle scenes, spirituals and all. For example, the skinny white woman who directed it, an elderly missionary type, would take a play whose characters were white, whose theme dealt with the Middle Ages, and recast it in terms of Southern Negro life with overtones of African backgrounds. . . .

What a waste of talent, I thought. Here was an opportunity for the production of a worth-while Negro drama and no one was aware of it. I studied the situation, then laid the matter before white friends of mine who held influential positions in the Works Progress Administration. I asked them to replace the white woman—including her quaint aesthetic notions. . . .

Within a month the white woman director had been transferred. We moved from the South Side to the Loop and were housed in a first-rate theater. I successfully recommended Charles DeSheim, a talented Jew, as director. DeSheim and I held long talks during which I outlined what I thought could be accomplished. I urged that our first offering should be a bill of three one-act plays; including Paul Green's *Hymn to the Rising Sun*, a grim, poetical, powerful one-acter dealing with chain-gang conditions in the South.

I was happy. At last I was in a position to make suggestions and have them acted upon. I was convinced that we had a rare chance to build a genuine Negro theater. I convoked a meeting and introduced DeSheim . . . he said that he was not at the theater to direct it, but to help the Negroes to direct it. He spoke so simply and eloquently that they rose and applauded him.

I then proudly passed out copies of Paul Green's *Hymn to the Rising Sun* to all members of the company. DeSheim assigned reading parts. I sat down to enjoy adult Negro dramatics. But something went wrong. The Negroes stammered and faltered in their lines. Finally they stopped reading altogether. DeSheim looked frightened. One of the Negro actors rose.

"Mr. DeSheim," he began, "we think this play is indecent. We don't want to act in a play like this before the American public. I don't think any such conditions exist in the South . . . Mr. DeSheim, we want a play that will make the public love us."

"What kind of play do you want?" DeSheim asked them.

They did not know. I went to the office and looked up their record and found that most of them had spent their lives playing cheap vaudeville. I had thought that they played vaudeville because the legitimate theater was barred to them, and now it turned out they wanted none of the legitimate theater, that they were scared spitless at the prospects of appearing in a play that the public might not like.

I felt—but only temporarily—that perhaps the whites were right, that Negroes were children and would never grow up. . . .

When I arrived at the theater a few mornings later, I was horrified to find that the company had drawn up a petition demanding the ousting of DeSheim. I was asked to sign the petition and I refused.

"Don't you know your friends?" I asked them.

They glared at me. I called DeSheim to the theater and we went into a frantic conference. "What must I do?" he asked.

"Take them into your confidence," I said. "Let them know that it is their right to petition for a redress of their grievances."

DeSheim thought my advice sound and, accordingly, he assembled the company and told them that they had a right to petition against him if they wanted to, but that he thought any misunderstandings that existed could be settled smoothly.

"Who told you that we were getting up a petition?" a black man demanded.

DeSheim looked at me and stammered wordlessly.

RICHARD WRIGHT

"There's an Uncle Tom in the theater!" a black girl yelled.

After the meeting a delegation of Negro men came to my office and took out their pocketknives and flashed them in my face.

"You get the hell off this job before we cut your bellybutton out!" they said.

I telephoned my white friends in the Works Progress Administration: "Transfer me at once to another job, or I'll be murdered." Within twenty-four hours DeSheim and I were given our papers. . . .

[Wright's story then turns to the inevitable trial of Ross by the Communist Party. They ask Wright to come, but he is suspicious that Ross's trial will also turn into his trial. He traces the Communist distrust of intellectuals back to the Russian Revolution's distrust of exploitive, "educated, arrogant noblemen." What baffles the party in the West, says Wright, is "the prevalence of self-achieved literacy. Even a Negro, entrapped by ignorance and exploitation . . . could, if he had the will and the love for it, learn to read and to understand the world in which he lived. And it was these people that the Communists could not understand." Wright then turns to Ross's trial. It is a long, exhausting event with speakers building "a vivid picture of mankind under oppression" as a background for accusing Ross of actions hurtful to the cause of lifting that oppression.]

Finally a speaker came forward and spoke of Chicago's South Side, its Negro population, their suffering and handicaps, linking all that also to the world struggle. Then still another speaker followed and described the tasks of the Communist Party of the South Side. At last, the world, the national, and the local pictures had been fused into one overwhelming drama of moral struggle in which everybody in the hall was participating. This presentation had lasted for more than three hours, but it had enthroned a new sense of reality in the hearts of those present, a sense of man on earth. With the exception of the church and its myths and legends, there was no agency in the world so capable of making men feel the earth and the people upon it as the Communist Party.

Toward evening the direct charges against Ross were made, not by the leaders of the party, but by Ross's friends, those who knew him best! It was crushing. Ross wilted. His emotions could not withstand the weight of the moral pressure. No one was terrorized into giving information against him. They gave it willingly, citing dates, conversations, scenes. The black mass of Ross's wrongdoing emerged slowly and irrefutably.

The moment came for Ross to defend himself. I had been told that he had arranged for friends to testify in his behalf, but he called upon no one. He stood, trembling; he tried to talk and his words would not come. The hall was as still as death. Guilt was written in every pore of his black skin. His hands shook. He held on to the edge of the table to keep on his feet. His personality, his sense of himself, had been obliterated. Yet he could not have been so humbled unless he had shared and accepted the vision that had crushed him, the common vision that bound us all together.

"Comrades," he said in a low, charged voice, "I'm guilty of all the charges, all of them."

His voice broke in a sob. No one prodded him. No one tortured him. No one threatened him. He was free to go out of the hall and never see another Communist. But he did not want to. He could not. The vision of a communal world had sunk down into his soul and it would never leave him until life left him. He talked on, outlining how he had erred, how he would reform.

I knew, as I sat there, that there were many people . . . who had been skeptical of the Moscow trials. But they could not have been skeptical had they witnessed this astonishing trial. Ross had not been doped; he had been awakened. It was not a fear of the Communist Party that had made him confess, but a fear of the punishment that he would exact of himself that made him tell of his wrongdoings. The Communists had talked to him until they had given him new eyes with which to see his own crime. And then they sat back and listened to him tell how he had erred. He was one with all the members there, regardless of race or color; his heart was theirs and their hearts were his; and when a man reaches that state of kinship with others, that degree of oneness, or when a trial has made him kin after he has been sundered from them by wrongdoing, then he must rise and say, out of a sense of the deepest morality in the world: "I'm guilty. Forgive me."

This, to me, was a spectacle of glory; and yet because it had condemned me, because it was blind and ignorant, I felt that it was a spectacle of horror. The blindness of their limited lives—lives truncated and impoverished by the oppression they had suffered long before they had ever heard of Communism—made them think that I was with their enemies. American life had so corrupted their consciousness that they were unable to recognize their friends when they saw them. . . .

I could not stay until the end. I was anxious to get out of the hall and into the streets and shake free from the gigantic tension that had hold of me. I rose and went to the door; a comrade shook his head, warning me that I could not leave until the trial had ended.

RICHARD WRIGHT

"You can't leave now," he said.

"I'm going out of here," I said, my anger making my voice louder than I intended.

We glared at each other. Another comrade came running up. I stepped forward. The comrade who had rushed up gave the signal for me to be allowed to leave. They did not want violence, and neither did I. They stepped aside. I went into the dark Chicago streets and walked home through the cold, filled with a sense of sadness. Once again I told myself that I must learn to stand alone. . . .

[As many writers in the Federal Writers' Project were members of the Communist Party, they soon make trouble for Wright, asking that he be removed from a supervisory role. One day, men and women on a picket line for higher wages for WPA artists and writers shout "There's Wright, that goddam Trotskyite . . . We know you . . . traitor!" "It shook me," says Wright, "as nothing else had." Over party members' bitter opposition, he is elected shop chairman of a union he has organized, and that union votes to march in the 1936 May Day parade. The essay closes with Wright arriving late, missing his union's ranks, and being pulled into the parade ranks of the Communist Party's South Side section by an old party friend.]

"You know the trouble I've had," I said.

"That's nothing," he said. "Everybody's marching today."

"I don't think I'd better," I said, shaking my head.

"Are you scared?" he asked. "This is *May Day*."

He caught my right arm and pulled me into line beside him. I stood talking to him, asking him about his work, about common friends.

"Get out of our ranks!" a voice barked.

I turned. A white Communist, a leader of the district of the Communist Party, Cy Perry, a slender, close-cropped fellow, stood glaring at me.

"I—It's May Day and I want to march," I said.

"Get out!" he shouted.

"I was invited here," I said.

I turned to the Negro Communist who had invited me into the ranks. I did not want public violence. I looked at my friend. He turned his eyes away. He was afraid. I did not know what to do. "You asked me to march here," I said to him. He did not answer.

"Tell him that you did invite me," I said, pulling his sleeve.

"I'm asking you for the last time to get out of our ranks!" Cy Perry shouted.

I did not move. I had intended to, but I was beset by so many impulses that I could not act. Another white Communist came to assist Perry. Perry caught hold of my collar and pulled at me. I resisted. They held me fast. I struggled to free myself.

"Turn me loose!" I said. Hands lifted me bodily from the sidewalk; I felt myself being pitched headlong through the air. I saved myself from landing on my head by clutching a curbstone with my hands. Slowly I rose and stood. Perry and his assistant were glaring at me. The rows of white and black Communists were looking at me with cold eyes of non-recognition. I could not quite believe what had happened, even though my hands were smarting and bleeding. . . .

Suddenly, the vast ranks of the Communist Party began to move. Scarlet banners with the hammer and sickle emblem of world revolution were lifted, and they fluttered in the May breeze. Drums beat. Voices were chanting. The tramp of many feet shook the earth. A long line of set-faced men and women, white and black flowed past me.

I followed the procession to the Loop and went into Grant Park Plaza and sat upon a bench. I was not thinking; I could not think. But an objectivity of vision was being born within me. A surging sweep of many odds and ends came together and formed an attitude, a perspective. "They're blind," I said to myself. "Their enemies have blinded them with too much oppression." I lit a cigarette and I heard a song floating out over the sunlit air:

"Arise you prisoners of starvation!"

I remembered the stories I had written, the stories in which I had assigned a role of honor and glory to the Communist Party, and I was glad that they were down in black and white, were finished. For I knew in my heart that I should never be able to write that way again, should never be able to feel with that simple sharpness about life, should never again express such passionate hope, should never again make so total a commitment of faith.

"A better world's in birth."

The procession still passed. Banners still floated. Voices of hope still chanted.

I headed toward home alone, really alone now, telling myself that in all the sprawling immensity of our mighty continent the least-known factor of living was the human heart, the least-sought goal of being was a way to live a human life. Perhaps, I thought, out of my tortured feelings I could fling a spark into this darkness. I would try, not because I wanted to but because I felt that I had to if I were to live at all.

RICHARD WRIGHT

I would hurl words into this darkness and wait for an echo; and if an echo sounded, no matter how faintly, I would send other words to tell, to march, to fight, to create a sense of the hunger for life that gnaws in us all, to keep alive in our hearts a sense of the inexpressibly human.

Cyrus Colter (1910–2002)

Born in Noblesville, Indiana, in 1910, Cyrus Colter received his law degree from Chicago-Kent College of Law in 1940 and began a successful career in business and government as a lawyer and, from 1950 to 1973, as commissioner of the Illinois Commerce Commission. He was sixty when his first collection of stories, *The Beach Umbrella* (1970), won the University of Iowa's School of Letters fiction prize. The success of his novels *The River of Eros* (1972) and *The Hippodrome* (1973) led to his appointment as the Chester D. Tripp Professor of Humanities at Northwestern University from 1973 to 1978. *Night Studies* (1979) won the 1980 Carl Sandburg fiction prize. In 1988, he published *A Chocolate Soldier* and his collected stories *The Amoralist and Other Tales*. In 1993, he published *City of Light*.

The stories in *The Amoralist* explore Black life, or the reaction to it, from the ghetto to the anxiety-ridden world of the Black middle class. In "The March," the book's most spectacular, outgoing story, a mother sees her eighteen-year-old son Archie off to the Army and an almost certain assignment to Vietnam, then returns home to deal with the indifference and bitterness of her second husband and the protests sweeping the neighborhood. Leaflets for an antiwar march read in part: "Join the thousands of protesters who will MARCH! Then hear speeches about the cruel hoax of our NEGRO BOYS fighting and dying in Vietnam.... Why are we sending NEGRO BOYS thousands of miles across the sea to fight for so-called DEMOCRACY when these same boys never shared in it right here at home?" Other stories are quieter and powerfully indirect, as in "A Chance Meeting," where an elderly house servant's identity and seeming closeness to his former high-society employer is undermined by chance, unwelcomed revelations. "Overnight Trip" is one of these quieter stories, and one of the most sensitive in all of Colter's work.

Overnight Trip

The street lights and the lights from the store windows shone gauzily through the rainy mist, as Amos slouched up Michigan Boulevard, peering now and then across the Chicago River to the matriarchal old Wrigley building, solitary, stark-naked white, and wet, against its glaring floodlights bursting up from the south bank. For just an instant the Taj Mahal flashed to his mind out of a colorful travelogue movie, but right off he realized it was very, very different; it had a *soft* glow—with placid, waxen tints. Ducking his head, squinting, and turning up his coat collar at the same time, he leaned his long skinny Negroid frame shrinkingly into the weather.

All day long, at his linotype machine, he had been in low spirits, and the miserable night didn't help any. Sometime during the afternoon he had vaguely decided to take the bus home, instead of the El. That way he wouldn't have to transfer; and, too, there wasn't so much commotion on the bus. He could think. Lately, he was always looking for opportunities to isolate himself—in order to think, to persist in this constant mulling over in his mind of matters that had, so far, completely foiled him.

He stopped and waited at South Water Street where he'd be sure of getting a seat—the ride out to 79th and King Drive was a long one. Soon he caught a No. 3 going south; all along Michigan Boulevard, down to the Illinois Central station at 12th Street, people were clambering aboard out of the near-freezing drizzle.

He settled back in his seat, tired; and, gazing out the window, his mind reverted to the thoughts that never seemed to leave him—slippery, confounding thoughts, and grimly anchored to the fate of his marriage. He thought of little else lately. But he never seemed to reach any solid conclusions—although he always started from the same point, the one premise he could be sure about: that he loved little Penny. To him, she was the near-perfect wife. But after that, his mind would stray off into connective dilemmas and motives—the whys and wherefores—and they were myriad and confused. She was many things to him: diminutive and shy, but straightforward and natural, too; so honestly herself, so lacking in cunning, and sweet—but, at times, thoughtful and uncommunicative. But, alas, it was the combination of these very qualities that had finally set up the extraordinary impulses tormenting his brain. For he now harbored a quiet, but fierce, urge to circumscribe and protect her—to shield her from what he considered a dangerous, seamy world. His rather set, channeled mentality could not see that the urge was fast growing into an obsession—even if suppressed, still a bizarre, whimsical, mad obsession. Actually, the soul-searching that occupied his days and nights was peripheral, for he could not bring himself to examine his odd purposes.

The big bus rocked and spattered along. He was now vaguely aware of the black woman sitting beside him, her eyes closed, nodding. Her chin occasionally dropped and rested on her chest, as she hugged a bulky, rumpled shopping bag on her lap. How wonderful, he thought, to be able to sleep on a bus.

His dismal day had begun that morning at breakfast when Penny mentioned that her friend, Bobbie, had invited her to go down to St. Louis with her—on just an overnight trip. Although Penny didn't say so, he knew she wanted to go—despite his cautious reminder that they hadn't spent a night apart in their whole six years of marriage. After that he had adopted an uneasy nonchalance. But all day long now he had seethed inside—Bobbie was a pert, saucy, friendly girl, and pretty too, but a divorcee and, he suspected, had been around. He could not understand Penny's really fine intelligence—the antithesis of her seeming naiveté; nor, for that matter, her frustration, her yearning for children—and her repressed sexual longings so puzzled by his once-a-fortnight ineptness. All this eluded his narrow, hedge-like mind—to him, she was a little girl (an orphan of eighteen when he married her) who required his sheltering, his craft, always.

He was forever cueing her on the precautions she must take for her own personal safety when he was not present: never cross the street without first looking both ways; always pull down the shades in the bedroom and bathroom at night—all the way down; never, for any reason, be out of the house alone after dark; make sure the apartment doors are locked all during the day; and never, never, under any circumstances, open the door to a salesman. But, although visions of harm befalling her from *any* quarter were to him unnerving enough, the image of harm to her from a *man* filled him with cold terror, drove him to cement up his mind against the very thought. It was more than jealousy. To him she was inviolate. And more extraordinary still—and quite beyond his comprehension—was his dark intuition that she was inviolate even against himself. Those fortnightly transgressions, he so regarded them, dismayed and saddened him—made him feel a ravisher.

The bus left 43rd Street—as his seatmate snored softly. Peering through the glass out into the wet night, he wondered what it was about life that made it so risky. You were always on the edge of trouble—at least, most of *his* life it had been like that. After graduation from high school, he had hopped bells and waited tables. Then along came the chance to learn linotyping. Being black, he knew the barriers existing then—from the union, as well as employers. But he went through it all—and succeeded; and for seven years now he'd had a job he prized—with a Chicago daily. And after he found little Penny and married her, he breathed easier, confiding to himself that he was finally "out of the woods." But now he realized you never were. This was hard to accept—although he was thirty—for his teachings had been the very opposite. His mother, now long dead, used to say to him, "Keep on agoin' fou-werd, Amos, and look to Jesus, an' everything will come out all right." It was a mild shock to regard this as possibly untrue. Still—he felt that Penny loved him. She always said so—that is, whenever he asked her. But he always had to ask her. He guessed that was just her way.

CYRUS COLTER

It was 6:20 when finally he got off the bus at 79th Street, and walked north, homeward—he always neared home with a warm pang of expectancy. He knew Penny was there, quiet and self-possessed—sometimes faintly sardonic—in her tiny rose apron. When he felt himself walking faster, he resolutely slowed his gait. He wondered if he shouldn't have brought her something—assorted nuts, maybe, or some dates. But he could never be sure what she liked; she never said.

Their apartment was on the second floor, and after using his key, and going up, he wiped his feet vigorously on the mat outside, and let himself in. The neat rooms were small and boxy—but there were soft colors everywhere; the modern furnishings still looked new, if rather miscellaneous, and the little sofa and two arm chairs were protected by plastic covers.

"Hi," he called toward the rear, pulling off his rubbers.

"Hi," the poised reply came back.

He walked into the bedroom and found Penny sitting on a velvet hassock, a blue dress draped across her knees, and a needle and thread in her hand. "What're *you* up to?" he grinned, reaching into the closet for a coat hanger.

"I'm taking up the hem on this dress. Can't you see?" She looked up at him and laughed softly. Like himself, she was medium brown-skinned, but small, even for a woman, and very cute. After hanging up his hat and coat, he bent down and kissed her on the forehead. Then it hit him—the dress and the trip to St. Louis.

"Hungry?" she asked.

"Oh, so-so." He was moody now.

She got up and went to the dresser and stuck the needle in a pin cushion, before hanging the dress in the closet. Then she started for the kitchen, and as always, he followed, slumping in a chair at the kitchen table, and, in a show of unconcern, began eating from the bowl of potato chips.

"You'll spoil your dinner," she said.

"Okay." He watched her turn the oven on, and sensed her preoccupation. "What'd you do today?" he asked.

After a short, busy delay, she turned around to him. Well, she'd stayed up after he left—she couldn't sleep anymore; she did the kitchen floor, as he could see; that was first; then started cleaning the two clothes closets—and what a job *that* turned out to be; then took a bath; and later, called Bobbie; after that, watched the two o'clock movie—it was pretty good today, for a change; then she took a nap; and about 5:30, started dinner. She crossed in front of him to open the refrigerator.

Quickly his long arm shot out around her waist, pulling her back onto his lap; her feet dangled off the floor. "Gimme a kiss," he whispered. She looked at him. "Come *on,* I said gimme a kiss." She turned her lips to his and closed her eyes, and he kissed her with abashed briefness. "Do you get lonesome sometimes—during the day?" he said.

She looked self-consciously over at the casserole just out of the oven. "Oh . . . not often."

After a silence he said, half to himself, "Maybe we ought to see the doctor again."

She swung her legs gently to and fro, and said nothing.

"Maybe next time would do it," he went on, still half in soliloquy. "Are you game?"

"Yes." But she faced him dubiously.

Then, as he kissed her dryly again, she suddenly with violence jerked her head and shoulders back from him, and viewed him sadly. "Oooooh, I want some kids so!" She closed her eyes with a little shiver.

"I pray every night," he said weakly.

"I *know,* but we don't give ourselves a chance!" The words came out first in exasperation, then pity. Conscious of her outburst, she slipped down off his knees, and pulled the refrigerator door open. When she took out the two salads and turned around again, he was staring gloomily at the door. "The rolls are almost ready." She was gentle now. "Go wash up."

He got up and followed her to the table and put his arm down around her shoulder. "D'you love me?" he said, and studied her profile.

"Sure."

"How d'you *know* you love me?"

"Oh, shoot . . . you just know things like that—you don't talk about 'em."

"I love *you.* Y'know *that,* don't you?"

"Yep," she grinned. He could see she was trying to be funny, but he caught the tenseness.

They finished a mostly silent meal. And afterwards, she lost no time in returning to the bedroom, and the dress, as, inevitably, he followed her. He sat in the bedroom chair, quietly smoking a big black pipe, and contemplating her. "What'd Bobbie say about going to St. Louis?" He could stifle the question no longer.

"She's going day after tomorrow, Thursday—and back Friday night."

"Has she got some relatives down there or something?"

"No, she's going to see some lawyer that's handling a case for her father. I didn't get it all. Something about her father's farm down in Missouri."

"D'you *want* to go?"

". . . I wouldn't mind. I've never been to St. Louis—just through there."

"Where would you stay?"

"At a hotel, Dopey," she laughed softly. . . . But then, after reflection, she said, "I don't just *have* to go—I didn't promise Bobbie for sure."

Her willing concession came so honestly, so childlike, it completely undermined him. Feelings of tenderness and remorse flooded him, and he longed to take her in his arms again. "Of *course* you can go," he said huskily. "If you want to . . . you can go."

At first she paused. Then tiny fires of elation jigged in her eyes. "I told Bobbie I wouldn't mind going—It'd be just the one night."

". . . Okay," he said, his voice now a dejected echo. "You'd better go pick up your ticket tomorrow."

"Oh, Bobbie'll get them!—I can pay her Thursday, on the train."

She sewed with purpose now, as he looked on helplessly. He hadn't expected such eagerness from her, and he tried to gulp the swelling in his throat. It was just a harmless overnight trip, he knew, but perhaps the beginning of something. She could like it. Next time she'd want to stay longer, maybe. He burned to seize her by the wrists, to wrestle her down, to beg her not to go. But he sat mute—ineffectual.

Thursday morning they were up before six o'clock. He sat on the side of the bed and rubbed his weary neck, waiting for Penny to clear the bathroom. He had pitched and tossed all night, and was jaded. If he'd had *his* way, this particular morning would have postponed itself—from day to day, perhaps—until he'd had a chance to think the whole thing out; for now he sat searching his past again, for reasons—he had a passion for reasons. The ache deep inside him—why? And why the fear? Was it punishment? What wrong had he done? But he could not make his plodding brain give answers.

He sighed and looked at his wristwatch—train time was 8:20; he was glad they wouldn't have to rush. They?—he realized it wasn't necessary for him to take her; he could put her in a cab. But he well knew he'd take her, in the end—even if it made him late for work.

Penny came out of the bathroom, in a robe too long for her, on her way to the kitchen to make coffee; she looked tired. As he entered the bathroom, he felt contrite for keeping her awake by his restlessness. He opened the door of the little white medicine cabinet to get a fresh razor blade, and saw her nail scissors on the bottom shelf; and there on the second shelf were two new powder puffs lying primly on a folded piece of pink Kleenex, next to a small can of tooth powder. He could never understand why she preferred tooth powder to tooth paste; it was probably due to that guff about the dentists using it; she *would* fall for a line like that; that's what worried him about her. In the left-hand corner of the second shelf there were a half dozen bobby pins, all placed in a careful row, and next to them were hand lotion, cold cream, and a lipstick. On the towel rack at his right he saw her spotless, bright-colored towels and wash cloths. He stood there holding the cabinet door open, studying the mute little articles, and reflecting how completely they all mirrored her personality—at least the part that could be mirrored; he felt he didn't understand the rest—he'd never really got inside her mind. How he hoped she didn't feel trapped with him. He knew you couldn't keep a woman trapped for long—even a good woman.

As he shaved, his mind soared back over and beyond his present state, to their first meeting—at a church picnic in Dan Ryan Woods. She was living with her grandmother then. He remembered he'd asked her for a date that very first day, and had felt some surprise at her ready "Yes"—he put it down to inexperience. They had four straight dates in two weeks, and she appeared to like every minute of it. Then—he couldn't wangle a date with her for two months; the only reason she gave was that she wasn't dating for a while. But after the two months they started again. And within eight months they were married. That all this was six whole years ago didn't seem possible. He had seen, before their marriage, how crazy she was for pretty clothes—she had very few of them—and one bright April Saturday afternoon, when they were still newlyweds, he took her downtown to a department store and bought her a beautiful, banana-colored spring coat. He would never forget her happy, earnest eyes, and her struggle against her natural reserve, when telling him how she adored it. And on their way home, she asked him if they could get a bottle of sparkling Burgundy—her grandmother always had it at Christmas dinner, she said—and when they got home and drank it, they were both giddy, and she giggled a lot. He recalled that a seam in her stocking was twisted, and that she wanted to make love on the day-bed—they didn't own a real bed yet—and afterwards (including the nap) she had teased him for what she called "stalling." He was still a little frightened, reliving it.

CYRUS COLTER

98

It was snowing lightly when, at eight sharp, they arrived in a cab at 63rd Street station. He had insisted on coming, despite her quizzical look when he told her. They walked stoically through the main station building out onto a long concrete platform that paralleled the tracks, where a small enclosure—with window walls—provided shelter from the weather. He was carrying her small off white bag—the one from the two piece luggage set he had bought her for their honeymoon trip to Detroit. They entered the enclosure and he set the bag down on the concrete floor, and they took seats on a bench along the wall and looked out at the lazily-falling snow—there was very little of it on the ground and the housetops, for it was just beginning. Penny looked calm, but he sensed her excitement. She wore a heavy grey coat and white gloves, but no hat, and he noticed how the tiniest particles of snow had melted in her hair.

"Gee, what a pretty snow," she said.

"Yeah." He was grave.

"Wonder if it's snowing in St. Louis?"

He did not answer right away; he took out his pipe and knocked it hard against the hot radiator along the wall, and patted his pockets for tobacco. "I wouldn't know, honey," he finally said. "That's three hundred miles from here."

"Oh," she said.

They sat without talking; he smoked his pipe and she watched the people entering. A blond sailor with a pimply face came in, with his girl. There were no seats left—at least twenty people were in the little enclosure now—and the two stood in a corner, only six feet from Amos. The girl's thin coat hung open down the front, so that, as they stood against the wall, the sailor ran his arm inside around her waist and pulled her to him, and they kissed wetly with open mouths. People pretended not to see. Penny kept her eyes out the window, and Amos sucked noisily at his pipe. A grinning black man with bloodshot eyes, slouching against the wall, and still reeking of his all night liquor, ogled the couple. "Hey, Daddy-O," he cackled, "cool it! *Cool it, man!*" Then he broke into a loud, gravelly, drooling laugh. Amos got up and stalked to the window, as Penny stole one more fleet glance at the pair. Then she looked at her wristwatch—and then toward the door.

"Oh, *there's* Bobbie!" she cried. Amos turned around.

"Hi!" Bobbie laughed, out of breath, as she shouldered her way, with purse and bag, through the stiff-swinging door. Penny and Amos called "Hi" at the same time—"How's everything?" he asked bravely.

"Fine, Amos! Howya doing, honey?" she said to Penny, panting and setting her bag down. She was wearing a red coat and a little white hat.

"You made it!" Penny said happily. "I was getting worried."

"You know *me*, honey—and I thought I gave myself plenty of time. Well, I'm here, anyhow."

Amos watched her with a grudging respect. Here, he thought, was a little girl who had married a big bruiser of a man, the fullback type, but who, whenever they got into one of their frequent brawls, was suddenly transformed into a she-puma—scratching, clawing, pummeling, shrieking; giving far more than she had to take. And she was so lithe and feminine—so frilly! That's what to him was so wacky about it. She was slightly taller than Penny, and a lighter brown—with a perky, cheerful radiance that explained her delight in the splashy colors of her clothes. But he recoiled from the heavy black eyebrow pencil she used. To him that spoiled everything.

"I got our hotel reservation," she said to Penny "—at the Jefferson."

"Oh, swell!" Penny said, as Bobbie sat down on the bench beside her; the two were soon lost in a busy, heedless chatter, as Amos stood.

The fine snow kept sifting down, for there was practically no wind. The big radiator against the wall started pounding and hissing—to Amos the heat was suffocating; he was wretched.

"Don't forget to take in the newspapers," Penny finally turned and said to him, glancing at Bobbie with a teasing little snicker.

"Okay, ma'm," he grinned. "Anything further?"

"Oh, I'll think up something else in a minute."

Suddenly the loud-speaker broke in raucously: "May we have your attention, please! Illinois Central train No. 21, *The Green Diamond,* for Springfield, St. Louis, and scheduled intermediate stops, is now approaching the platform. Please stand back of the white line, and watch your step as the train approaches!"

Penny had already grabbed up her bag off the floor, and Amos had to wrest it from her. Then he picked up Bobbie's bag, and slowly pushed outside ahead of them. All the people were coming out now, as the snow kept falling lightly. The giant orange and green Diesel unit came sliding in, as the rails and cross-ties settled heavily, sending tremors throughout the concrete platform. The bespectacled old engineer, wearing starched beige coveralls, sat two stories up, and looked bored as he eased the heavy coaches to a stop. The people were walking briskly down the platform toward the coaches, which looked nearly full already—most passengers had boarded downtown at the main station. When Amos and the girls reached their coach, he set the bags down for the porter.

"St. Louis?" the porter asked.

"Yes," Amos said. "So long, kids." He could barely speak.

Bobbie, now ahead, was climbing aboard, the porter just touching her elbow. "Bye-bye, Amos!" she cried. "See you tomorrow night!"

He did not hear her, as he bent down and took Penny in his arms. He had never seen her eyes so bright—like a ten-year-old child's—as she kissed him with embarrassment before the crowd. Then she hurried up the steps and, turning to wave, disappeared after Bobbie. He stood docilely aside. The ache had never been like this—he kept opening his eyes wider and wider, stretching them grotesquely to prevent the stinging, the brimming over. He dared not look.

But when all the passengers had boarded, his eyes searched the windows of Penny's coach. All the seats he could see were filled. Now the porter reached down and picked up his little portable step and swung aboard, and the train was moving—slowly, smoothly, silently, inexorably; her coach was slipping away. Then he saw her! She was leaning awkwardly over two seated people, waving to him, and smiling her childlike, artless, sad smile. He waved frantically just in time, as the stone station building ruthlessly cut off the view.

He stood there for a moment. And then he turned and slowly walked back toward the street. He knew she'd return tomorrow night, but that really she was gone.

William Attaway (1911–1986)

With the appearance of his first novel *Let Me Breathe Thunder* in 1939, and especially *Blood on the Forge* in 1941, reviewers were predicting a great future as a novelist for William Attaway, one on the level, perhaps, of Richard Wright. Like Wright, Attaway himself took part in the mass migration from the South—again, like Wright, from Mississippi to Chicago. Robert A. Bone called *Blood on the Forge* "by far the most perceptive novel of the Great Migration," but the book was to be Attaway's last novel. Perhaps because of poor sales, Attaway turned instead to more lucrative screen and music writing and would probably be best known today as the composer of Harry Belafonte's big hit "The Banana Boat Song" (Day-O-Day-O). Though such luminaries as Ralph Ellison and Addison Gayle found fault with *Blood on the Forge* for its pessimism and incomplete handling of the implications of Black violence, they agreed on the novel's impressive style and ambition. The book tells the story of the three Moss brothers—Melody, Chinatown, and Big Mat. Several critics (Ellison chief among them) saw them as three sides of Black consciousness: the artistic, the pagan, and the religious—though Big Mat's anger towards whites marked him as similar to Wright's Bigger Thomas. Leaving the South and the land, they come to an ill-fated life of work in a Northern steel mill. This excerpt describes one of their first nights in town and is notable in part for its portrayal of ethnic violence against Blacks, whom the steel mill owners bring in every time there is any strike talk. Further consequences of the Great Migration are touched upon in the Ronald L. Fair selection later in this book.

From *Blood on the Forge*

They hunched against one another, whispering and wondering, and big drops of rain, grayed with slag and soot, rolled on the long wooden bunkhouse. Passing the makings back and forth, they burned cigarettes until their tongues felt like flannel in their jaws. There was a crap game going on in the bunkhouse, but the newcomers didn't have any money to put on the wood. There was nothing for them to do that first day, except smoke and keep walking the rows of bunks. Windows stretched in the long wooden walls around them. And outside they could see the things that they would see for a long time to come.

A giant might have planted his foot on the heel of a great shovel and split the bare hills. Half buried in the earth where the great shovel had trenched were the mills. The mills were as big as creation when the new men had ridden by on the freight. From the bunkhouse they were just so much scrap iron, scattered carelessly, smoking lazily. In back of them ran a dirty-as-a-catfish-hole river with a beautiful name: the Monongahela. Its banks were lined with mountains of red ore, yellow limestone and black coke. None of this was good to the eyes of men accustomed to the pattern of fields.

Most of the crap shooters had been in the valley a long time. Some of them took time from the game to come back and talk with the green men.

"See them towers? That's where I works. The iron blast. Don't take the blast if you kin help it. It ain't the work—it's the head blower. Goddamn tough mick. Why, I seen the time when the keeper on my furnace mess up the blast, and the furnace freeze before you know it. That head blower don't stop to find who the fault go to. Naw, he run up and right quick lays out three men with a sow. One of the hunkies yanks a knife on him, but that hunky gits laid out too. I reckon somebody would a got that mick 'fore this. Only a man ain't much fer a fight when he's makin' four hundred tons of fast iron from one sun to the other."

The men from the hills were not listening. They were not talking. Their attitude spoke. Like a refrain:

We have been tricked away from our poor, good-as-bad-ground-and-bad-white-men-will-let-'em-be hills. What men in their right minds would leave off tending green growing things to tend iron monsters?

"Lots of green guys git knocked out by the heat—'specially hunkies. They don't talk nothin' but gobbler talk. Don't understand nothin' else neither. Foreman tell one old feller who was workin' right next to me to put leather over his chest. Foreman might jest as well been whistlin', 'cause when the heat come down there that hunky lays with a chest like a scrambled egg."

Yes, them red-clay hills was what we call stripped ground, but there was growing things everywhere and crab-apple trees bunched—stunted but beautiful in the sun.

. . . magnet lift the steel ball thirty feet up and drop her. Steel ball weigh nigh eight tons. That eight tons bust the hell out of old scrap metal. Got to be keerful not to git some of it in your skull. . . .

What's the good in strainin' our eyes out these windows? We can't see where nothin' grows around here but rusty iron towers and brick stacks, walled up like some body's liable to try and steal them. Where are the trees? They so far away on the tops of the low mountains that they look like the fringe on a black wear-me-to-a-wake dress held upside down against the sky.

Melody and Chinatown went out into the wet. The door closed behind them. The rain had lessened to a drizzle. They could hear the clank of the mills over the steady swish of the rain. Melody led the way. He turned away from the river and walked toward the town.

"Boy, this here North don't seem like nothin' to me," complained Chinatown. "All this smoke and stuff in the air! How a man gonna breathe?"

The drizzle stopped. Thin clouds rolled. Melody looked up. "Sun liable to break through soon."

"Won't make no difference to us if the sun don't shine."

"How come?"

"There won't be no crop to make or take out."

"Sun make you feel better," said Melody.

"Couldn't shine through the smoke, nohow. Long time ago a fella told me a nigger need sun so's he kin keep black."

Melody kicked Chinatown with his knee. Chinatown kicked back. Soon they were kicking and dodging around the ash piles. They were laughing when they came to the weedy field at the edge of town. Both men stopped. The laughter died.

Quivering above the high weeds were the freckled white legs of a girl. She struggled with a small form—a little boy who wanted to be turned loose. Other children were peeping through the wet grass. They began to chant, "Shame, shame! Mary and her brother—shame!"

Chinatown and Melody wheeled and hurried away. They had no need to speak to each other. In both of them was the fear brought from Kentucky: that girl might scream. Back in the hills young Charley had been lynched because a girl screamed.

Breathing hard, they followed the path until it became a dirt street. In front of them was a long line of women waiting in front of a pump shed. A few boys crouched underneath one corner of the shelter, held by a game with a jackknife.

"Look—more hunkies!" breathed Chinatown.

"Keep shut," warned Melody.

The pump at the edge of town watered about fifty families. Every Saturday the women were here in line. . . .

Then one of the boys spied the three strangers. He was on his feet in a second.

"Ya-a-a . . ."

A rock whizzed between Melody and Chinatown. The two men halted, confused. In the eyes of all the Slavs was a hatred and contempt different from anything they had ever experienced in Kentucky. Another rock went past. Chinatown started to back away.

"We ain't done nothin'," cried Melody. He took a step toward the pump shed. The women covered their faces with their shawls.

"We ain't done nothin'," he cried again.

His words were lost in the shrill child voices: Ya-a-a . . . ya-a-a . . . ya-a-a . . .

Melody backed after his half brother. A little distance away they turned and trotted riverward.

"So this how the North different from the South," panted Chinatown.

"Musta mistook us for somebody," said Melody.

"When white folks git mad all niggers look alike," said Chinatown.

"Musta mistook us," insisted Melody.

It should have been easy for them to find the bunkhouse. The river was a sure landmark. But, in turning in among a series of knolls, they lost direction and found themselves back at the town. . . .

"Maybe if I climbs that garbage . . ."

Chinatown started at a run down the road. At the top of the garbage pile he got his bearings. To the west the gray was tinged with faint streaks of orange.

"Over yonder apiece," he yelled, pointing westward.

At the cry, white faces appeared in the doorway opposite him. Nothing was said. Little faces grimaced between the overalled legs of the bearded father. . . . An old Slav bent like a burned weed out of the window. Great handle-bar mustaches dripped below his chin. With eyes a snow-washed blue, he looked contempt at Chinatown . . .

Chinatown slid down the pile of wet garbage. Hardly daring to hurry, he walked the middle of the road to the place where Melody waited.

"These here folks ain't mistook nobody." They made quick tracks in the mud to the west.

St. Clair Drake (1911–1990) and
Horace R. Cayton (1903–1970)

Cayton and Drake will forever be bound together for their collaboration on the ground-breaking *Black Metropolis: A Study of Negro Life in a Northern City* (1945). Drake was born in Suffolk, Virginia, graduated from Hampton Institute, and enrolled at the University of Chicago, focusing on the sociology and cultural anthropology of Black Chicago. He became one of the first Black faculty at Roosevelt University, moving to Stanford in 1973 to chair its African American studies program. A prolific lecturer and writer, his other most important book was *Black Diaspora* (1972). Horace R. Cayton was born in Seattle, the son of that city's pre-eminent Black couple, Horace Cayton Sr. and Susie Revels Cayton. His father, an ex-slave, settled in Seattle in the late 1880s and published the *Seattle Republican*. Aimed at both Black and white readers, it became the city's second largest paper. Yet even in the seemingly enlightened northwest, racism proved a decisive factor in housing and labor, and at one point the senior Caytons were served an eviction notice for lowering property values in their neighborhood. Horace Cayton Jr. soon became an activist and staged, among many things, a 1924 one-man sit-in at the segregated Strand Movie Theatre. His association with St. Clair Drake began when he worked under Drake as a researcher for the WPA in Chicago's Black Belt in the 1930s. He became deeply involved in Chicago's writing and art community, numbering Chester Himes and Richard Wright as close friends. Cayton's other major works were the 1939 *Black Workers and the New Unions* and his 1970 autobiography *Long Old Road*. This small excerpt from the massive *Black Metropolis* focuses on Bronzeville, Chicago's "City within a city," the importance of which I have already suggested in the introduction.

From *Black Metropolis*

Stand in the center of the Black Belt—at Chicago's 47th St. and South Parkway. Around you swirls a continuous eddy of faces—black, brown, olive, yellow, and white. Soon you will realize that this is not "just another neighborhood" of Midwest Metropolis. Glance at the newsstand on the corner. You will see the Chicago dailies—the *Tribune*, the *Times*, the *Herald-American*, the *News*, the *Sun*. But you will also find a number of weeklies headlining the activities of Negroes—Chicago's *Defender, Bee, News-Ledger*, and *Metropolitan News*, the Pittsburgh *Courier*, and a number of others. In the nearby drugstore colored clerks are bustling about. (They are seldom seen in other neighborhoods.) In most of the other stores, too, there are colored salespeople, although a white proprietor or manager usually looms in the offing. In the offices around you, colored doctors, dentists, and lawyers go about their duties. And a brown-skinned policeman saunters along swinging his club and glaring sternly at the urchins who dodge in and out among the shoppers.

Two large theaters will catch your eye with their billboards featuring Negro orchestras and vaudeville troupes, and the Negro great and near-great of Hollywood—Lena Horne, Rochester, Hattie McDaniels.

On a spring or summer day this spot, "47th and South Park," is the urban equivalent of a village square. In fact, Black Metropolis has a saying, "If you're trying to find a certain Negro in Chicago, stand on the corner of 47th and South Park long enough and you're bound to see him." There is continuous and colorful movement here—shoppers streaming in and out of stores; insurance agents turning in their collections at a funeral parlor; club reporters rushing into a newspaper office with their social notes. . . . Today a picket line may be calling attention to the "unfair labor practices" of a merchant. Tomorrow a girl may be selling tags on the corner for a hospital or community house. . . . This is Bronzeville's central shopping district. . . . At an exclusive "Eat Shoppe" just off the boulevard, you may find a Negro Congressman or ex-Congressman dining at your elbow, or former heavyweight champion Jack Johnson, beret pushed back on his head, chuckling at the next table. . . .

Within a half-mile radius of "47th and South Park" are clustered the major community institutions: the Negro-staffed Provident Hospital; the George Cleveland Hall Library (named for a colored physician); the YWCA; the "largest colored Catholic church in the country"; the "largest Protestant congregation in America"; the Black Belt's Hotel Grand; Parkway Community House; and the imposing Michigan Boulevard Garden Apartments for middle-income families.

As important as any of these is the large four-square-mile green, Washington Park—playground of the South Side. Here in the summer thousands of Negroes of all ages congregate to play softball and tennis, to swim, or just lounge around. Here during the Depression stormy crowds met to listen to leaders of the unemployed. . . .

If you wander about a bit in Black Metropolis you will note that one of the most striking features of the area is the prevalence of churches, numbering some 500. Many of these edifices still bear the marks of previous ownership—six-pointed Stars of David, Hebrew and Swedish inscriptions, or names chiseled on old cornerstones which do not tally with those on new bulletin boards. . . . Nowhere else in Midwest Metropolis could one find, within a stone's throw of one another, a Hebrew Baptist Church, a Baptized

Believers' Holiness Church, a Universal Union Independent, a Church of Love and Faith, Spiritual, a Holy Mt. Zion Methodist Episcopal Independent, and a United Pentecostal Holiness Church. . . .

Churches are conspicuous, but to those who have eyes to see they are rivaled in number by another community institution, the policy station, which is to the Negro community what the race-horse bookie is to white neighborhoods. In these mysterious little shops, tucked away in basements or behind stores, one may place a dime bet and hope to win $20 if the numbers "fall right." Definitely illegal, but tolerated by the law, the policy station is a ubiquitous institution, absent only from the more exclusive residential neighborhoods.

In addition to these more or less legitimate institutions, "tea pads" and "reefer dens," "buffet flats" and "call houses" also flourish, known only to the habitues of the underworld and to those respectable patrons, white and colored, without whose faithful support they could not exist. . . .

In its thinking, Black Metropolis draws a clear line between the "shady" and the "respectable," the "sporting world" and the world of churches, clubs, and polite society. In practice, however, as we shall see, the line is a continuously shifting one and is hard to maintain, in the Black Metropolis as in other parts of Midwest Metropolis.

Getting Ahead

The dominating individual drive in American life is not "staying alive," nor "enjoying life," nor "praising the Lord"—it is "getting ahead." . . . For thousands of Negro migrants from the South, merely arriving in Bronzeville represented "getting ahead." Yet Negroes, like other Americans, share the general interest in getting ahead in more conventional terms. The Job Ceiling and the Black Ghetto limit free competition for the money and for residential symbols of success. Partly because of these limitations (which are not peculiar to Chicago) it has become customary among the masses of Negroes in America to center their interest upon living in the immediate present or upon going to heaven—upon "having a good time" or "praising the Lord." Though some derive their prestige from the respect accorded them by the white world, or by the professional and business segments of the Negro world, most Negroes seem to adopt a pattern of conspicuous behavior and conspicuous consumption. Maintaining a "front" and "showing off" become very important substitutes for getting ahead in the economic sense. . . .

ST. CLAIR DRAKE AND HORACE R. CAYTON

Leaders in Bronzeville, like Negro leaders everywhere since the Civil War, are constantly urging the community to raise its sights above "survival," "enjoying life," and "praising the Lord." They present "getting ahead" as a racial duty as well as a personal gain. When a Negro saves money, buys bonds, invests in a business or in property, he is automatically "advancing The Race." When Negroes "waste their substance," they are "setting The Race back. . . ."

. . . Negroes feel impelled to prove to themselves continually that they are not the inferior creatures which their minority status implies. Thus, ever since emancipation, Negro leaders have preached the necessity for cultivating "race pride." They have assiduously repeated the half-truth that "no other race has ever made the progress that Negroes have made in an equivalent length of time." . . . "Catching up with the white folks" has been developed as the dominating theme of inspirational exhortations, and the Negro "firsts" and "onlies" are set up as Race Heroes. "Beating the white man at his own game" becomes a powerful motivation for achievement and explains the popularity of such personalities as Joe Louis or Jesse Owens, George Washington Carver or outstanding soldier-heroes. A myth of "special gifts" has also emerged, with Negroes (and whites also) believing that American Negroes have some inborn, unusual talent as dancers, musicians, artists and athletes.

In the period between the First and the Second World Wars, this emphasis upon race pride became a mass phenomenon among the Negroes in large urban communities. Race consciousness was transformed into a positive and aggressive defensive racialism. . . .

But Bronzeville is also a part of Midwest Metropolis, and Negro life is organically bound up with American life. Negroes attend the same movies, read the same daily papers, study the same textbooks, and participate in the same political and industrial activity as other Americans. They know white America far better than white America knows them. . . .

John Hope Franklin (b. 1914)

One of America's great historians, John Hope Franklin taught at the University of Chicago from 1964 to 1982, chairing the history department from 1967 to 1970, and serving as the John Matthew Manly Distinguished Service Professor until retiring and moving to Duke University to found the John Hope Franklin Center for Interdisciplinary and International Studies. Among his classic works are *From Slavery to Freedom: A History of African-Americans* and *Reconstruction After the Civil War. Race and History* collected major essays from 1938 to 1988. He served as president of at least five major history associations, including the American Historical Association, and sat on the boards of the Chicago Public Library and the Chicago Symphony. Recipient of over one hundred honorary degrees and many prizes, including the W. E. B. DuBois Award, Dr. Franklin also served on President Clinton's Race Advisory Panel. Yet all these distinctions never dulled his sense of the tenuous "citizenship" accorded African Americans. After a famous 1995 incident in which a hotel patron took him for a parking valet, he marveled again at how at any age any Black man could still be perceived as a boy. He was eighty-one at the time. The excerpt below comes from the Jefferson Lectures, which he delivered for the U.S. Bicentennial in three cities, including Chicago. Published as *Racial Equality in America,* it won the Clarence Holte Literary Prize.

From *Racial Equality in America*

As one views the problems of racial equality over the last two or three centuries, it becomes clear that a prime concern of the policy makers was to create distinctions between those who were regarded as equals and those who were not. To put it another way, many of the policy makers were committed to the idea that it was entirely possible to divide equality. The attempt to do so . . . would become not only one of the major preoccupations of Americans in the twentieth century but a major policy problem at every level of American society and government. The story as well as the problem of racial equality in twentieth century America is essentially the story of the struggle to divide a privilege or a right whose indivisibility would become more and more apparent.

. . . When Dr. A. L. Nixon, the black dentist in El Paso, Texas, brought suit in 1927 to challenge the white primary there, he began the drive to achieve political equality for blacks. The drive would be punctuated by court cases that put white primary officials on the run in all states where blacks were excluded. It would tax the ingenuity and creativity of those officials until they were finally brought to bay in 1947. It would culminate in the Voting

Rights Act of 1965 and the election of thousands of blacks to public office in the decade that followed.

The step that Dr. Nixon took was more than a challenge to a respected and venerated practice of race orthodoxy in the South. It was a signal to white Americans, North and South, that there were educated, articulate, and courageous black Americans who were no longer willing to accept the inequality that by this time had become as American as apple pie or major league baseball. Even in the complex and difficult field of economic life, they showed a remarkable determination to fight for racial equality. The New Negro, said A. Philip Randolph in his magazine *The Messenger,* would not be "lulled into a false sense of security with political spoils and patronage." He must have the full product of his toil that was being consistently denied him by management and white organized labor. And he stood for "absolute social equality, education, physical action in self-defense, and freedom of speech, press, and assembly." If they could not even aspire to these modest goals that would mark them as equals in the American system, then they would embrace more radical approaches, such as socialism as advocated by the Friends of Negro Freedom or even Black Zionism as advocated by Marcus Garvey.

But it was not radicalism that so many blacks embraced unless it was the radicalism of equal protection of the laws, which was guaranteed by the Constitution but was neither honored nor enforced. This was the radicalism of Ossian H. Sweet, the Negro physician in Detroit who together with friends had to protect his newly purchased home from the assault of a white mob in 1925. When he was indicted for murder for killing a member of the mob as it charged toward the entrance of his home, the question was whether the preservation of an "ethnic treasure" or "ethnic purity" was more important than the protection of one's life and property that the police had declined to protect. The jury thought it was not, and Dr. Sweet was exonerated.

No political party wanted to take notice of the problem of race, but the fear that its rival might do so prompted statements or actions that no leaders really wanted to take seriously. Political platforms that paid lip service to traditional American concepts of equality and fair play were to be forgotten, or at least the platform writers hoped they would be. And each major party seemed to be content if by its pious platitudes it merely neutralized the effects of the other's pious platitudes in the racial sphere. Nowhere was the plain assertion made that blacks were entitled to complete political equality. Rather, there was the hope that they would remain as inferior and as inconsequential in politics as they were in other areas.

One of the remarkable consequences of the effort to keep blacks politically impotent and generally degraded was the initially unnoticed black backlash to white intransigence which inevitably resulted in the erosion of that intransigence. Blacks reacted to the revived Ku Klux Klan, the white citizens' councils, and the other terrorist organizations with an equanimity that was somewhat disconcerting to whites. They laughed at the Klan parades as they recognized the swagger of Mr. Jones or the limp of Mr. Smith under their white sheets. And they began quietly but firmly to stand their ground in their demand for greater consideration as American citizens. Equally remarkable were the relatively modest demands that blacks made of white officials. They did not demand public office, but merely fair treatment in the administration of justice and an opportunity to participate in the political process. They did not even demand the same public accommodations.

One wonders what would have happened if blacks who wanted to register and vote in the 1950s had been permitted to do so. It is possible that they would have been more inclined to trust the white candidates for public office, voted for them, and manifested no undue interest in holding public office themselves. That is, of course, mere speculation. One wonders what would have happened if Montgomery whites had met the first demands of Dr. Martin Luther King and his associates-to-be permitted to enter the front door of the bus and to sit in seats reserved for whites when those seats were vacant. It was white intransigence that caused black voters to conclude they must vote and must hold public office in order to enjoy the first fruits of equality. It was white intransigence that caused Dr. King and his followers to decide they must have desegregated buses and must have black bus drivers in order to ride in dignity.

One supposes that the whites who were resisting the efforts of blacks to enjoy equality were actually operating from the premise that equality could not be shared. Since they assumed that blacks occupied an inferior position in the social order, they believed that equality could not and, indeed, should not be divided between blacks and whites. To the extent that they believed equality could not be divided they were perhaps correct. To the extent that they believed equality could be arrogated to one segment of society and withheld from another segment, they were woefully mistaken. Equality could be shared, but it could not be divided in a way that some would be more equal than others. For some three hundred years those in power in this country have confronted this problem and for most of that time they have succeeded in achieving the democratically incongruous feat of designating who should be equal and who should not be. Offhand, it reminds one of the paintings of Audubon's birds. They are attractive and even plausible, but some of the postures are anatomically impossible.

The incongruity has always been noted by some Americans, if only in passing. Some of the Founding Fathers noted it, but its solution had no priority on their agenda. The abolitionists were quite aware of it, but emancipation, not equality, was their main preoccupation. Partisan politicians were aware of it, but they were unwilling to run the risk of doing anything about it, lest their adversaries take advantage of their move, even for selfish and sinister reasons. Running through every consideration of the matter was the feeling that somehow this was not central to the survival or even to the progress of the country. Hence, one could not get too excited about it. This was a safe, comfortable position to take until about two decades ago, but it did not last. Indeed, it could not last in the face of a growing awareness on the part of an increasing number of Americans that equality was indivisible. . . .

It was one thing to deal with a few Negro leaders and reach some compromise arrangement with them, or buy them off or seek to discredit them and, failing in these efforts, to engage in combat with them and win. That was essentially the pattern for two centuries and more. It reached its climax in what I choose to call the Booker Washington Syndrome in which whites would deal with one Negro leader and having brought that leader under their control had no further worries or concerns. Although a leader like Martin Luther King was abhorrent to them, they at least could focus on him and try to control him, feeling that he was the key to controlling the entire range of Negro aspirations. The Federal Bureau of Investigation had this perception, and this led to its despicable and thoroughly un-American methods of seeking to discredit Dr. King. It was quite another thing to confront not one leader or a few hundred or even a few thousand blacks whose very size made them vulnerable, but to confront several million angry, impatient, aggressive blacks who were willing to risk everything in the battle to achieve equality.

By the 1950s the movement to achieve equality was no longer an elitist movement directed from the offices of the National Association for the Advancement of Colored People and the National Urban League, but a

JOHN HOPE FRANKLIN
113

mass movement; and the very numbers themselves dramatically changed the character of the movement. It was now the Movement for the Liberation of Black People or it was the Black Revolution. It was a movement that took to the streets in Alabama as well as New York to express the chagrin and outrage that blacks felt at having been denied equality for so long. It had more educated, articulate blacks than any earlier egalitarian movement could boast. There were teachers, physicians, lawyers, clergymen, and businessmen. But it also had enormous numbers of common laborers, maids, artisans, union members, and farmers. This not only provided a greater cross-section of the black population than had ever participated in a drive for equality, but it also presented to the general public a picture of solidarity that was hitherto unknown.

From the time of the founding of the National Association for the Advancement of Colored People in 1909, there had been whites in the movement for equal rights for blacks. Indeed, from the beginning, they had assumed leadership roles. Now, they were present in larger numbers than ever before. Some were leaders of interracial groups, others were leaders of religious or labor groups, while others came representing white organizations—friends of the court, as it were—willing to cast their lot with blacks for the common cause. But there were more than white leaders. There were hundreds of thousands of white followers, volunteering to assist in the struggle for equality. Held in suspicion by numerous blacks, they were frequently confined to yeoman service by those blacks who feared that the motivations and the aspirations of the whites might be different from their own. Indeed, some whites were driven out of the movement by some blacks whose paranoia, born of bitter experience, made it impossible for them to work with whites and trust them.

Some whites were doubtless motivated by fear and self-interest. If the movement got out of control and became violent, they did not want to be among those from whom Negroes felt alienated. There were many others, however, who were deeply moved by the opportunity, at long last, to participate in the realization of the long-deferred dream of equality. Some had even come to feel that equality was indivisible and that their own enjoyment of equal rights was a tenuous arrangement so long as equality was not shared by all. It was entirely conceivable that if the equal rights movement became explosive, an unsympathetic government might take drastic steps to repress it. In doing so, it could well assume the posture of a police state and jeopardize the equal rights even of whites. The example of the absence of freedom in those communities where racial orthodoxy demanded that all whites stand together against all blacks was a frightening spectacle to some. The example of South Africa, as the logical extension of that repression, was there for all to see.

Margaret Danner (1915–1984)

Margaret Danner began winning poetry awards in the eighth grade. In 1945 she won second prize in the Poetry Workshop Award at Northwestern, and went on to win such awards as a John Hay Whitney Fellowship (1951), the Harriet Tubman Award (1956), and the Native Chicago Literary Prize (1960). In 1953 *Poetry* published a series of her poems, and in 1956 she became the first Black to become assistant editor of the prestigious magazine. She was also Wayne State's Poet in Residence. One of the beloved figures of the Negro Renaissance, Danner published, among several books, *Poem Counterpoem* (1966), in which she and Dudley Randall wrote alternating pairs of poems on similar themes. The wonderful "Beautiful? You Are the Most," for Josephine Baker, comes from this collection. Her dedication to African culture brought her a grant from the American Society of African Culture and filled many of her later poems with African images. "The Bells of Benin," "The Christmas Soiree and the Missing Object of African Art," and "To A Nigerian Student of Metallurgy" are among best of these poems, as is "These Beasts and the Benin Bronze," which comes from the oddly titled *Impressions of African Art Forms in the Poetry of Margaret Danner* (1961), and opens with an allusion to Chicagoan Dave Garroway's monkey. Danner's poetry is noted for its delicate, beautiful complexity, and a quirky conversational style that suddenly gives way to insights into the nature of, and need for, beauty.

These Beasts and the Benin Bronze

Dave Garroway's Mr. J. Fred Muggs often thumps
quite a rhythmical thump with his feet,
doesn't he? Sometimes he seems pretty clever.

But irrespective of his Fauntleroy and other neat
and obviously dear apparel, have you ever
wondered whether he, if his very life

depended on it, could take a stave from a barrel
and curve a small, smooth, round stick? And while
it is evident (from the ever growing strife

resulting from the wider scope of guile)
that a talking snake is working overtime
not even in the bible did a dragon

horse or serpent use a sculpturer's knife
nor can as sacred a thing as a Hindu cow carve or
even draw one of those lovely Hindu girls, or a wagon

for that matter. And I've studied Bushman for years
and can, along with the thousands of others who
loved the big brute, attest to his dignity and near

human intelligence, but he couldn't have fashioned one true
free form, or if given a knife, whittled one whistle.
No history has chronicled a four legged sculpturer,

so how can we reconcile this beast epistle
to this pure Benin bronze for with all
the contraptions that moderns have to aid them
their skill doesn't compete
with these masques, so what beast made them?

Beautiful? You Are the Most

To Josephine Baker's stage appearance and her all nations adoptions

If to do is to be, take this lovely cat, here.
This elegant Siamese, take you and her,
with a purr.
Elegy?
It draws close,
but you melody the most.

Take this cat, here and you
with a flow, saunter, stroll.
It is there, too,
but
you are the whole.

This sweet little kitten's soft purr
nearly matches your cheek
in its grain, its contour, but this meek
little kitten, when its mittens unsheathe, cannot match
your lightning-like scratch.
Or
if this cat had the vision

would the ice in its blood
let it probe to the sore,
slit an incision,
and pour in this balm
that you pour?

Richard Durham (1917–1984)

Today most people would recognize Richard Durham as the author of *The Greatest*, the autobiography of Muhammad Ali. He also worked to analyze the Black press in Chicago for the Illinois Writer's Project in the 1930s, wrote a column for the *Chicago Defender* in the 1940s, and between 1948 and 1950 was the script writer behind the groundbreaking radio series *Destination Freedom* produced at Chicago's WMAQ. Ninety-one different scripts dramatized the lives of famous Blacks, including Crispus Attucks, Frederick Douglass, Joe Louis, Ida B. Wells, Gwendolyn Brooks, Jean-Baptiste Pointe DuSable, Buddy Bolden, Nat King Cole, Louis Armstrong, and more. "Nowhere else in radio history," writes J. Fred McDonald, "did a single series, written by a single talent over as long a period, project such a strident reminder of liberties denied and rights abused." It always began something like this:

> ANNOUNCER: *Destination Freedom*—dramatizations of the great democratic traditions of the Negro people—is brought to you by station WMAQ as a part of the pageant of history and of America's own *Destination Freedom!*

The excerpt below, from "Premonition of the Panther," is about another boxer, the great Sugar Ray Robinson, born Walker Smith. Focusing more on the inner turmoil of his subject, Durham deals less directly with Black history and social issues than in his other scripts. As this excerpt makes clear, however, Durham wants us to ponder the questions, What is Robinson's price? and Who really owns him?—questions with deep echoes of the slave past. The drama opens with Robinson dreaming he has knocked out and killed his next opponent, a kid named Doyle. His trainer, Gainsford, shakes him out of his nightmare, and talk turns to whether Robinson will make weight. He starts jumping rope and the rope's rhythm takes him on a flashback recounting his rise to fame. Briefly, his mother, Mrs. Smith, wants her graceful son to be a dancer. There's too much violence and brutality in the world, she says, and she especially wants him to stay away from the big bully boxer boy next door, who turns out to be Joe Louis. Robinson can't, of course, and one night after he watches Louis knock someone out, Louis gives him his gym bag, a symbolic mantle of boxing greatness. Robinson begins his career, hiding it from his mother. This excerpt begins just after he comes home with $3,000 made in boxing and tells his mother to send back all the laundry she does for others. She is furious. She knows he's been boxing. He says he likes it and has seen Joe Louis and their boyhood idol Henry Armstrong "pulling in a night what no poor man makes in a lifetime." Mrs. Smith remains defiant. After his she throws him out, Robinson, on Gainsford's suggestion, goes to meet "the Tycoon," his first big patron.

From "Premonition of the Panther"

> (*Sound: Then buzzer of an apartment, off, door opened*)
> TYCOON: (*A gigantic, florid frame. The secure arrogance of the ignorant*) Come in, come in, my man, we've been waiting

for you. *(Calls)* Middleburry—our Mr. Robinson a drink—please.

VALET: Yes, sir!

RAY: *(Coming in)* No thanks. I don't drink, sir.

TYCOON: Endangers your professional standing? *(Chuckles)* of course. Then let your trainer have one for you. *(Florid waving)* Mr. Gainsford—help yourself. Now we can conclude our deal for the—er—services of this , young panther. *(Appraises. him, chuckles)* Stand out there where I can see you! So you are the notorious "Sugar." Never lost a fight?

RAY: I—don't believe I know you—Mr.—

TYCOON: *(Brush aside)* It's not important that *you* know me. It's only important that *I* know you—and I'm willing to buy you.

RAY: *(Stung)* Who said I was for sale?

TYCOON: *(Cut in)* Of course you're for sale. Everything's for sale, depends on the price. Now—

GAINSFORD: Er—Sugar—he just means your boxing contract.

TYCOON: Exactly. Now I suppose you're curious as to why a man of my position would want you—

RAY: *(Correct)* Would want my contract—

TYCOON: It's all the same. Well—to put it bluntly—you're so fortunate because big-game hunting happens to be my hobby. *(Florid)* Look on the walls there, a tiger I bagged in Bengal. That elephant's from Ceylon. There's a python—gorilla, leopard, lions from Africa.

RAY: *(As before)* Where do I fit in?

TYCOON: Aha! Now—on the other wall you see my hunting guns: the best rifles, pistols, shotguns. Well—to put it bluntly—I'm seeking another kind of game: men—specifically prizefighters. For that I need a weapon, the best. You can punch, they say, faster and sharper than any man living or dead. You are such a weapon.

RAY: *(Aside)* George—I don't like this guy.

TYCOON: Affection doesn't matter! *(Goes on)* Now—in return for bringing me certain victories—mostly by knockout—I will assure you that no boxing club in the country will bar you. You will have clear channel to the title—as long, of course, as you—bring in victories. I must have excitement. Boredom kills me!

VALET: *(Uneasy)* Sir—remember what the doctor said about your heart?

TYCOON: Forget the heart—I want to talk business with these gentlemen. You'll sign? Of course you will! Now there a certain blow you use, young man, a sort of slashing, looping uppercut I especially like.

RAY: You mean the bolo?

TYCOON: *(Ecstacy)* Ahhhh I love it, I love it! Use it in your next fight—for I must have excitement, and nothing excites me as much as blood. *(Fade slowly to background, continuing)* I'll want to have action, action, plenty of action! None of your tame stuff, give me blood.

RAY: *(Close, wondrous)* So I entered the gilded gates of the professionals with my peculiar pilot always occupying . . .

(Sound: Sneak in under the stadium crowd sounds and sustain)

RAY: . . . two ringside seats and pounding his fist in fury throughout my bouts. And while I was throwing punches in the ring, I could hear his shout above the crowd.

TYCOON: *(Through crowd but close and clear)* Harder, Sugar, harder. Hit harder.

(Sound: Sneak out)

RAY: I often dreamed of his pounding fist until the night in June when we went to his penthouse to negotiate a new contract.

TYCOON: *(Ecstacy, chuckles)* An excellent performance tonight, my panther, excellent. I haven't had as much excitement since I hunted the wild buffalo in Mozambique. We'll discuss the future contract—but what blood you drew last night! What— arms. *(Begins to cough)* Middleburry! Help! *(Cough)*

RAY: He suddenly staggered and slumped with his head striking the tusk of his stuffed Ceylon elephant.

(Sound: Slump)

GAINSFORD: Maybe we can take up the contract another time.

VALET: *(With some dignity and regret)* Gentlemen, you've lost your contract. Mr. Dumbarton is dead.

(Music: Punctuate with drum impact)

GAINSFORD: *(Impression of some time passed)* I suppose—we'll look for another manager, Sugar.

RAY: No, another manager may be like the last—better, or worse. . . . If I go on—I intend to keep some of the fruits.

GAINSFORD: Good. Let's climb together.

(Sound: Sneak crowd)

RAY: And from Buffalo to Cleveland we climbed in the ring to-gether. In Pennsylvania, Illinois, Ohio, Indiana, Massachusetts, New Jersey, Florida we kept on the trail of the welterweight title. Tracked it down through forty fights in a dozen states. I kept on the trail, climbing up the ladder until I took the welterweight title. And as I climbed, I met many of my idols on the way down.

REF II: The winnah: Ray Robinson!

REF I: Winnah! Sugar Ray!

(Sound: Crowd out)

(Sound: Door opened)

GAINSFORD: *(Eases in)* Sugar—a gentleman here to see you.

RAY: George brought one to my apartment.

HENRY: *(As though his lips are split)* I'm Henry Armstrong—you remember me?

RAY: You know I do!

HENRY: My manager's been trying to get you.

RAY: *(Cut in)* And I turned it down because I can't stand fighting you—my friend—I couldn't do it!

GAINSFORD: Listen—the newspapers might say—

RAY: I don't care what the newspapers say! Since I was a kid dancing in school I looked up to Henry Armstrong as my idol—I don't want to help tear him down—

HENRY: Ray!

RAY: *(Stops, quiet)* Yes, Henry.

HENRY: Do you think I want to fight you, kid? Don't you think I want to see you go on and stay up there? Why do I come here begging for you to fight me? The way you punch, a man who's not in condition could get killed. Why do I ask? *(Quieter)* Be-cause I'm busted, kid. Because I need the money, and this is the only way I know how to get it. Don't ask me what happened to my dough. Who got it?—the gamblers, the promoters, the racketeers, the managers? Don't ask me. Fight with you'll draw plenty—enough—maybe to help me—get started again *(Pause)*. Will you fight me—pal? *(Music: Sting and under)*

RAY: *(Throaty)* I—fought him. I beat him. I kept clear of the gamblers and kept climbing, looking for middleweights, catching their 170 pounds in the criss-cross of my lefts and rights—listening to my trainer from the corner. Learning to outspeed and outpunch the bigger ones, scale myself down to make weight for the lighter boys.

(Music: Out)

GAINSFORD: Next fight's a welterweight, Ray.

RAY: What's his name?

GAINSFORD: *(Notices him)* Usually you don't even bother.

RAY: What's his name?

GAINSFORD: Kid named Doyle from out in Los Angeles. Fast. Got a good record. The commissioner made us put up fifty-thou-sand guarantee. They don't think you can make the weight.

RAY: Don't I always make it?

GAINSFORD: *(Nods, but is worried)* Yea—you make it. Someday you'll weaken yourself too much—you're ten pounds over the limit now. *(Up)* Mike! Get out the ropes and the sweat shirt. We're going to take some pounds off this panther.

(Sound: Rope in under)

GAINSFORD: *(Begins whistling "Big Noise from Winnetka")*

RAY: *(Low, working)* So the ordeal of trimming down to the strict one-hundred-forty-seven-pound limit was on again. I skipped until I felt sweat washing my torso, and I kept pushing back into my brain the dream I'd had that morning. But every hour when I stepped on the scale, I had trouble keeping the dream away from me.

(Sound: Scale clanks)

GAINSFORD: *(Whistles his characteristic whistle)* You'd better get what's in your mind out—Sugah! We got one day to go, and you're still four pounds over!

RAY: I can lose it! Send Mike after the gum, lemons, talcum powder, seltzer magnesia.

GAINSFORD: OK. *(Up)* You hear that, Mike?

RAY: *(Terse)* The gum was for chewing all day and splitting out all the saliva that came up. The lemon was to dry me out. The talcum powder was to be rubbed along my shanks while George's fingers hunted down any excess ounces of fat. The seltzer magnesia was to drink before lying down and sleeping ten hours and hoping that on the day of weighing, when I came into the boxing commissioner's office at twelve noon, the scales would bear me out.

(Sound: Under above, establish the sound of a rather large and busy room)

RAY: When I got there—I saw the boxer I was to fight, grinning at me self-consciously. He stepped on the Scales.

(Sound: Clank of scales)

COMMISSIONER: Ummmmmm Doyle you're under the wire. One-hundred-forty-six even. How about you Robinson?

(Sound: Clank of scales)

COMMISSIONER: *(Peering closer)* Ummmmm—well now—let me see—almost almost—Over—nope—on the head!

CAST: *(Relieved murmurs from onlookers)*

COMMISSIONER: OK, you men. Be in the stadium at eight P.M. The fight's on.

CAST: *(Murmurs from spectators while)*

RAY: I had eight hours to eat beef broth and steak, gain my strength and bearing, and at three—I lay tossing about on my hotel bed—afraid to sleep.

GAINSFORD: *(Concerned)* Look—Sugar, if there's anything wrong, we can cancel.

RAY: I just don't wanna sleep.

GAINSFORD: You got to rest!

RAY: I—was thinking about that dream!

GAINSFORD: Awww—that kid looks as healthy as an ox—You see his biceps?

RAY: *(Comforted)* Yea—

GAINSFORD: *(Sighs)* You took off six pounds in two days, and you're worried about—hurting him.

RAY: That dream—

GAINSFORD: Go to sleep *(Fade)*.

(Music: Sneak in with dream effect and sustain throughout)

RAY: It was three o'clock. My habit of sleeping three hours before a fight caught up with me. And I had the dream again. It was eight o'clock. The stadium was packed.

(Sound: In under with stadium crowd

RAY: I heard the fight bell and . . .

(Sound: Gong! Scuffling under)

RAY: . . . the crowd's growl. I whirled out of my corner, saw Doyle's tense face telegraph his punches and I *(in action)* slipped two fast left hooks under his heart, hammered my right home to his head, and when he ducked, slashed him with a bolo blow that spun him like a compass without a pole. He clinched, and for an instant I was looking into his startled eyes, so deep I could see my own soul. He slipped from my grip and hit the canvas.

(Sound: Crowd up)

RAY: *(Hushed)* I knew I was dream-ing—I'd dreamed the same thing twice before—but this time— the referee stopped at ten, not thirteen.

REF: One. Two. Three. Four. Five. Six. Seven. Eight. Nine. Ten.

(Sound: Crowd up)

RAY: This time my opponent's handlers jumped through the ropes and took him out of the ring. I fought my way to his dressing room:

DOCTOR: Are you—Sugar Ray?

RAY: A doctor looked at me for long time and at my fist. "Yes."

DOCTOR: I'm afraid—he is hurt.

RAY: How—much!

DOCTOR: All the way. Cerebral hemorrhage. I'd say—in a few hours—he'll be dead.

(Music: Sting and out. Hold music before cuing)

RAY: I put my arms around his bruised face, kissed him, and for the first time in my life wept—without shame—not only for him—but for myself, for my fellow fighters—fallen, stricken, climbing the ladder or trying to cut their niche in a blood and

RICHARD DURHAM

leather world. When I swore I'd quit, a wiser-older trainer shook his head.

GAINSFORD: No—you won't quit. And I'll tell you why. You belong to the crowds out there. They're your brothers. You're the keeper of their savagery and fighting skill. You're the weapon they hunt with. There's no quitting.

(Music: Sneak curtain)

RAY: He was right. I was made up of everything the crowd needed and screamed for. They had become my manager.

RAY: Maybe if another kind of crowd had molded me, had let me carry their magic bag, I would have been what Mrs. Smith wanted. But my crowd pays off to the panthers that climb the ladder without rings: the prizefight game. And they like to see their panthers—sharpen their claws. That is what I found when I threw away dancing shoes—for Joe Louis's magic bag.

Margaret T. Burroughs (b. 1917)

Writer of essays, children's books, and poems, Margaret Burroughs is best known for her art and her involvement in Chicago culture. In 1961, she and her husband, Charles, opened the DuSable Museum of African American History. It began in their home and has grown to become one of Chicago's most important cultural institutions. Virtually every poem in her 1968 *What Shall I Tell My Children Who Are Black?* (from which the poem below comes) urges the importance of Black pride and Black history. In "To Non-African American Brothers and Sisters" she attacks slanted, lying white history by extolling Blacks who invented the blood bank, performed the first open-heart surgery, "proportioned the Sphinx," and achieved other great accomplishments. "Homage to Black Madonnas" is one of several poems (along with a lecture titled "Message to Soul Sisters") cultivating Black feminist pride by uniting Sheba, Nefertiti, and Cleopatra with Margaret Walker, Mahalia Jackson, Rosa Parks, and Ida B. Wells in an expansive Black history. If this anthology needs a smaller, sweet piece of writing, the piece below is it; and even here Burroughs's sense of the importance of history still filters in.

For Eric Toller

Age 10 months, 7/3/1966

As soon as the first delicious chortle smacked the air,
I became a wiser, smarter, and more intuitive person.
Now I know all, see all, and sense all since you came, Eric.
I find that now I grasp ideas more easily
And am able to cut quickly through all kinds of red tape.
I extract that which is useful and discard the superfluous.

Acquisition of things for things' sake is not important.
I find that I am now able to dress smartly, but yet
I am unembarrassed by the conventional fiddle faddle of fashion.
My clothes are most comfortable now and most of all my shoes.
My patience, too, has developed to a very high degree
And I have discovered founts of understanding which I never
    knew.

I have become highly conscious of our folk heritage and lore
For I realize that it is my duty to pass it on to you.

So lately, I have been going over songs and rhymes and games
Of our people, and the stories of our great heroes and heroines.
Like Tubman and Truth, Douglass, Gannet and Wheatley and
     more.
For it is up to me to acquaint you with these noble ancestors.

I am more serene. I do not need to be up front at all times,
I now enjoy sitting in the background, observing, and meditating.
No longer do I need to run hither and thither, I find
It is pleasurable to sit at home, to reflect and to remember.
I enjoy sitting in sunshine or shade in parks or playgrounds.
Time has become very precious. I dare not waste it.

I plan most carefully my day and my work, to get the most of it.
I ponder what I have tried to do to make a better life for all.
And vow to try and do more, for when you ask me about it
I must be able to answer you truthfully, to be approved.

Now Eric, I find that wrinkles, a few gray hairs,
A slower gait, unexplained aches and pains, cease to be
Factors that frighten me any more for I know you would
Want me to have crinkles. Especially around the eyes and
     mouth.
So how does it feel to be a grandmother? Great! Simply great!

Gwendolyn Brooks (1917–2000)

Born in Topeka, Kansas, in 1917, Gwendolyn Brooks moved to Chicago as a youngster and stayed. At the time of her death in November 2000, she was one of the most celebrated poets in American history, a professor at Chicago State University, and the recipient of more than fifty honorary doctorates and a host of other honors, including the Lifetime Achievement Award of the National Endowment for the Arts, a long tenure as the poet laureate of Illinois, and induction into the National Women's Hall of Fame. For her dedication to others, especially the young, she was legendary and beloved in her own community and the world. From her stunning debut collection, *A Street in Bronzeville* (1945), through *Annie Allen* (1950, for which she became the first Black to win the Pulitzer Prize), and in nearly twenty other volumes of poetry, she maintained an astonishing ability for finding the perfect subject and language to explore, critique, and celebrate Black life and American life in general. The poems selected here speak to her championing of the young and are the second and third of a three-part sequence she called "Young Heroes." Brooks also wrote children's books, an autobiography (*Report from Part One*, 1972), other non-fiction, and the novel *Maud Martha* (1953), which follows Maud Martha's life in short, pungent, and highly lyrical passages from her youth through her brother Harry's return from the war. In between, she sorts out what she wants to be "on the inside," starts a home, observes neighbors, spares a pesky mouse, has children, works as a maid, and goes to a movie house where she and her husband are the only Black people there. Her marriage to Paul Phillips is central. Maud Martha accepts his kindness, endures his often misguided ambitions to climb in society, and suffers torments about the entwining of love, attraction, and race. In chapter 13, entitled "low yellow," she says to herself just before he proposes: "I know what he is thinking . . . That I am really all right. That I will do . . . But I am certainly not what he would call pretty." In chapter 19, entitled "if you're light and have long hair," they are invited to the Foxy Cats Ball, probably as a prelude to Paul's being invited to join the Foxy Cats Club, "the club of clubs," though Maud Martha notes that its main business seems to be just "being 'hep.'" Mixing with the glittering but shallow guests, watching Paul dance with the glamorous Maella, she says: "it's my color that makes him mad. I try to shut my eyes to that, but it's no good. What I am inside, what is really me, he likes okay. But he keeps looking at my color, which is like a wall. He has to jump over it in order to meet and touch what I've got for him." To be cherished, to be loved is "the dearest wish of the heart of Maud Martha Brown." "It oughta be that simple . . . It oughta be that easy," she says at the ball. But it's not. It's just possible—if you yourself endure, and love, and decide you will be joyous on the inside. From this wonderful book we have room for just a small taste, two very short chapters, 6 and 31.

To Dón at Salaam

> I like to see you lean back in your chair
> so far you have to fall but do not—

your arms back, your fine hands
in your print pockets.

Beautiful. Impudent.
Ready for life.
A tied storm.

I like to see you wearing your boy smile
whose tribute is for two of us or three.

Sometimes in life
things seem to be moving
and they are not
and they are not
there.
You are there.

Your voice is the listened-for music.
Your act is the consolation.

I like to see you living in the world.

Walter Bradford

Just As You Think You're "Better Now"
Something Comes To The Door.
It's a Wilderness, Walter.
It's a Whirlpool or Whipper.

THEN you have to revise the messages;
and, pushing through roars
of the Last Trombones of seduction,
the deft orchestration,
settle the sick ears to hear and to heed and to hold;
the sick ears a-plenty.

It's Walter-work, Walter.
Not overmuch for

brick-fitter, brick-MAKER, and wave-
outwitter;
whip-stopper.
Not overmuch for a
Tree-planting Man.

Stay.

From *Maud Martha*

6: AT THE REGAL

The applause was quick. And the silence—final.

That was what Maud Martha, sixteen and very erect, believed, as she manipulated herself through a heavy outflowing crowd in the lobby of the Regal Theatre on Forty-seventh and South Park.

She thought of fame, and of that singer, that Howie Joe Jones, that tall oily brown thing with hair set in thickly pomaded waves, with cocky teeth, eyes like thin glass. With—a Voice. A Voice that Howie Joe's publicity described as "rugged honey." She had not been favorably impressed. She had not been able to thrill. Not even when he threw his head back so that his waves dropped low, shut his eyes sweetly, writhed, thrust out his arms (really *gave* them to the world) and thundered out, with passionate seriousness, with deep meaning, with high purpose—

———Sa-WEET sa-oooo

Jaust-a Yooooooo———

Maud Martha's brow wrinkled. The audience had applauded. Had stamped its strange, hilarious foot. Had put its fingers in its mouth—whistled. Had sped a shininess up to its eyes. But now part of it was going home, as she was, and its face was dull again. It had not been helped. Not truly. Not well. For a hot half hour it had put that light gauze across its little miseries and monotonies, but now here they were again, ungauzed, self-assertive, cancerous as ever. The audience had gotten a fairy gold. And it was not going to spend the rest of its life, or even the rest of the night, being grateful to Howie Joe Jones. No, it would not make plans to raise a hard monument to him.

She swung out of the lobby, turned north.

The applause was quick.

But the silence was final, so what was the singer's profit?

GWENDOLYN BROOKS

131

Money.

You had to admit Howie Joe Jones was making money. Money that was raced to the track, to the De Lisa, to women, to the sellers of cars; to Capper and Capper, to Henry C. Lytton and Company for those suits in which he looked like an upright corpse. She read all about it in the columns of the Chicago *Defender*'s gossip departments.

She had never understood how people could parade themselves on a stage like that, exhibit their precious private identities; shake themselves about; be very foolish for a thousand eyes.

She was going to keep herself to herself. She did not want fame. She did not want to be a "star." To create—a role, a poem, picture, music, a rapture in stone: great. But not for her.

What she wanted was to donate to the world a good Maud Martha. That was the offering, the bit of art, that could not come from any other.

She would polish and hone that.

31: ON THIRTY-FOURTH STREET

Maud Martha went east on Thirty-fourth Street, headed for Cottage Grove. It was August, and Thirty-fourth Street was in bloom. The blooms, in their undershirts, sundresses and diapers, were hanging over porches and fence stiles and strollers, and were even bringing chairs out to the rims of the sidewalks.

At the corner of Thirty-fourth and Cottage Grove, a middle-aged blind man on a three-legged stool picked at a scarred guitar. The five and six patched and middle-aged men around him sang in husky, low tones, which carried the higher tone—ungarnished, insistent, at once a question and an answer—of the instrument.

Those men were going no further—and had gone nowhere. Tragedy.

She considered that word. On the whole, she felt, life was more comedy than tragedy. Nearly everything that happened had its comic element, not too well buried, either. Sooner or later one could find something to laugh at in almost every situation. That was what, in the last analysis, could keep folks from going mad. The truth was, if you got a good Tragedy out of a lifetime, one good, ripping tragedy, thorough, unridiculous, bottom-scraping, *not* the issue of human stupidity, you were doing, she thought, very well, you were doing well.

Dempsey J. Travis (b. 1920)

Born in Chicago in 1920, Dempsey J. Travis became a self-made millionaire, one of the country's most successful Black entrepreneurs. He is president and CEO of Travis Realty Company, but his many interests and his intense commitment to the community has taken him to board positions in the Chicago Historical Society, the Museum of Broadcast Communications, the New Regal Theater Foundation, and Northwestern Memorial Hospital. He is on the governing committee of the Film Center of the School of the Art Institute of Chicago, has been president of the Society of Midland Authors, and is the author of seven books. *I Refuse to Learn to Fail*, his autobiography, combines a nostalgic naiveté with an unflinching look at social obstacles as it swings back and forth between Travis's absolute faith in the promise of success and the difficulty of fulfilling that promise in the face of racism. The book begins with his first hard experience of racism at age five and his mother's tender response: she pulls out a beautiful black velvet jacket and says he is her beautiful black velvet boy. This sows in him the resolve never to fail. Much later, after experiencing such things as the brutal racism of the army, he gains his first major position as head of the Dearborn Real Estate Board. "At last," he says, "I had gained the attention of both the white and Black press in Chicago." Yet he soon realizes that "Prominence in the Black community and professional standing provided no immunity from discrimination by the insurance industry." His response? Launch a multilevel campaign against red-lining.

But Travis himself might quibble with the term "self-made." Undergirding his autobiography is, as Harvette Grey says in the introduction, "the conviction that African American communities can be strong . . . that African American heritage supersedes other issues, such as class." Chapter 5 begins: "DuSable High School nurtured many talents, including Mayor Harold Washington, Judge William Cousins, Dr. Allen Wright, Dr. Alice Blair and comic Redd Foxx, whose real name was John Elroy Sanford. Nat 'King' Cole was in my Spanish class." Travis is extraordinarily proud of this heritage of success, and thus self-making is always tied to pride in, and commitment to, the Black community.

From *I Refuse to Learn to Fail*

From Chapter 2: "My First Business Ventures"

1925 was a silver year for me; the year I decided to enter the business world at age 5. The idea of being a boy in business was inspired by the sight of a brand-new red tricycle, which was owned by Charles Murray Jr., an African-American lad my age. His father, Charles Murray Sr., drove a 1925 pale green Buick with side mount tires on both front fenders. The car was new, just like the tricycle.

Charles senior manufactured and distributed hair pomade out of five storefronts across the street from where we lived. Murray's Hair Pomade was to African-Americans in the 1920s and '30s what Fashion Fair and Soft Sheen are today.

I did not know if my father would ever own a new Buick, but I knew that one day I would use Murray's Hair Pomade, and I did. I tried to look like the handsome man pictured on the pomade's orange tin container.

A few weeks after I first saw young Charles and his tricycle, a man opened a barbershop in a storefront in our neighborhood. I asked him if he needed a young barber. He replied, "No, but I need someone to pass out my business cards," and said he would pay me 50 cents. I accepted his offer without telling my parents and started work immediately.

I was not satisfied with simply distributing the barber's cards in front of his shop as he had instructed me; I had to cover both sides of Cottage Grove which was a busy thoroughfare. While running across the street to give a man a card, I spied a streetcar, "Big Red," headed straight at me. I dodged it just in time—just in time to be hit by a black open-top Model T Ford coming up on my blind side.

When I woke up, I was in Provident Hospital at 36th and Dearborn Avenue. My mother and a man dressed in a white smock were standing at the foot of the bed.

My mother was crying and wringing her hands and asking, "Is he going to be all right?"

"He doesn't seem to be too badly injured," the doctor assured her. "All he seems to have suffered is a fractured left leg."

Mom began to smile a little, but didn't seem convinced until she leaned over the bed and tickled the bottom of my right foot. I giggled and her broad smile lit up the room. She turned to the doctor and said, "Yes, he's going to be all right."

My first business venture ended with me colliding with a car and my sponsor bringing me a basket full of apples, oranges and pears, and an extra dollar for service rendered beyond the call of duty.

My next entrepreneurial excursion began several months later, three weeks before Thanksgiving. The Sunday comic strips carried an advertisement that offered a toy electric train to any boy or girl who could sell 200 miniature, multicolored bottles of perfume.

My mother mailed the newspaper coupon to the company and I received a shipment of perfume on December 1. I was determined to sell enough to win an electric train for Christmas.

My sales efforts were riddled with problems. Almost everyone I approached sniffed from a bottle of the perfume and frowned. However, for reasons I did not understand at the time, some people smiled at me, handed me 10 cents, and told me to keep the perfume. I was unable to sell enough bottles to be awarded the train.

Disappointed, but not downhearted, I took on the task of selling the *Chicago Defender* weekly newspaper. During those days, paperboys had to pay for their papers in advance. I purchased the newspapers for 6 cents each and sold them for a dime. I usually sold at least 10 *Defenders* every Friday afternoon on the southwest corner of 35th and Cottage Grove, across the street from Walgreen, the second in the chain that currently boasts more than 1,000 stores. My weekly profit of 40 cents enabled me to go to the theater every Saturday and Sunday afternoon and have enough change left to buy candy and peanuts. I continued this successful operation until I was 9 years old.

From Epilogue

The Chicago of my yesteryears was 100 percent Black after sundown when the white landlords and merchants closed their offices and shops and went home to the suburbs.

The late Chicago Mayor Harold Washington crystallized the period between 1920 and 1942: "I went through the same Jim Crow nonsense that most Black people experienced in Chicago. I lived in an incubator. The South Side was my world. I would get on my bike and ride all over the entire South Side and not come in personal contact with a single white person."

In those years, the best and the brightest African Americans lived within a stone's throw of people who by 1990s standards would be classified as the underclass. Proximity to the middle-class Blacks provided a wide window of opportunity from which to watch and learn.

Some of the most powerful and successful of today's African Americans were yesterday's urchins. Their springboard from the streets to the suites came through observing or adopting as mentors, even vicariously, the Black achievers who lived next door, down the block, across the street or around the corner.

Although restrictive housing covenants, rather than individual preferences, defined where African Americans could live until 1948, the mobility of successful Blacks during the past three decades has created a void in leadership for those who stay in the old neighborhoods. There are few role models left to meet urban youth on the streets of their own communities and encourage them to stay in school and study hard so that they, too, can achieve financial security through legitimate avenues.

Role models in the 1990s spring not from the neighborhood, but from TV and movie screens. Young people watching *In Living Color* see Willie, the coke dealer, looking cool as he drives a Jeep Grand Wagoneer around the school. They identify with Baby Wimp the Pimp, who rides through the streets in his Mercedes Benz 560 SEL to monitor his girls. Who among their elders point out that the real role model on that TV show is Keenen Ivory Wayans, whose comedic talents and fiscal savvy are founded in self-discipline, determination and dedication?

Many big-money athletes live in white suburbs or in some sections of a city where they are oddities rather than role models. The Black idols jumped ship early, taking their talents, and investment capital away from communities that needed them both. They focus their future on the suburbs in spite of overwhelming evidence that the central urban areas will be the new frontiers of the 21st century.

Chicago Planning Commissioner Charles Thurow announced plans in September 1991 for the first phase of a $3 billion, 72 acre neighborhood development on the Near South Side, the second largest in Chicago history. Black gladiators are missing out on investment opportunities like these, in part because many of their white agents advise them to live and invest in more affluent and currently "acceptable" white communities.

Chicago Bulls home games are played in a stadium on the Near West Side near hundreds of acres that have laid dormant since the riots of 1968. The twist is a Black entertainment mogul, and not a sports star, has carved out a permanent financial presence in that community.

I arrived at this fact in late 1991 when I made a windshield appraisal of the exterior of Oprah Winfrey's Harpo Studios, Inc., which occupies a square city block on the Near West Side. Although I am not privy to Ms. Winfrey's investment plans, there is no doubt in my mind that her choice of location was a deliberate and very astute business decision.

Ms. Winfrey's entrepreneurial accomplishments and sensitivity have placed her in a class beyond category. She is to America in the last decade of the 20th century what Madame C. J. Walker was in the first decade of the 1900s. Madame Walker, a cosmetics manufacturer, was one of the first

American women of any race to become a millionaire independent of inheritance. Like Madame Walker, multi-millionaire Winfrey saw some old bricks and proceeded to mold them into a castle from which she and her multiracial staff produce first-rate entertainment.

The new Comiskey Park is an example of restoring a historic neighborhood—in this case, a Black community on the Near South Side where Scott Joplin lived in 1900. The White Sox players cannot reach their park without passing through the area. How many of the Black kings of swat have let down their buckets in the tradition of Booker T. Washington.

Buppies flee the Black community faster than rabbits run from a forest fire. The generation whose slogan is "I Got Mine" is too busy to be reminded they owe a lifetime tax to the thousands of Black and white Americans who bled and died in the mud holes of the South and mean streets of the North. The neo-establishment Negro is blind to the sacrifices that made it possible for them to cross over into Buppieland.

Clarence Thomas, Thomas Sowell, Stanley Crouch, Shelby Steele and other Black conservatives in ivory towers may philosophize about the plight of African Americans, but they cannot understand and empathize with the less fortunate citizens who must look like aliens from another planet when they are viewed from the prism of prejudice.

The stains of racism have been woven deeply into our national fabric. Had the impurities of racism been implanted or stamped, there might be an outside chance that they could be washed away by the tides of justice.

Hoyt W. Fuller (1923–1981)

One of the most revered figures in Chicago literary culture, Hoyt W. Fuller published articles and criticism for *Negro Digest* and *Black World;* the *Chicago Defender, Tribune,* and *Sun-Times;* the *Nation,* the *New Republic,* and many other periodicals. He published poetry and fiction, and the non-fiction book *A Journey to Africa* (1971), from which the following excerpt comes. But it was as an editor for *Ebony,* and especially as the founder of *Negro Digest* (which later became *Black World*), and through his tireless championing of Black writers and writing that he made perhaps his greatest contributions. Many see him as a father figure, the "main man" not only of Chicago writing, but for much of American Black writing and cultural production from 1960 on, including rap and hip-hop. Addison Gayle has called Fuller's "Towards a Black Aesthetic" (1967) "one of the seminal documents in Black American criticism." "The great bard of Avon," wrote Fuller in that enormously influential essay, "has only limited relevance to the revolutionary spirit raging in the ghetto." His goal was to "set in motion the long overdue assault against the restrictive assumptions of the white critics." "In Chicago," he wrote,

> the Organization of Black American Culture has moved boldly towards a definition of a black aesthetic. In the writers' workshop sponsored by the group, the writers are deliberately striving to invest their work with the distinctive styles and rhythms and colors of the ghetto, with those peculiar qualities which, for example, characterize the music of a John Coltrane or a Charlie Parker or a Ray Charles.

In this and many other articles, Fuller defined a Black cultural mission that gave direction and assurance to an extraordinary number of artists and writers. Robert L. Harris wrote that "Hoyt W. Fuller lived as a beacon in the murky waters of race that challenge the identity, if not the sanity, of every Afro-American." But as the excerpt below shows, Fuller could issue such clarion calls because he himself was perhaps the most restless seeker of them all. Fuller begins. *A Journey to Africa* with a profile of Sekou Toure, president of the Republic of Guinea, as well as the French West African–wide Union of Black African Workers, then 700,000 strong. He makes much of his subsequent meetings with Toure, probing through him and other leaders both the immensity of many African dilemmas, as well as the real power that Black men have to solve them, socially, technologically, politically. The prospects are a real mixed bag. "I could rhapsodize . . . and marvel at the incredible energy of the people," he writes, "but the overwhelming fact about Africa is its helplessness, the staggering task to be performed in transforming potential into power." On a return trip in 1969, he notices progress, and the book ends with some optimism in an African "coming of age"—which is nonetheless tempered by his clear-eyed assessment of "the staggering task." In the end, Africa fulfills his "desire for rootedness" and gives him international insight into the position of American Blacks.

Often during my first year of voluntary exile in Europe in 1958, thinking with ambivalent feelings about the inevitable time when I would have to go home again, lines from a poem by the French poet Charles Pierre Baudelaire would haunt me . . .

> "You'll not find another place, you'll not find another sea.
> This city is going to follow you. You'll stray
> In the same streets. In the same suburbs you'll grow gray;
> Amid these same houses you'll reach old age.
> You'll always find this city. Another?—It's a mirage."

I had run away from America. It was an old, many times told story. In the year before I packed up and sailed to France I had spent much of the time futilely trying to find some slot in which I could fit with a reasonable degree of comfort and satisfaction. I had quit *Ebony* magazine, for the magazine did not seem to be moving in any direction that it seemed important for me to go, and it was extremely difficult in 1957 to find meaningful work that also would not threaten my sense of racial integrity in the white publishing world. I could adjust neither to what seemed to me irrelevance nor to "tokenism" in employment, and that meant that my alternatives were effectively exhausted. I could not play the game of "making it" when the cost of winning was the loss of my self respect.

My failure to find an acceptable job was not the most important reason for my flight to Europe. It was merely the ultimate spur. Every single day in America had brought moments when there was need to find some refuge from the nerve-wrenching reality of the omnipresent war of race. A report of some incident in the papers, the rudeness of some waiter in a restaurant, a walk through the Black slums, or a drive (it had to be a drive) through a white suburb, an encounter with some unwittingly patronizing "liberal"—any of these things, and countless others. But even more than these things, the terrible apathy of "educated" and "affluent" Black people plunged me into impotent rage. Three years after the Supreme Court had ruled school segregation to be unconstitutional, bigots had unleashed a virtual reign of racist terror against Black people all over the country, and the response of the ablest, most articulate and resourceful segment of the Black population was pathetic: they either tucked their tails and said nothing, fearing to risk their jobs or their status; or else they mouthed the same old cliché about "discrimination" and "justice" and "equality" that Black people had been safely echoing for 300 years. In Chicago, where a unified stand of a few hundred influential Blacks would have turned the political machine into panic, the reaction against police brutality and economic colonialism was shameful silence. And Chicago was merely prototypical. Black people seemed to lack the courage to act in their own self-interest. I had seen Europe before, and I knew it was not "another place." Still, in Europe there was at least temporary escape from the poisonous climate of hate and oppression that threatens to smother America.

For more than a year I lived in a salmon-colored miniature villa that sits in the middle of a huge garden off the main street of Terrene, one of the foreign-occupied subdivisions of Palma de Mall Orca. It is a lovely, romantic house, surrounded by flowers and fruit trees, and I was happy there. Sometimes as I sat in the living room and gazed out at the people and traffic beyond the garden, the realization would crowd in on me that in no similar resort city in my own country would I be able to live unhorsed in such a setting. On these occasions the old rage would stage its abortive riot in me and I would turn for relief to pleasanter thought than home. I found myself thinking more frequently of Africa. I had for years nursed a vague ambition to go there. Why not now?

The decision then—not the desire—was sudden. I knew that, being so close to the African continent as the mid-Mediterranean, I would forever regret it if I did not, whatever the difficulties, make the effort. I also thought that I would—if I liked it and if it was possible—try to find some work there, perhaps tutoring English privately. I thought I would like to spend a year in Africa, if no longer. Perhaps what talents I possessed would be needed. I decided on the new Republic of Guinea for two reasons: first, because I wanted practice in the French language; and second, because the country was now independent and it was not necessary to apply for a visa to France which ordinarily makes certain restrictions on visits by foreigners to its African territories.

When I mentioned to a French friend in Palma that I was planning a trip to Guinea, he said: "Africa is not what you think. You will be disappointed." This was four months after a muscular, iron-jawed Mailman with a legendary ancestry had led the territory to sever its political links with France. In rejecting Charles de Gaulle's crucial new constitution, Sekou Toure had found appropriately dramatic words with which history could record the moment. "We prefer poverty in freedom," he had orated, "to riches in slavery."

My French friend, being understandably patriotic, was unimpressed with Toure's brave rhetoric. "They'll find out there's more to independence than a lot of hot air," he said. "Before a year has passed they'll be crying for the French to come back."

And then he told a Guinea story currently making the rounds among Palma's French nationals. The story went that the day following the fact of independence, a block-long queue had formed outside the Conakry railroad station awaiting the through train to Niger. Guineans who had never been able to afford a train ride flocked to the station. But when told that they would still have to buy tickets, just as before, a roar of disillusioned protest ran through the crowd. "What good is independence," they demanded, "if you can't ride free?"

Algiers loomed in the distance when I mounted to the deck early the next morning. It was a fabulous sight. In the pre-dawn darkness the city lay like a dazzlingly jeweled mound against the sky. It was, of course, illusory. When I came up again after breakfast Algiers in the daylight was no jewel. It was impressive, though. Built on hills, the city rises from the sea and stretches out on both sides so that from the sea, it looks like a giant octopus in repose. An octopus scourged with cancer. The left side of the giant head is bright and healthy; the right side gutted and ravaged like a diseased cheek.

Casablanca, unlike Algiers, does not rise up from the harbor. . . . As its name denotes, it is a white city, while Algiers strikes the eye as gray, and it seems spacious rather than cramped. It is an attractive city and, like Algiers, quite French. The medinahs, the Moroccan versions of the Casbah, are equally teeming and squalid. Many Moroccans are "Black," I was surprised to see. An unusual number of the bus drivers and civil Servants might have been refugees from Chicago's South Side. A friendly Frenchman, a merchant who had no plans to quit the city, treated me to a drive through the villa-thick suburbs and along the new white beach where many of the pastel houses and hotels are occupied by American Air Force personnel.

All along the avenue leading from the harbor, and in the heart of town, flashily dressed young hustlers called out, "Hey, man!", and sidled up to peddle anything from watches to women in the latest jive jargon. This breed had been noticeably absent on the streets of downtown Algiers.

At Algiers, when I stepped off the gangplank onto the ground, I had paused, marking with a secret moment of solemnity the touch of my feet upon the soil of Africa. There was not, as I would have liked, some significant emotion to be afterwards associated with the occasion. And, indeed, except for the brief excursion into the Casbah, Algiers might have been a city in France or some other country along the north shore of the Mediterranean. Casablanca was more African, but only because the Moroccans were more in evidence in the streets and shops and ordinary service jobs. The bazaars and markets and medinahs, like tourist traps, did not appreciably alter the French—and therefore European—character of the city.

But Dakar, for me, was Africa. Perhaps not the Africa of Solomon and Abyssinia and Egypt, of Hannibal and the old Roman Empire, but the Africa evoked by the word as it is popularly used in America. The "dark" continent, the source of slaves and tribes and beasts and jungles and fever. A word rife with negative connotations. At first I could see only the people. There was about them a surpassing serenity. A serenity and a sureness. It began to be clear to me that an element of their visual mysteriousness was the absence in their faces of the indelible imprint of harassment and fear and of their counter reactions, sullenness and combativeness, emotions that haunt the Black American. It was with joy that I watched the women on the streets, moving like so many ebony monarchs, their heads high, their shoulders straight, their backs slightly swayed, their hips swinging free and sinuously as if to some voluptuous inner music. Of course, I knew the origin of their grace. There they were on the streets and in the markets, balancing burdens effortlessly on their heads. And the vivid, almost screeching colors that they bustled and skirted and draped like saris about their bodies were right for them, perfect. Dark-skinned Black American women are intimidated by brilliant colors. They turn their backs on them. For the aquamarines and tangerines and fuchsias would call attention to their skin, and that would never do! In America, one does not accentuate one's blackness; one tries to hide it beneath creams and paints and powders. And failing that, one plays it down with quiet, dark and neutral colors, appropriately matched with a bland, apologetic manner.

But one understands their shyness. For the Black American, all his years on the American continent, has been fleeing the color he associates with his shame. He has been running from the color which forever marks him, in his imposed language and religion, as not quite a man. One understands this. One understands when a friend's mother, learning her son wants to marry a dark-skinned girl, threatens to take poison if he does. "Think of the children," she moaned. "They will be black." And one understands when a co-worker, regarding a fair-skinned, straight-haired little girl, says, "Now that's a fine example of selective breeding." And what he meant, what Blacks in America go on proving, is that the fairer the skin and the straighter the hair the closer they come to feeling whole. . . .

From "The African Actuality: A Personal Journey"

It was five years later after I had come home, in 1965, that I decided again to go to Africa, this time under the auspices of a John Hay Whitney fellowship. It had been my plan to return to Guinea, to tour the country, check out its economic problems and progress, and perhaps write about the country and its valiant struggle for survival. Much had happened in Guinea since my visit there, and a great deal of what had happened had soured the Government even further on America and Americans. Unhappily, the suspicion which the Guineans directed at Americans also included Black Americans, for some so-called "soul brothers" had been prominent in the clandestine activities which had successfully undermined African leadership unacceptable to the West. My overtures and inquiries were met with general coldness, or even with silence, and so I elected to visit Senegal again instead. I was in Senegal when the word came, in February 1966, that Kwame Nkrumah, on a mission to the Far East to persuade battling Indo-Chinese brothers against murdering each other for the benefit of the Western vulture, had been deposed as president of the country he had led to independence from the British. Black representatives of the American government, so the reports say, played key roles in plotting Nkrumah's fall. Sekou Toure, in a brotherly gesture and in the spirit of Pan-Africanism, gave Nkrumah refuge in Guinea. I understood perfectly then why Guinea had not rolled out the welcome mat for me.

Senegal was (is) something else. On my first visit to the country, Senegal was one of the territories which made up French West Africa (the other territories were Upper Volta, Niger, the Ivory Coast, Dahomey, Mauritania and the Sudan-the latter now Mali), and Dakar was the administrative capital of that branch of the French African empire. Leopold Senghor, the eloquent poet-statesman who was now president of the republic had been territorial delegate to the French Parliament in Paris. The French were omnipresent and omnipotent, and the bud of nationalism among the Senegalese gave little indication that it might burst into bloom. In fact, it was not easy to discover among the black intellectuals in Dakar in 1959 voices raised against the French presence and French dominance. Senegalese intellectuals glowed with pride at their status as *evolues* and at the French reputation for racial tolerance. They were French Africans, moving with some ease in French society in Dakar and looking to Paris as their cultural and spiritual capital with no less fervor and dedication than the white men whose heritage was installed there. When I returned to Senegal in 1965, the color of the man who occupied the governmental palace had changed—that man was, in fact, Leopold Senghor himself—but the French remained omni-present and omnipotent although political independence had come to the country in 1960. Nationalism had blossomed briefly, and Senghor—the great patron of freedom and patriarch of Negritude—had found it expedient, as a matter of practical politics, to slap good and patriotic brothers in prison. Clamor for black control shook up the lovely little university nestled beside the sea, but those students and professors who agitated learned quickly enough the overriding fact of Senegalese—and Black African-reality: the fuel that powered the machinery of government came from storerooms owned by white men.

Nor had Senegal's rather large Black intellectual community undergone any significant ideological conversion. Most of these astonishingly vital and attractive men and women still thought of themselves as French Africans, and if they never questioned their loyalty to France it was because, in their view of things, the idea of the necessity of choice between the two countries was never conceivably an issue. There was little discernible difference between the Frenchman's attitude toward Senegal and its problems and the attitude of many Senegalese intellectuals toward his country and its problems. . . .

What the Senegalese intellectuals suffer from is the Black skin-white mask syndrome so brilliantly delineated by Franz Fanon. Having accepted colonialism and the values and images of the colonizers, they are incapable of acting as free men, as Africans who hold in their hands the fate, first, of their nation and, finally, of their ravaged and debased continent. "In underdeveloped countries, we have seen that no true *bourgeoisie* exists;" Fanon wrote, "there is only a sort of little greedy caste, avid and voracious, with the mind of a huckster, only too glad to accept the dividends that the former colonial power hands out to it. This get-rich-quick middle class shows itself incapable of great ideas or of inventiveness. It remembers what is has read in European textbooks and imperceptibly it becomes not even the replica of Europe, but its caricature. . . . For 95 % of the population of underdeveloped countries, independence brings no change. . . . These hands of government are the true traitors of Africa, for they sell their country to the most terrifying of its enemies: stupidity. . . . In fact, the *bourgeoisie* phase in the history of underdeveloped countries is a completely useless phase. When this caste has vanished, devoured by its own contradictions, it will be seen that nothing new has happened since independence was proclaimed, and that everything must be started again from scratch. . . . The truth of the latter observation was never so evident as in Senegal, where everything remains to be done. At the university, of course, a vanguard of students know this, inevitably, and they are anxious to begin, first by Africanizing their university, by making it relevant to their true situation and to their real needs, and then by taking over the institutions which control the country, transforming or demolishing them if they do not serve the interests of the people. And several times in recent years, the government has cracked down on the students, making some small concessions in the process but leaving the university, for all practical purposes, a bastion of European ideas and outlook fully in the control of Europeans.

My months in Senegal taught me another dreary lesson: that the American black *bourgeoisie* was not merely content to serve out its useless existence emulating white people in America but that now its members had embarked on far more dangerous and demeaning adventures. They were scattered all over Africa—in the Peace Corps, in the various embassies, as agents of international aid organizations, as teachers, consultants, specialists and representatives of American industries—using their black skins as a shield behind which they carried out schemes calculated to keep Africa weak, exploited and dependent. In Dakar, I met several such people who were conscious agents, blacks who wore their rank with an open arrogance, who lived in a kind of splendor they had never known in America, and who reveled in the fact that they were "making it" on the international scene. As far as I could tell, they made no identification with Africa and its enormous problems beyond a patronizing expression of intellectual sympathy. There were, of course, black Americans in Senegal who had the interests of the Africans at heart—Mercer Cook, the ambassador at that time and an old hand at relating with Africans, among them—but there were enough of the others to lead one to the edge of nausea.

One of these days, the full, awful story of the American Secret Service's role in the First World Festival of Negro Arts at Dakar in 1966 will be told, stripping of honor certain esteemed Black Americans who lent their prestige to the effort to hold to the barest minimum the political impact of that unprecedented event. . . . Almost alone, it seemed, I raged against the lack of interest in involving Black Americans in the Festival. . . . On one occasion, weary at my repeated implications of conspiracy in keeping Black America ignorant of the great Festival, an agent of the American Government (and of the CIA?) finally let his red hair down. *Yes,* he told me, with a sneer that expressed all his racist feelings, *we are keeping Black radicals away from the Africans, and we will succeed. There's a damned good chance that we'll have the French back in control here after a few years!*

I remembered that man's explosion every time I entered a shop in Dakar or stopped in an airline office or entered a restaurant or a movie or a hotel, for all these places, and others like them, are owned by Frenchmen. His words haunted me every time I saw Leopold Senghor at a public event, his smiling Norman wife beside him. *Senegal still belongs to France . . . Senegal still belongs to France. . . .*

The American bigot's words were still with me a year later in Paris when, in exasperation, I stalked out of a party, unable to bear the pretensions of a group of vigorous young Senegalese hustlers who found existence in the *demi-monde* of Paris preferable to the life of building a nation at home. It was all of a part, of course. Fanon had said it all.

But there had been other times and other men at Dakar. I remembered spending a quiet evening at the home of a Paris-educated professor, a superior man then out of favor with the Senghor regime. He trusted me enough to include me in a conversation with a colleague, a young man who taught in the local *Ecole Superiere*. These men understood how important it was that Senegal—that Africa—be truly free. They knew that power in Africa would liberate Black men in the Americas and that, together, Black men in Africa and Black men in the Americas could alter the shape of the world. . . .

Herman Cromwell Gilbert (1923–1997)

Among many jobs, Herman Cromwell Gilbert worked as a farm hand, a union coordinator, a congressional chief of staff (for Chicagoan Gus Savage), the administrator of the Illinois Bureau of Employment Security, a community organizer, and the executive vice-president of Path Press, an important publisher of Chicago Black writing. His first novel, *The Uncertain Sound* (1969), was well received, and his second, *The Negotiation: A Novel of Tomorrow*, a near sensation. Set amid racial tensions brought to a head by the Reagan administration, it imagines the struggles of setting up a separate Black state. Filled with the kinds of political and business intrigues Gilbert witnessed firsthand in several of his jobs, the book also sharply etches the power plays attending personality politics. Ultimately, what is clashing are visions of America as fundamentally different as those fought out in the Civil War. The excerpts below come from a prologue, and then a dream-like interlude (in italics here as in the original) that occurs in the head of Preston Simmons, the computer-selected chief negotiator of the separate state. It sums up much of the action and some of the main ideas of the novel while also showing how the larger political situation intersects with relationships between individuals.

From *The Negotiation: A Novel of Tomorrow*

PROLOGUE ONE

It was shortly after 8:00 P.M. on Tuesday, September 1, in the Year of Our Lord 1987. The polls had just closed in the most unusual election ever held in the United States of America. Unlike in times past, white Americans had not participated in this election. Only black Americans had been eligible to vote, and they had flocked to the polling places in unprecedented numbers. Later an analysis would reveal that of those black citizens registered to vote, eighty-five percent had voted.

It was not an election of candidates to public offices. Neither was it a vote to approve bond issues for the construction of buildings, bridges, roads or other physical structures. Rather it was a referendum, through a yes or no vote, to ratify or reject the following proposition:

> The Black American Council is hereby authorized to negotiate with the United States of America for the creation of a separate and independent state, within the continental limits of the United States, for American citizens of African descent.

CHAPTER 20: 10:00 A.M., SUNDAY, OCTOBER 11, 1987

Long ago, in a past so distant it seems like a dream, when you were absorb-

ing the precise theories of computer logic and convincing yourself that the strict disciplines of the physical sciences were not the domain of the white world alone, you developed a disdain for the occult, harbored contempt for the mystic, and closed your ears to the voices of the spirit calling to you from the land of your fathers. But you were blessed, as few are blessed, and soon learned—or at least permitted yourself to feel you had learned—that the atoms of the body, the molecules of the mind and the elements of the spirit are parts of the same world, and that the mysteries of one will not be unraveled until the door shutting out knowledge of the others is finally unlocked. And it is for this reason you feel in the secret recesses of your being that nothing is ever lost, that each thought, each act somehow influences everything that occurs in the universe.

So, now, Sunday again, calmed by the quiet hours of morning, sitting in the living room of your suite in Hotel Washington, a room which is more a place of refuge than of abode, you tell yourself that although in one sense you have lived two lives during the past week, in another sense it has been only one life, probably more inextricably intertwined by the apparent contradictions. One life has been concerned with directing the nationwide demonstrations to make the powers that be more susceptible to the demands for a separate state, while the other has been aimed at forging a relationship with a woman who is both familiar and strange, new and old, in the eternal battle between man and woman. And because you have been occupied with both at the same time, you realize that both lives have suffered, yet have been immeasurably enriched by the influences of the one on the other. Nevertheless, during the hectic week just passed, neither life has progressed to your satisfaction. But you accept this, for your experience has taught you that nothing is ever as definite as wishing expects nor as fulfilling as hoping demands.

But your acceptance carries with it a feeling of guilt because the balance, the tidy evenness by which you govern your existence, has not been maintained; for in this hour of calm you are reflecting more on what has happened between you and Hilda Larsen, the woman, than on what has occurred in the struggle for your people.

It is Tuesday night in Los Angeles, following a session with Albert James to assess the results of a street demonstration which has extended from a long afternoon into a tiring evening. Dinner completed, you are sitting in a quiet restaurant talking to her, having permitted analyses of specific incidents to transform themselves into a discussion of things in general.

HERMAN CROMWELL GILBERT

"It might not be a good idea to value things too highly," you say; "for when you do, it is too painful to give them up."

"Is that your formula for living," she asks—"don't get into things for fear you will have to give them up? It seems like a plastic way to live, or rather, to not live."

"I know," you reply, smiling. "But believe me, it's better to have never loved than to have loved and lost."

She shakes her head. "There is another way. You don't have to let them take the things you want away from you. You don't have to give them up."

"That calls for clarification," you say.

"You are talking about going on living after your loss," she says. "There is another way, you know. You don't have to go on living. You can die fighting to keep the things you want."

You laugh. "It always comes back to the basic question," you say. "Whether living at any price is preferable to dying."

Then, after a few more cocktails and slightly more intimate talk, the conversation returned to the same general theme.

"Only fools apply revolutionary tactics to evolutionary situations," you say.

She smiles sweetly. "Probably true. But on the other hand, cowards are the ones who keep revolutionary situations from coming into existence by constantly engaging in evolutionary tactics. Am I correct in assuming that you are not a coward?"

The next night, in San Francisco, you are feeling poetic. The demonstrations have gone well. At her urging, a number of women's groups have joined the demonstrations, not to support your demands but to voice their support of your right to make them. You are in a taxicab, returning to your respective hotels from a session with a newspaper editor, and in your poetic mood you are strangely reflective, putting into words something you have not thought about in a long time.

"I believe," you say, "we exist simultaneously at different levels of consciousness. And each level of consciousness has its own continuity."

Her leg brushed against your leg, momentarily breaking your trend of thought. "How's that?" she asks.

"How's what?"

"What proof do you have for what you have just said?"

"The best proof in the world," you reply. "From my own experience. For example, often when I get a fever from a cold or some other bacteria or virus,

I go back and connect with thoughts I had and experiences I went through the last time I had a fever. Things I don't think about at all when I don't have a fever. It is also the same with dreams. In dreams I often complete philosophical analyses I have started in other dreams, continue experiences I have begun nights or months before."

She leans against you. "Ummm," she says, "I understand what you mean. The same things happen to me. But tell me, Preston, have you ever gotten the impression that you were on the verge of a major breakthrough in communication, that if you could just get past a certain barrier, you could experience things that few persons have experienced before?"

"In what way?"

"That you are about to free yourself from self-entrapment, almost have the ability to move vertically from the present into the past or future, and horizontally into the minds of other people."

"Yes," you reply, aware of the eagerness in your voice. "My most vivid impression of having lived before relates to a recurring dream. In this dream I am a slave trying to escape from a plantation by way of the Mississippi River. For some unknown reason, I am tied to the propeller of a boat and I am stifling from the murky waters swirling about me. That's where all the dream sequences end. I suppose in an earlier life I drowned trying to escape. "

She touches your leg, ever so lightly. "You poor dear," she says in a soft voice.

In St. Louis, on Thursday, the demonstrations do not go well at all. The march from the black neighborhoods to the federal building is impeded by mobs of angry whites. Hundreds of blacks join the whites and violence erupts on a massive scale. Scores are injured. In the forefront of the march, you miraculously escape with only few scratches. After the legal maneuvers of charges and countercharges are out of the way, you decide to have dinner in your hotel room. Since she has a room in the same hotel, after genteel bickering, the decision is reached that she will have dinner with you. But the soft moods of the other nights have flown before the violence, and when the time for the inevitable self-revealing conversation arrives, you are filled with a strange harshness.

"A person who looks upon the possession of power as an end in itself," you say, "is much more difficult to deal with than a person who aspires to power for a specific purpose. If you can somehow accommodate the latter's viewpoint, convince him that you support his philosophy, then you can work with him and be relatively free from his suspicions. However, on the other hand, the only

way you can safely coexist with a person who yearns for power for itself is to inhabit that person's skin."

"Yes, but is that an advantage?" she asks. "I mean, if you are dealing with a person whose ideas are repugnant to you?"

"Of course not. Not if you really want to advance a certain point of view. However, although the guy who wants power for a specific reason might be more dangerous to your cause, you at least know where he stands. But the other guy will cut your throat for no rhyme or reason. "

Again, a little later, you say: "To believe that the creation was as it is described in the Bible is to do a disservice to the wonder and majesty of the universe."

"Why do you say that?"

"The creation as described in the Bible is extremely simplistic. Beautiful. But simplistic. The story in the Bible doesn't begin to approach the grand scope of the physical universe, to say nothing of the wonder of the human creation."

"Maybe that's the reason why the story is so simple," she says. "Because words and ideas could not be found to depict the complexity and grandeur of the subject matter."

You smile at her. You can tell she has gotten your point.

"Exactly," you say. "We don't understand these things. And until we do, we should say we don't. Not go around creating images for a knowledge we don't possess. All else is hypocrisy on the grandest scale."

She looks at you, her eyes consuming. "What you say might sound logical," she says, "but it stops short of truth, and you know it. To follow what you say to its logical conclusion would also say that since the mystery of the human existence is so complex and so frightening, the most compatible person is one who can keep us from looking into ourselves; that the most rewarding experiences are those which keep us distracted, prevent us from probing into the core of our being."

You smile at her. "I suppose you have me there, because if what I said was true," you reply, "by implication things like making love, having children, building governments, etc., are only make-believe artifacts with which man has surrounded himself to keep from looking into the hell, or heaven, of himself; because he cannot look too deeply into himself and still live, or at least, remain sane. Such logic would doom humans to a life of inaction."

She holds up her hand in a manner which indicates that she is ignoring what you just said, although both of you know she isn't. You realize she has grasped a thought which she must state before it eludes her. "As an indication that a person doesn't know where the core of his/her being is located," she says, "consider just what part of you you are talking to when you speak to yourself. Are you talking to your face, eyes, forehead? Or to your brain, or heart? Or some other inner repository of yourself? Or are you talking to all of these things at the same time?" Her eyes are sparkling.

Now, it is your turn to hold up your hand. "You talk too much," you say. "This is neither the time nor the place for me to answer that."

When you arrive in Chicago on Friday afternoon, Rubye has everything under control. She has scheduled a rally for one o'clock at the Dirksen building on South Dearborn in the Loop and a solidarity parade through the black neighborhoods for Saturday morning. Things, however, are not going well at all in New York City. According to newscasts and confirmed by a phone call to Marcus Jackson from O'Hare Airport, police are battling your demonstrators in that city. Jackson swears the police are acting like they have orders to go on the attack.

When you, with Hilda at your side, arrive at the Dirksen Building shortly after three o'clock the rally is winding down. The moderate-sized crowd is surprisingly good-natured and you are wondering how the reaction can be so different in New York and Chicago on the same day. Rubye is standing on the sidewalk surrounded by a knot of dignitaries when you join her. After the dignitaries have dispersed and you, Rubye and Hilda are alone, Rubye says teasingly, but somewhat sharply: "The last I saw you two you were together in a hotel room. Have you been together ever since?"

You are surprised at the depth of Hilda's blush. "Don't be silly," she says. "I'm not really with Preston. I'm observing the demonstrations for my organization."

Rubye chuckles. "And the best way to observe them is up front with the head man, ain't that right, now?"

Hilda glances at you, but you deliberately avert your eyes, so she replies: "Right. I always heard that the front seats were the best seats."

Rubye gives Hilda a sideways glance. "Are you making any headway in your campaign?" she asks.

"What campaign?" Hilda asks.

"Have you forgotten so soon? The campaign to get us to forget about the separate nation and join you?"

Before Hilda can answer, you enter the conversation. "Hilda hasn't been proselytizing since her initial efforts failed Sunday night. All week she has been the courteous guest."

"And you have been the gracious host," Hilda says.

Rubye looks intently at the two of you, then she laughs. "A person would think I'm jealous," she says. "And how could I be? After all, I was the one who brought you to his hotel room. Right?"

"Right," Hilda replies.

And you take them by their arms, Rubye on your right and Hilda on your left, and guide them to the waiting car for the trip to your hotels.

In the early hours after nightfall, the three of you, in the company of two body-guards, tour the city, you and Rubye pointing out to Hilda sights of general interest and places you revered in a time long past. You even take her across 79th Street and show her the Brown Girl Lounge, but you do not enter.

And when the night grows relaxing with October coolness, you pick up junk food—hamburgers, ribs and shrimps—and, giggling like teenagers, go to your home. And there amid the memories of Margaret, the three of you eat and talk and drink under the aura of a soothing companionship, bask in a soothing relationship, almost eerie because of its intensity and intimacy. And in the atmosphere of this relationship, you recount to them a dream you have never before revealed to a living soul.

"In this dream, shortly before Margaret's death," you say, "I had a vision of Margaret and Preston Junior at a funeral, supposedly my own. Margaret is leaning on Preston Junior's arm. The only trouble is, Margaret looks much younger than she was at the time and Preston Junior much older—so that they appear to be about the same age."

"How do you figure that?" Rubye asks.

"I have thought and thought about it," you say. "I have finally come to the conclusion that in Margaret's mind, something important in our relation-ship died long ago—long before her physical death and, of course, long before mine."

When you finish speaking you are observing them closely. Rubye laughs, hysterically, and covers her face with her hand. Hilda is looking straight ahead, almost as though transfixed, but her eyes are glistening with tears.

"I'm so sorry," she says. "So sorry for her, and for you."

So now, in the sweet solitude of Sunday morning, savoring the memory of the wanderings of the spirit and the cleverness of the tongue which the new relation-ship has brought forth, you realize that the harsh things of the past week—the feet-numbing marches, the throat-parching shouts, the head-cracking attacks—

are somewhat reduced in your remembering, like muddy water made almost clear by the sieves of a filter. And this, you know, despite philosophizing to the contrary, is not as it should be.

Suddenly, you are filled with a consuming sadness which tingles the nostrils and blurs the eyes, for you realize that surrender to reality-altering reflection is a luxury you no longer can afford; that though tendency toward such reflection will follow you all the days of your life, you must bar your mind against its beguiling entrapment, like a curtain shutting out a glimpse into an enchanted land. So placing your head in your hands and closing your eyes tight against intruding visions, you feel a shudder go through your body; then the shudder passes, like a person shaking off a chill which has run its course.

And when you open your eyes, the world is real again.

Frank London Brown (1927–1962)

So well-received was Frank London Brown's first novel, *Trumbull Park* (1959), that critic Sterling Stuckey wrote: "along with Lorraine Hansberry's *Raisin in the Sun* and Ossie Davis' *Purlie Victorious*, [it] signaled the advent of a new and brilliant flowering of creative effort on the part of Negro writers." Also praised by Stuckey as that rare combination of writer and activist, Brown had based *Trumbull Park* on his real-life experience of moving from Chicago's South Side into the Trumbull Park housing project near Gary, partly as a show of solidarity with poor people. In blunt, straightforward style, he tells the all-too-familiar tale of a family who endures not just the harassment and "Get out, nigger!" taunting, but also stone after stone, bomb after bomb of mobs and individuals trying to drive them away. The novel revealed to thousands of people the degrading racism and living conditions of slums. Unfortunately, as the dates above show, Brown, like Hansberry, died terribly early. His second novel, *The Mythmakers*, was published posthumously. During his life, he published many articles and stories in such periodicals as *Downbeat, Ebony,* the Chicago *Tribune* and *Sun-Times, Negro Digest,* and the *Chicago Review.* Besides writing, he worked as a machinist and union organizer and was director of the Union Leadership Program at the University of Chicago. He enjoyed some fame as a jazz singer as well, appearing with Thelonius Monk not only in Chicago but also at New York's legendary Five Spot. Of all his work, the short story "McDougal" has received unanimous high praise. Here Frank London Brown's gift for dialogue and precise, dramatic scene-setting reached its peak. The story also explored the possibilities that people could indeed relate and empathize across those same terrible racial boundaries he spent his short life not only writing about, but also trying to help everyone overcome in daily life.

McDougal

The bass was walking. Nothing but the bass. And the rhythm section waited, counting time with the tap of a foot or the tip of a finger against the piano top. Pro had just finished his solo and the blood in his neck was pumping so hard it made his head hurt. Sweat shone upon the brown backs of his fingers and the moisture stained the bright brass of his tenor where he held it. Jake, young eyeglass-wearing boy from Dallas, had stopped playing the drums, and he too was sweating, and slight stains were beginning to appear upon his thin cotton coat, and his dark skin caught the purple haze from the overhead spotlight and the sweat that gathered on his flat cheekbones seemed purple. Percy R. Brookins bent over the piano tapping the black keys but not hard enough to make a sound.

Everybody seemed to be waiting. And the bass was walking. Doom-de-doom-doom-doom-doom-doom!

A tall thin white man whose black hair shone with sweat stood beside the tenorman, lanky, ginger-brown Pro.

Pro had wailed—had blown choruses that dripped with the smell of cornbread and cabbage and had roared like a late "L" and had cried like a blues singer on the last night of a good gig.

Now it was the white man's turn, right after the bass solo was over . . . and he waited and Pro waited and so did Jake the drummer, and Percy R. Brookins. Little Jug was going into his eighth chorus and showed no sign of letting up.

DOOM-DE-DOOM-DOOM-DOOM-DOOM-DOOM!

Jake looked out into the audience. And the shadowy faces were hard to see behind the bright colored lights that ringed the bandstand. Yet he felt that they too waited . . . Pro had laid down some righteous sound—he had told so much truth—told it so plainly, so passionately that it had scared everybody in the place, even Pro, and now he waited for the affirming bass to finish so that he could hear what the white man had to say.

McDougal was his name. And his young face had many wrinkles. And his young body slouched and his shoulders hung round and loose. He was listening to Little Jug's bass yet he also seemed to be listening to something else, almost as if he were still listening to the truth Pro had told.

And the bass walked.

Jake leaned over his drums and whispered to Percy R. Brookins.

"That cat sure looks beat don't he?"

Percy R. Brookins nodded, and then put his hand to the side of his mouth, and whispered back. "His old lady's pregnant again."

"Again?! What's that? Number three?"

"Number four," Percy R. Brookins answered.

"Hell I'd look sad too . . . Is he still living on Forty Seventh Street?"

The drums slid in underneath the bass and the bass dropped out amid strong applause and a few "Yeahs!" And Jake, not having realized it, cut in where McDougal was to begin his solo. He smiled sheepishly at Percy R. Brookins and the piano player hunched his shoulders and smiled.

McDougal didn't look around, he didn't move from his slouched one-sided stance, he didn't stop staring beyond the audience and beyond the room itself. Yet his left foot kept time with the light bombs the drummer dropped and the husky soft scrape of the brushes.

Little Jug pulled a handkerchief from his back pocket and wiped his cheeks and around the back of his neck, then he stared at the black, glistening back of McDougal's head and then leaned down and whispered to Percy R. Brookins.

"Your boy sure could stand a haircut. He looks as bad as Ol' Theo." And they both knew how bad Ol' Theo looked and they both frowned and laughed.

Percy R. Brookins touched a chord lightly to give some color to Jake's solo and then he said.

"Man, that cat has suffered for that brownskin woman."

Little Jug added.

"And those . . . three little brownskin crumb-crushers."

Percy R. Brookins hit another chord and then he said.

"Do you know none of the white folks'll rent to him now?"

Little Jug laughed.

"Why hell yes . . . will they rent to me?"

"Sure they will, down on Forty Seventh Street."

Little Jug nodded at Jake and Jake made a couple of breaks that meant that he was about to give in to McDougal.

Percy R. Brookins turned to face his piano and then he got an idea and he turned to Little Jug and spoke with a serious look behind the curious smile on his face.

"You know that cat's after us? I mean he's out to blow the real thing. You know what I mean? Like he's no Harry James? Do you know that?"

Little Jug ran into some triplets and skipped a couple of beats and brought McDougal in right on time.

At the same time McDougal rode in on a long, hollow, gut bucket note that made Percy R. Brookins laugh, and caused Pro to cock his head and rub his cheek. The tall worried looking white man bent his trumpet to the floor and hunched his shoulders and closed his eyes and blew.

Little Jug answered Percy R. Brookins question about McDougal.

"I been knowing that . . . he knows the happenings . . . I mean about where we get it, you dig? I mean like with Leola and those kids and Forty Seventh Street and those jive landlords, you dig? The man's been burnt, Percy. Listen to that somitch—listen to him!"

McDougal's eyes were closed and he did not see the dark woman with the dark cotton suit that ballooned away from the great bulge of her stomach. He didn't see her ease into a chair at the back of the dark smoky room. He didn't see the smile on her face or the sweat upon her flat nose.

FRANK LONDON BROWN

Lerone Bennett Jr. (b. 1928)

Born in Clarksdale, Mississippi, October 17, 1928, Lerone Bennett Jr. came to Chicago in 1953 to become associate editor of *Jet* magazine, then associate and senior editor at *Ebony* starting in 1954. He has also held positions as a visiting professor of history at Northwestern, a senior fellow of the Institute of the Black World, and a member of the board of directors of the Chicago Public Library. Author of many articles, short stories, and poems, he was a mainstay of Chicago's Johnson Publishing Company, writing ten books for them, including *Pioneers in Protest* (1968) and *The Challenge of Blackness* (1972). Hailed as one of the country's best popular historians, he has played an enormous role in conveying the power of the Black presence in American history, as well as showing the way to better communication between Blacks and whites, and Blacks and their own constituencies, as he did in *Confrontation: Black and White* (1965). Considered his most influential book, *Before the Mayflower* was first published in 1962. In chapter 3, "The Founding of Black America," Bennett tells the story of the crucial role Black patriots played in the American revolution, including the legendary Crispus Attucks, who, as the first person to die in the revolution, has been a source of immense pride for Black Americans. Bennett distinguishes four "recognizable types" in the founding of Black America: Jupiter Hammon, who "went over to the enemy . . . producing intellectual products that . . . buttressed their world view"; Phillis Wheatley, a founder of American poetry, who "subtly challenged" the premises of American society "by the authority of her work"; the anonymous Othello, outright militant; and Richard Allen, who "spoke in muted tones but created big sticks of organization," including the AME Church and, with Absalom Jones, the Free African Society. This excerpt from the end of chapter 3 begins by focusing on Allen and moves on to DuSable, the founder of Chicago.

From *Before the Mayflower: A History of the Negro in America*

By withdrawing from the white Methodist church, the band of protestants affirmed the new forces moving within them. But the withdrawal raised large questions of identity, which were discussed at several heated meetings of the Free African Society. Certain members of the society suggested affiliation with the Quakers, while others held out for an entente with the Episcopalians or Methodists. Behind this debate was another question: What relation, if any, should blacks have with white institutions?

After a protracted and somewhat acrimonious debate, the Free African Society split into two groups. The larger group followed Absalom Jones, an affable, easy-going former slave, into the Episcopal church. In 1794 the African Church of St. Thomas was erected in Philadelphia and eleven words were engraved in the vestibule: "The People Who Walked in Darkness Have Seen a Great Light."

But had they—really?

Richard Allen didn't think so. The new black communicants were denied full status in the Episcopal church and were barred from annual conferences and governing boards. This, to Allen, was rank discrimination. . . . In his mind, in an unmanifested seed state, was an image of *Negritude,* of Negro being and becoming.

Who was Allen?

He was a former slave who started his career with an act of extraordinary symbolic significance: the conversion of his master. Shrewd and hardworking, Allen accumulated enough money to buy his freedom and migrated to Philadelphia. After the split in the Free African Society, he formed an independent black Methodist church. In 1816 he became the first bishop of the African Methodist Episcopal Church, the first national organization created by blacks. During the whole of this period, according to contemporary witnesses, his house was never shut "against the friendless, homeless, penniless fugitive from the house of bondage." So persuasive was Allen's image, so dynamic was his example, that author Vernon Loggin nominated him for the title of "Father of the Negro . . ."

Men and women made in Allen's image dominated the second phase of the Black Pioneer period, creating a tier of independent black churches that spanned the North. By 1830 there were black churches of almost every conceivable description, including an Ethiopian Church of Jesus Christ in Savannah, Georgia, and a black Dutch Reformed Church in New York City.

On the foundation of these churches rose a third tier of social and fraternal organizations. The leading spirit in this movement was Prince Hall, a leather-dresser and Revolutionary War veteran who organized the first black Masonic lodge. Like Richard Allen, like Absalom Jones, like all leaders of the period, Prince Hall tried first to enter white American institutions. Rebuffed on this front, he turned to England and was granted a charter by the Grand Lodge of England. On May 6, 1787, African Lodge No. 459 was formally organized in Boston with Hall as Master. In 1797 Hall helped organize lodges in Philadelphia and Providence, Rhode Island, thereby becoming a pioneer in the development of black interstate organizations.

While Hall and other leaders were pressing forward on this level, they were at the same time creating the fourth tier of the Black American structure, the perennial movement for equal rights. From the beginning that movement was based on internal development and external protest. In succeeding years different protest leaders would emphasize different dimensions of this concept. Booker T. Washington, for example, would make an artificial distinction between external protest and internal development. But in the beginning black leaders articulated a total concept, involving a double and reciprocal struggle *for* black development and *against* white restrictions on that development.

True to their rhetoric, these leaders founded black schools and organized the social capital of the community. A major leader in this effort, as in so many others, was Richard Allen, who opened a day school for children and a night school for adults in Bethel AME Church in Philadelphia. In Boston, in the same decade, Prince Hall opened a school for black children in his home. This movement was supported by Quakers like Anthony Benezet, who organized a black school in Philadelphia, and the New York Manumission Society, which organized the famous Free African Schools of New York City. According to some authorities, the opening of the first African Free School in November, 1787, marked the beginning of free secular education in New York.

All the while, on another level of existence, black leaders were pressing an increasingly sophisticated campaign against discrimination and segregation. In a 1794 pamphlet Richard Allen and Absalom Jones attacked slavery and its Northern twin, bigotry. Six years later Jones and other Philadelphians sent an antislavery petition to Congress. Allied with Jones and Allen in the Philadelphia protest movement was industrialist James Forten, who attracted national attention with a series of letters that demolished the arguments of whites who wanted to limit the number of free blacks entering Pennsylvania.

Along with equal rights, blacks pressed the equal education movement. On October 17, 1787, Prince Hall and other Boston blacks filed one of the first public petitions in this field, telling the Massachusetts legislature that "we . . . must fear for our rising offspring to see them in ignorance in a land of gospel light, when there is provision made for them as well as others and [they] can't enjoy them, and [no other reason] can be given [than that] they are black. . . ." In a different but allied development, Paul Cuffe raised the issue of black suffrage. When, in 1780, he was barred from the ballot box in Dartmouth, Massachusetts, he refused to pay taxes and filed a defiant petition of protest. After a long controversy, it was decided that taxation without representation was tyranny in America. The case was widely regarded as establishing a precedent for black suffrage.

Buttressed by the four tiers of these ascending levels of expressiveness, the horizons of black pioneers expanded in widening circles that, in some cases, overlapped the efforts of white pioneers. Not only in the South but also in the North black pioneers contributed to the common effort, building schools and roads and extending the social capital of America. In one characteristic transaction, Paul Cuffe donated a school to his town and built a meeting house for the Quakers.

There were also black pioneers who extended the boundaries of America, founding new communities and towns. The most celebrated of these pioneers was Jean Baptiste Pointe DuSable, who founded Chicago, Illinois. There is abundant evidence—a deed in the Wayne County courthouse, the contemporary reports of British officers and the journals and records of travelers and traders—that DuSable settled in the area in the 1770s and created the foundations of Chicago, building the first home there and opening the first business.

The contributions of DuSable and other black founding fathers had no appreciable effect on the level of racism in America. There are even indications that DuSable the founder was isolated and pushed to the sidelines of Chicago life in the 1790s when large numbers of white Americans settled in the area, bringing with them traditional American perceptions. If, as seems probable, DuSable was indeed the victim of his own creation, he shares that mournful distinction with thousands of other black pioneers who found themselves under increasing attack in the last decade of the eighteenth century.

What did it mean to be black in the America of that period?

Prince Hall, the activist and Revolutionary War veteran who organized the first black Masonic lodge, provided one answer in his charge to Boston's African Lodge.

"Patience, I say; for were we not possessed of a great measure of it, we could not bear up under the daily insults . . . we [are] shamefully abused, and that to such a degree, that we may truly be said to carry our lives in our hands, and the arrows of death are flying about our heads."

A similar answer came from Colonel Middleton, another Revolutionary War veteran. During a Boston riot, a group of whites attacked blacks in front of his home. The old soldier stuck a musket out of his door and threatened to kill any white man who approached. One of his neighbors, a white man, asked the whites to leave. Then he approached Colonel Middleton and begged him to put away his gun. Colonel Middleton stood silent for a moment. Then he turned and tottered off, dropping his gun and weeping as he went.

Colonel Middleton's America, Prince Hall's America and Thomas Jefferson's America tottered into the nineteenth century, divided and afraid.

Lorraine Hansberry (1930–1965)

Born in Chicago on May 19, 1930, Lorraine Hansberry died in New York of cancer in January 1965. In her brief thirty-four years, however, she became one of the most luminous figures in Black America and American letters, primarily through the enormous success of *A Raisin in the Sun*. The play made its debut in Chicago in February 1959 at the Blackstone with a cast that included Sidney Poitier, Ruby Dee, and Louis Gossett. A month later, it became the first play by a Black woman to open on Broadway. Universally praised, it won the New York Drama Critics Circle Award. Hansberry thus became the youngest American playwright, and the first Black playwright, to win that award. As the powerful Chicago theater critic Claudia Cassidy wrote, the play—besides being remarkable in itself and in its gifted cast—had "the fresh impact of something urgently on its way." In 1961 Poitier starred in the successful film adaptation, and a musical version won the Tony Award for best musical in 1973. Even today, the play manages to maintain a kind of "on-its-way" urgency, partly because the social and personal dramas it portrays seem to connect with social and personal problems still at the heart of American society. "Never before, in the entire history of American theater," wrote James Baldwin, "had so much of the truth of black people's lives been seen on the stage."

Among Hansberry's other works are *The Sign in Sidney Brustein's Window* (1964), about the awakening of a Jewish intellectual, and several posthumous works: *Les Blancs, The Drinking Gourd,* and *What Use Are Flowers?* The selections below are from chapters 1 and 3 of *To Be Young, Gifted and Black: Lorraine Hansberry in Her Own Words*, a collage of her fiction, letters, journals, and plays published in 1969. The stage version, scripted by her husband, Howard Nemiroff, had premiered in New York earlier that year, on January 2. In the prologue, a projection of Lorraine Hansberry's recorded voice says, "I suppose I think that the highest gift that man has is art . . . I want to reach a little closer to the world, which is to say people, and see if we can share some illuminations together about each other." *To Be Young, Gifted and Black* contains many moments of Hansberry's best work. In it, we catch glimpses of where *A Raisin in the Sun* came from and where she was hoping to take her work, and us, from there.

From *To Be Young, Gifted and Black*

FROM CHAPTER 1: CHICAGO: SOUTHSIDE SUMMERS

(2)

All travelers to my city should ride the elevated trains that race along the back ways of Chicago. The lives you can look into! I think you could find the tempo of my people on their back porches. The honesty of their living is there in the shabbiness. Scrubbed porches that sag and look their danger. Dirty gray wood steps. And always a line of white and pink clothes scrubbed so well, waving in the dirty wind of the city.

My people are poor. And they are tired. And they are determined to live. Our Southside is a place apart: each piece of our living is a protest.

(4)

I was born May 19, 1930, the last of four children.

Of love and my parents there is little to be written: their relationship to their children was utilitarian. We were fed and housed and dressed and outfitted with more cash than our associates and that was all. We were also vaguely taught certain vague absolutes: that we were better than no one but infinitely superior to everyone; that we were the products of the proudest and most mistreated of the races of man; that there was nothing enormously difficult about life; that one *succeeded* as a matter of course.

Life was not a struggle—it was something that one *did*. One won an argument because, if facts gave out, one invented them—with color! The only sinful people in the world were dull people. And, above all, there were two things which were never to be betrayed: the family and the race. But of love, there was nothing ever said.

If we were sick, we were sternly, impersonally and carefully nursed and doctored back to health. Fevers, toothaches were attended to with urgency and importance; one always felt *important* in my family. Mother came with a tray to your room with the soup and Vick's salve or gave the enemas in a steaming bathroom. But we were not fondled, any of us—head held to breast, fingers about that head—until we were grown, all of us, and my father died.

At his funeral I at last, in my memory, saw my mother hold her sons that way, and for the first time in her life my sister held me in her arms I think. We were not a loving people: we were passionate in our hostilities and affinities, but the caress embarrassed us.

We have changed little.

CHAPTER 4: QUEEN OF THE ETHIOPES!

(1)

My High School Yearbook bears the dedication: "Englewood High trains for citizenship in a world of many different peoples. Who could better appreciate this wonderful country than our forefathers who traveled hundreds of miles from every known nation, seeking a land of freedom from discrimination of race, color or creed?" And in illustration, there is this:

The Great Branches of Man at Englewood High: in front, Mangolia Ali of East Indian Mohammedan descent; second couple, Nancy Diagre and

Harold Bradley, Negroid; middle couple, Rosalind Sherr and William Krugman, Jewish religion, not a racial stock; next, Eleanor Trester and Theodore Flood, Caucasoid; extreme right, Lois Lee and Barbara Nomura, Mongoloid; rear, left, Mr. Thompson, principal.

(2)

I was reminded of Englewood by a questionnaire which came from *Show* magazine the other day . . .

THE SHAKESPEAREAN EXPERIENCE

SHOW POLL #5, February 1964

Some Questions Answered by: Robert Bolt, Jean Cocteau, T. S. Eliot, Tyrone Guthrie, Lorraine Hansberry, Joan Littlewood, Harold Pinter, Alain Robbe-Grillet, Igor Stravinsky, Harry S. Truman.

QUESTION: *What was your first contact with Shakespeare?*

High School. English literature classwork. We had to read and memorize speeches from *Macbeth* and *Julius Caesar* all under the auspices of a strange and bewigged teacher who we, after this induction, naturally and cruelly christened "Pale Hecate"—God rest her gentle, enraptured and igniting soul!

> PALE HECATE *enters, ruler in hand, and takes her place in the classroom.* SHE *surveys the* CLASS. THEY *come to attention as her eye falls on* EACH *in turn.*

PALE HECATE

Y'do not read, nor speak, nor write the English language! I suspect that y'do not even *think* in it! God only knows in what language y'do think, or if you think at all. 'Tis true the *English* have done little enough with the tongue, but being the English I expect it was the best they could do.

> *(They giggle)*

In any case, I'll have it learned properly before a living one of y'll pass out of this class. That I will!

> *(Waving a composition book and indicating the grade marked in red at the top)*

As for *you*, Miss—as for you, indeed, surely you will recognize the third letter of the alphabet when y'have seen it?

STUDENT

"C."

PALE HECATE

Aye, a "C" it 'tis! You're a bright and clever one now after all, aren't y'lass?

LORRAINE HANSBERRY

(The class snickers)

And now, my brilliance, would you also be informing us as to what a grade signifies when it is thus put upon the page?

STUDENT

Average.

PALE HECATE

"Average." Yes, yes—and what else in your case, my iridescence? Well then, I'll be tellin' you in fine order. It stands for "cheat," my luminous one!

(The class sobers)

For them that will do *half* when *all* is called for; for them that will slip and slide through life at the edge *of* their minds, never once pushing into the interior to see what wonders are hiding there—content to drift along on whatever gets them by, *cheating* themselves, *cheating* the world, *cheating* Nature! That is what the "C" means, my dear child—

(She smiles)

—my pet

(They giggle; in rapid order she raps each on the head with her ruler)

—my laziest *Queen of the Ethiopes!*

SHE *exits or dims out.*

QUESTION: *Which is your favorite Shakespeare play and why?*

Favorite? It is like choosing the "superiority" *of* autumn days; mingling titles permits a reply: *Othello* and *Hamlet.* Why? There is a sweetness in the former that lingers long after the tragedy is done. A kind *of* possibility that we suspect in man wherein even its flaw is a tribute. The latter because there remains a depth in the Prince that, as we all know, constantly re-engages as we mature. And it does seem that the wit remains the brightest and most instructive in all dramatic literature.

QUESTION: *What is the most important result of your familiarity with Shakespeare? What has he given you?*

Comfort and agitation so bound together that they are inseparable. Man, as set down in the plays, is large. Enormous. Capable *of* anything at all. And yet fragile, too, this view *of* the human spirit; one feels it ought be respected and protected and loved rather fiercely.

Rollicking times, Shakespeare has given me. I love to laugh and his humor is that of everyday; of every man's foible at no man's expense. Language. At 13 a difficult and alien tedium, those Elizabethan cadences; but soon a balm, a thrilling source of contact with life . . .

LORRAINE HANSBERRY

166

But Shakespeare notwithstanding, neither "Pale Hecate" nor Mr. Thompson ("rear, left, principal") could do much with: the Great Branches of Man at Englewood High—"Negroid, Mongoloid, Caucasoid" *or* "Jewish"—on the day of the race riot and strike at school.

Oh, yes, she remembered! She remembered, and would never forget, how, on that day, the well-dressed colored students like herself had stood amusedly around the parapet, staring, simply staring at the mob of several hundred striking whites, trading taunts and insults—but showing not the least inclination to further assert racial pride.

Then had come the veterans—volunteers from Wendell Phillips High School and DuSable, carloads of them, waving baseball bats and shouting slogans of the charge. The word had gone into the ghetto: *The ofays are out on strike and beating up and raping colored girls under the viaduct out South!* And the summary, traditional and terse: WE BETTER GO 'CAUSE THEM LITTLE CHICKEN-SHIT NIGGERS OUT THERE AIN'T *ABOUT* TO FIGHT!

And so they had come, pouring out of the bowels of the ghetto, the children of the unqualified oppressed: the black working class in their costumes of pegged pants and conked heads and tight skirts and almost knee-length sweaters and—worst of all—*colored* anklets, held up by rubber bands!

Yes, they had come and they had fought. It had taken the Mayor and the visit of a famous movie star to get everyone's mind back on other things again. He had been terribly handsome and full of speeches on "tolerance" and had also given a lot of autographs. But she had been unimpressed.

She never could forget one thing: *They had fought back!*

LORRAINE HANSBERRY

167

Sam Greenlee (b. 1930)

Born in Chicago on July 13, 1930, Sam Greenlee has written poetry, fiction, plays, and screenplays, and has been a teacher, producer, director, and actor. He traveled the world as a first lieutenant in the U.S. Army in the early 1950s, then through a long career as an officer in the U.S. Information Agency, where he served in Iraq, Pakistan, Indonesia, and Greece. These experiences have led to a unique literary vision, which deals with race issues in a military and "spy" context, especially in his two novels *The Spook Who Sat By the Door* (1969) and *Baghdad Blues* (1976). Accepting a literary award for the former in 1999, he said, "I had no idea when I wrote the book on the island of Mykonos during the summer of 1966 that one day Black people would call it a classic." *Spook* tells the story of Dan Freeman, who tries to climb the CIA ladder after being recruited to work in an elite espionage program. Blocked and plagued by race, however, he drops out to train young Chicago Blacks as "Freedom Fighters," the FF, and spread revolution throughout the United Staes. The excerpts below come from four chapters. For the sake of smoother reading, I have rearranged the passages from chapter 5 to give the background of his relationship to his girlfriend Joy first. Chapters 12 and 13 begin with wonderful evocations of Chicago weather as a prelude to talking about the growth and spread of the Freedom Fighters. Chapter 20 then describes the beginnings of a nation-wide revolution. Few books have dealt with race, civil rights, and Black militancy in so focused and unusual a way as this book, which *Time* magazine described as blending "James Bond parody with wit and rage." For a February 2005 forum at the Carter Woodson Library in celebration of OBAC, Greenlee read a prose poem written for the occasion. Called "Weary Warrior Blues," it bemoans the disappearance of "warriors, revolutionaries devoted to a solution of the global pollution of Western Imperialism." Almost four decades after *Spook,* Greenlee's wit and rage seem undimmed as he casts a suspicious eye towards those who are "doing all right and without a fuss dropped back into the system they used to cuss."

From *The Spook Who Sat by the Door*

FROM CHAPTER 5

Freeman had met Joy years before in East Lansing, Michigan, when they were both students at Michigan State University. They were both slumbered, bright, quick and tough and considered a college degree the answer to undefined ambitions. They had much in common: they were both second-generation immigrants of refugee families from the Deep South. Their grandparents had migrated as displaced persons to the greater promises of the urban North; Joy's grandfather from Alabama to the Ford plant during the first war; Freeman's to the Chicago stockyards about the same time. Both Joy and Freeman had been born during the bleak depression years and had known the prying, arrogant social workers, the easily identifiable relief clothing, the relief beans, potatoes, rice and raisins wrapped in their forbidding brown paper bags. But poverty had done different things to them.

Joy had become determined she would never be poor again; Freeman that one day to be black and poor would no longer be synonymous. She regarded his militant idealism and total identification to his race first with amusement, then irritation and finally, growing concern. Joy had no intention of becoming her black brother's keeper. Slowly, she convinced Freeman he could best use his talents to help Negroes as a lawyer dedicated to the cause of civil rights. Could joint legal staff of one of the established civil-rights bureaucracies; one day argue precedent-making cases before the Supreme Court.

She convinced him and he began preparing himself for law school while working toward an undergraduate degree in sociology. Life was being very kind to Joy. She had never felt she would marry the man she loved. But she knew she would have to be very careful because Freeman could be a very stubborn man and the mere idea of his becoming a member of the black bourgeoisie was enough to enrage him. Joy intended not only that he become a member, but one of the leaders. She felt that she could manage this essentially unmanageable man because he loved her. The greatest potential danger was that she loved him as well, but she thought that she could control that emotion. She would have to, because there was far too much at stake.

Joy made an unfortunate strategic error. She insisted that Freeman attend the national convention of the civil-rights organization they thought he would join. Because she had to work that summer to replenish her wardrobe for the fall, Freeman went to the convention alone. He returned bitter and disillusioned.

"Baby, there ain't no way I can work for those motherfuckers. They don't give a damn about any niggers except themselves and they don't really think of themselves as niggers.

"You ought to hear the way they talk about people like us. Like, white folks don't really have much to do with the scene. It's that lower-class niggers are too stupid, lazy, dirty and immoral. If they weren't around, all them dirty, conkheaded niggers with their African and down-home ways, why, everything would be swinging for the swinging black bourgeois bureaucrats, their high-yellow wives, their spoiled brat kids, and their white liberal mistresses. Integration, shit! Their definition of integration is to have their kids the only niggers in a white private school."

SAM GREENLEE

169

***

Late one spring evening they were lying in his bed in Washington. They had eaten a seafood dinner in a restaurant not far from his apartment, just north of the junction of the Anacostia and Potomac rivers; they had been seated by the kitchen as usual. Later they had listened to Sonny Stitt in a small jazz club just off U Street in the heart of the big Washington ghetto. They made love when they returned but had not slept and lay silently sipping scotch and smoking, listening to the music of a late-night jazz station from the transistor radio which stood on the bed table.

Joy arose to one elbow and gazed into Freeman's face. "Dan, I think it's time to have a talk about the two of us. This kind of thing can't go on forever. It's time I started thinking about a home, family, security."

"OK," he said, "let's get married."

"Dan, you know I'd love to marry you, have your children, but this part of you, your bitterness, your preoccupation with the race thing—it frightens me, shuts me out. I feel threatened."

Freeman sat up in bed and looked at Joy in some surprise. "But why should you feel threatened? Hell, the way I feel doesn't even threaten whitey."

"Dan, how much longer are you going to stick with this job? You haven't had a promotion in four years and you're the only Negro officer they have."

"Once I prove myself, they'll recruit more Negroes; I'm certain of it. We can't all join the demonstrations; some of us have to try quietly to make integration work."

"Are you going to prove yourself by taking a bunch of bored housewives on guided tours?"

They were on shaky ground and Freeman had to be careful; Joy knew him too well and one false move, a statement which didn't ring true, and he might expose himself. He arose, walked to the dresser to light a cigarette, regarding her in the mirror as he did so.

"I'm hoping I can move into something else soon; something more substantial." He returned to the bed, sat on its edge and lit a cigarette for her. "If I left now, before they began hiring other Negroes, I'd always think I'd give easy continuing with this jive job, but it's little enough sacrifice for the cause of integration."

"Baby, I'm sorry, but I can't sacrifice my life for a cause. I admire the way you feel, but I fought too hard to get out of the slums and you continue to identify with the slum people you left behind."

"I never left them behind."

She placed her hand on his knee and smiled gently. "Honey, whether you admit it or not, the day you left Chicago for college, you left the block and the people on it. Besides, what's wrong with wanting to live in a decent neighborhood, to want the best for our kids?"

"Who do you think pays for those nice things if not the people we ought to be helping because nobody ever gave them a chance to help themselves? Joy, have you forgotten you came off those same streets? Except for your college degree, those people are just like you."

"Not me, baby! I left that behind me: all those hot, stinky rooms, those streets full of ghosts. Junkies, whores, pimps, con men. The crooked cops, the phony, fornicating preachers. And the smells: garbage, stale sweat, stale beer, reefers, wine and funk. That bad, hand-me-down meat from the white supermarket, the price hiked up and two minutes this side of turning a buzzard's stomach. I've had that shit and going back won't change things."

"Somebody has to try and change things."

"You can't change whitey. He needs things just the way they are, like a junkie needs shit. Whitey's hooked with messing with niggers and you want him to go cold turkey. It's not going to happen. We can be happy, Dan; we can be anything we want."

She wants that title, he thought, Mrs. Lawyer Freeman, then Mrs. Congressman Freeman. "I can go to law school; the kids only hang out at night."

"Stop kidding yourself, Dan: you don't want to go to law school, you never did like it, and you hate Negro lawyers. You hate all the Negro middle class because you think they don't do enough to help other Negroes. You forget something, honey; I'm middle class, too, but you're still on the block in spirit. You've made your choice and I have a right to make mine."

He looked at her but she dropped her head and stared morosely at the glowing tip of her cigarette, its smoke lightly veiling her face.

"Yes," he said softly, "you have."

"I'm not coming to Washington anymore. I'm going to get married."

He picked up his drink and took a sip. The ice had melted and it was weak, watery and warm. "The doctor or the lawyer?"

"The doctor," she answered. He drew a deep breath, let it out slowly.

"Seems like a nice cat." He thought of her never being his again and thrust the thought from his mind. He listened to the radio, Miles Davis playing a ballad. It didn't help, it was from a record Joy had given him as a present.

How many other things had she given to him in their years together, how much of her was a part of him? Suddenly, he was afraid she would cry.

"I'm sorry, Dan, but I'm not getting any younger, and—"

"It's all right, baby," he said, taking her cigarette and snuffing it out in an ashtray. "I guess it had to happen one day. Look, this is our last night together; let's say goodbye right." He reached for her.

She sent him an invitation to the wedding and he sent them a wedding present, but he did not go to Chicago for the ceremony because he thought you could carry being civilized too far.

From Chapter 12

It had been a harsh winter, with subzero temperatures a regular thing. There would be an occasional respite while the big, soft snow covered the city and for a short time covered the grime and dirt and ugliness of Chicago with its virginal whiteness, but within hours after the last flake fell, the virginal snow would be a greasy, dirt-grimed whorelike snow and then the temperature would drop and film the streets with mirrorlike glaze, turning the city snow into something that crunched underfoot like an old cereal in a new box labeled super and all-new. There was nothing super and all-new about Chicago and it is not a place for people who concern themselves with the weather, winter or summer. The wind would whip in from the lake, bearing airborne razors of ice that sliced the flesh. There were regular gray skies and little sun. The sky seemed to sit just above the Tribune Tower and it would sometimes descend to the city streets when the warm-air masses moved up across the plains from the Gulf of Mexico to turn the city into a fog-bound, slushy swamp full of mud-splattered people who groped their way in the dense muck, mire and moody low-sitting cloud, like amoebas in search of a guide to nowhere.

When there was sun, it would come from afar in a hazy, cloudless sky, giving a harsh, cold and biting light, the lack of clouds permitting what little warmth remained to flee toward the planets above, the people below creating little clouds of their own as they breathed and gasped, moving through the brutal city. Because the weather was so menacing, the Cobras were not missed from their usual haunts and there was no need to interrupt training by having some of the gangmembers on the block. It was too cold to be there and the police and social workers did not worry where they might be since the word was that the Cobras were no longer a bopping gang. And since lower-class Negroes are visible only when convenient or menacing, the Cobras disappeared and no one concerned themselves with what they might be doing that cold and forbidding winter.

They were learning the lessons of the oppressed throughout history in striking back at their oppressors; the linguistics of deception; subterfuge, to strike when least expected and then fade into the background; to hound, harass, worry and weaken the strong and whittle away at the strength and power that kept them where they were. Just before the rumble near the railroad tracks, the winter ended as abruptly as it had begun and spring was in Chicago with no warning, the flowers blooming, the trees suddenly budding, the grass turning green, the dirty snow melting and disappearing into the sewers. Spring meant baseball and track, walks in the parks for young lovers and examinations for the students reluctant to remain in the libraries and overheated apartments with textbooks that had become symbolic of the prison of a nasty Chicago winter.

It was time for examinations for Freeman's small band of revolutionaries-in-training.

From Chapter 13

Spring ended abruptly. A hot, moist air mass moved up from the Gulf of Mexico across the plains and into Chicago, smothering the city and turning the night into a furnace, the brick buildings radiating the heat collected from the sun during the day. Life in the ghetto moved outside, onto the door steps of the houses, into the air-conditioned bars and the cinemas that sold cool air and Doris Day dreams. On the South Side there was Washington Park, and families moved at night into its cool greenness, sleeping on blankets under the stars until the first rays of sun, returning to their stifling rooms to snatch a few more minutes of sleep before meeting the hot, humid day. Beer, watermelon, ice cream, anything cool, but there was no way to leave the engulfing heat. The city lay gasping like a big beast. Tempers shortened, and the ghetto lay like a bomb waiting to explode.

From Chapter 20

Oakland blew first, then Los Angeles, then, leapfrogging the continent, Harlem and South Philadelphia. After years of crying conspiracy, the witch hunters found, to their horror, there was a conspiracy afoot among the black masses. Every city with a ghetto wondered if they might be next. The most powerful nation in history stood on the brink of panic chaos. The Freedom

Fighters fought first the po lice, then the National Guard and finally, the elite troops of the army and marines. Within a week there were major guerrilla uprisings in eight major cities in the United States and efforts to eliminate them had proven futile.

Several days of heavy rain, followed by a cool air mass moving down from Canada, broke the Chicago heat. The city lay under a bright warm sun and at night there was a cool breeze from the lake. The birds began their southern journey—and the leaves of the cottonwood, poplar and maple trees began to change color, some of them reluctantly releasing from the limbs to trace a lazy descent to the ground, to be gathered and burned at the curb and produce the pungent smell of autumn come to Chicago. At night the city's silence would be broken by the explosion of grenades, the staccato message of automatic fire. The FF moved easily and silently through the ghetto which offered them affection and support, their coloration finally protective.

The curfew had silenced the streets below and a cleansing breeze from the lake stirred through Freeman's apartment. Miles Davis, mute meeting mike in a sexless kiss, blew bittersweet chocolate tones through the speakers, "My Funny Valentine" becoming a poignant poem of lonely love.

Ronald L. Fair (b. 1932)

Many Thousands Gone, published in 1965, brought Ronald L. Fair considerable critical acclaim, and that novel was quickly followed the next year by *Hog Butcher.* In 1970, Fair published two novellas as *World of Nothing,* which received the National Institute of Arts and Letters second highest prize, and 1972 saw the publication of the autobiographical novel *We Can't Breathe.* For several years, aided by several writing grants, Fair traveled abroad, pursuing a writing life of great ambition. In the early 1970s, critic Shane Stevens called him "one of the two best black writers in the country." The selections below come from *Hog Butcher,* a novel that revolves around the shooting by Chicago police of an innocent Black basketball star, Corn Bread. Though some have commented on the novel's humor and, in particular, on two adolescent protagonists through whom some of the action is seen, the novel, in fact, is a serious exploration of social class. The first excerpt is an essayistic interlude halfway through the book, which sets the novel's particular action against a history of social class. The second excerpt illustrates that history by focusing on Larry Atkins, a Black Chicago police officer close enough to the killing to be a decisive factor in uncovering the truth that is being obscured by a clumsy cover-up. Will Atkins rise to the challenge? That is the question that occupies much of the book's second half.

From *Hog Butcher*

They came to Chicago forty, fifty years ago like a school of black minnows frantically dashing away from danger; running to the great symbol of freedom up North. . . . Any improvement would be better than the state of enslavement they had left in the forgotten, vicious parts of Mississippi, Georgia, Alabama, Tennessee, and Louisiana. They came . . . bursting with industry, screaming to the world that it needed hands and minds and souls to help it grow. . . . They came up from the deep, deep, dead, hidden valleys of the South and they shouldered their way in and mingled with the foreigners and fought the aliens for jobs, and won the jobs as they won the negative respect of the established citizens. They squeezed their way as close to the existing social structure as they were allowed to go, and then they settled back and prospered and raised children and taught their children not to fight, not to resist, but to accept their limited progress as the end of the evolutionary pattern. They grew weak and mellowed from their success, and their children never developed hearts or shoulders or minds, and were gutless.

Their children refused to involve themselves with trivial things like politics or social improvements and pulled in the fences that surrounded their tiny ranch houses. Their children tightened the requirements for entrance into their sick social clubs. At first they only wanted light skin and straight hair. Then they added a college degree to the light skin and straight hair. Then they added a minimum salary. Then they added the possession of a Buick. Then they added the Cadillac. They had arrived; they had reached the top of their limited world and they were scared shitless.

And when they lost their will to fight, they lost their progress, and sank beneath the high levels their parents had attained. And since they were incapable of fighting, incapable of resisting oppression, totally defenseless in the face of opposition, they just sat there and waited for someone to pull them back up.

And then in the 'forties and 'fifties a new wave of proud black men invaded Chicago. They came over the same sets of tracks as their forerunners, and they came just as penniless. . . . They were not light-skinned and they didn't have straight hair and they spoke like Southerners . . . and their black brothers with seniority and the desire to be white were ashamed of them and ignored them and ran, ran, ran away from them and hid behind their cyclone and redwood fences, behind the security of their Martinis and social clubs. So the new immigrants first clustered in old areas that were being vacated by their brothers who had established themselves and were moving, now, into their own homes farther out south that white people were vacating in their flight to the suburbs. And once they had filled up these small areas on the south side, they began to assault the massive rambling west side of Chicago, as one hundred black people a day fled the inhuman South and journeyed to the Chicago of their dreams, to the Chicago that no longer had jobs for blacks, but would now rather substitute public aid than fair employment.

They came by the thousands and quadrupled the black population within less than twenty years. They came and pried their way into the city of no shoulders, into the vicious, lying, deceiving, corrupt Chicago that tried to deny their existence. But these people were not like the children of the giants. These people were hungry and they were alive. They wanted to see the Chicago of their dreams and they were willing to fight for it. They were ill informed and they were loud and they were sometimes vulgar, and sometimes they didn't have much respect for the law because the law had no respect at all for them, but they were vibrant with a will to belong and they were not afraid to fight for what they knew to be their right to remake Chicago.

RONALD L. FAIR

But their opposition was even greater than that of the founders of the city, and their ultimate mastery of it will be longer in coming. When it does come the city will be a richer place; it will be the place poets dreamed of . . . it will breathe again, it will be alive.

***

It was four days before Larry Atkins opened his eyes and the doctor sighed and drew three lines through the word "critical" on his chart. During those four days he had many visitors; people he had not heard from in years. They came out of friendship for him. They came out of respect for his wife. . . .

But those who knew him best came to offer their condolences for the death of his spirit; to mourn the loss of a man who had once been an idealist, but who had mellowed, as a man often does because of the security that money and position bring, or because he weakens and allows the system to overcome him and consume and destroy the dreams that are rebellious in nature and have no place in a patent, sterile society. Hidden beneath a firm crust—layers upon protective layers of bitterness and self-hate—brought about by his acceptance of the way of life he had chosen, of the middle-class standards, there still remained a slight flicker of the flame of rebellion. But so well hidden was his idealism, his constructive anger, his belief in his fellow man, that even he was not aware of it. They had come, these select few, who knew how devoted he had been to the old neighborhood, and wept inwardly for the death of his dream.

The dream was that when he finished school next year he would return to the old neighborhood and teach in the very same school where he had received his basic education. . . . He had been on the police force eight years. He had attended night school the last six of those eight years. So many times he had been tempted to quit, but always he and his wife would find a way to get the tuition together. . . .

She was a clever woman, his Beatrice. Often, when he was really down, she would trick him into believing that his mere presence had so stimulated her that she couldn't resist him and would all but plead with him to take her, to make wild, painful love to her although she seldom derived any pleasure from it, and with her body and her soft words and gentle sounds she would bring him out of his depression and transform him into a sedated but determined man of purpose.

But sometimes loving and being loved was not enough for someone as sensitive as Larry, and she would have to resort to other means. Occasionally she would pick a fight, deliberately, to get his mind off what was bothering him. Sometimes it worked; sometimes it only made life more unbearable for both of them. But she was always trying, always truly concerned. . . . Sometimes she played what she knew to be a game, the "professional game," she called it. . . .

"When you become a teacher," she'd say, "I'll be so proud of you. I'll come by the school every day and look up at your classroom and stop people on the street and say: 'That's my husband's room up there.' And they'll look at me and think I'm crazy, but I won't care because you'll be up there and we'll have made it."

He'd grumble something about the price of textbooks and she'd touch his arm, or the slight bald spot at the back of his head, sigh, and say, "Larry Atkins, a teacher?. . ." . . . It never sounded right, but that was the idea the children of his old neighborhood had planted after he had been on the force only two years. He had never thought of himself as being smart enough to get through college, but once he started he found he could pass . . . and on rare occasions when everything broke right he could even make the Dean's list.

When he came home from the Navy at the end of the Korean War his only plans for the future were to marry Beatrice and get a job and buy a home out on the far south side of Chicago. . . . They would have children and their children would play in their own yard. Larry would build a barbecue pit in that yard. They would have friends over and drink Martinis and eat barbecue and laugh as loud as they wanted to and play the record player as loud as it would go. . . .

When he got home he found that strange things had happened in Chicago. He found that many jobs were open to him that had been restricted to whites before he left for the service three years earlier. Of the jobs he considered, the police force seemed to offer two things the others lacked: a suitable pension plan that could be put into effect long before he reached the old age of sixty-five, and a position of respect in the community. . . .

Within eighteen months he and Beatrice had saved enough money for a down payment . . . on a six-room house in a neighborhood that was in transition. They were lucky to get the house at such a low price. The owner was anxious to sell, because, as he told Larry: "I got three girls, and all of their little girl friends have moved, and you know how girls are. . . . I've got to sell quick because the place I want in the suburbs—the guy says he'll only hold it off the market a little longer" . . .

Larry had driven halfway down the block, rushing to get to the bank before it closed, talking rapidly about the infinite advantages of this house and how lucky they were to be one of the first Negro families on that particular block, before he noticed that [Beatrice] was crying.

He stopped the car quickly. "Are you all right?" he asked anxiously. . . .

"No, no, darling. I'm happy. That's all. I'm just too happy. I pray to God we can get that house . . ."

They moved a week later and Larry found when he returned to his beat that his determination to have a home had had far-reaching effects. To his amazement, the people of the old neighborhood not only understood his desire to move but cheered his accomplishment and urged him on to higher goals. He was shocked to find that they considered him as something of a success symbol and wished all the best for him. . . . And since he had been placed in such an extremely high position in their minds, he found himself responding to it with a genuine concern for those who felt so much warmth for him. The children loved him, too, and he found that he had become the father image for a great many of them, even some of those who had fathers. The little ones tugged at his trousers and played cops and robbers with him, and sometimes, against his will, rode on the fender of the squad car until he chased them away in pretended anger.

One Saturday afternoon Larry stopped to play handball with some of the younger boys. The games were played across the street from the school store against the red brick wall of the school auditorium, directly under a sign that read NO HAND-BALL PLAYING ALLOWED.

After the game a boy of about eight came up to Larry and said, "You know, Officer Atkins, it'd be great if you was a teacher, 'cause then you could tell us 'bout the war and all that, you know, and we could have some real honest-to-goodness fun in school, you know, and I bet you could teach us a lotta other things, too, you know, and I bet you'd be a good teacher, too, and I bet you could be principal, too, and . . ."

The idea seemed to explode inside his head and Larry thought about it for weeks, fighting it with every reasonable argument he could muster. . . . They needed him because he knew where they were weakest and they would respect him and they would either learn or else!

But all that was six years ago. That was when he and Beatrice were much younger. That was when they were not afraid to be dreamers. . . . That was

RONALD L. FAIR

when they were young enough to think that they could erase their past by beautifying the future. . . . That was all before he began to see the world with the cold, sick eyes of the materialist. The dreams were all before he had forgotten the reasons behind the seemingly uncalled-for actions of the people of his neighborhood. That was before the crime rate there took such a sharp turn upward, and before he had been shot while trying to break up a fight between a woman and a man. It was before he was knifed four times—the last time in the thigh, by a drunk, when he and John stopped at a tavern and walked right into a dozen knives.

John had become his partner only two years ago when the new superintendent had issued orders to integrate all aspects of the force, and when John joined him, Larry began to feel ashamed of these people he had known all his life. . . . He found himself wanting to be something other than a black man and finally succeeded in convincing himself that he had nothing in common with these people except color, which was purely an accident of birth. . . . He would finish school and he would become a teacher, but not because he was dedicated, not any longer. . . . He would take up teaching because he wanted to break all ties with that animalistic world, and becoming a professional man would make the break final. This would put him at the very pinnacle of his middle-class society, and he would never look back again.

Useni Eugene Perkins (b. 1932)

In his introduction to Perkins's latest book, *Images and Memories: Selected Poems,* Haki Madhubuti says, "Of the Chicago writers to emerge out of the dynamic sixties, [Perkins] is one of the few who embraced the mission of cultural worker/artist/activist." He has published, besides *Images and Memories* (2002), seven other poetry volumes, including *An Apology to My African Brother* (1965), *Black Is Beautiful* (1968), and *Midnight Blues in the Afternoon* (1984). Among his more than twenty-five plays are *Cry of the Black Ghetto* (1970) and *Pride of Race* (1984), as well as plays on the lives of Fred Hampton, Leadbelly, and Cinque. In 2000, he was inducted into the National Literary Hall of Fame for Writers of African Descent, and in 2002 received the Black Theater Network Playwriting Award. But beyond these literary honors, Perkins has long been beloved for his involvement in the Black community as a proponent of institutions like Third World Press, and especially as a social worker and champion of youth, these latter roles manifesting themselves not only in the everyday lives and struggles of young people, but also in three highly regarded books of social investigation: *Home Is a Dirty Street: The Social Oppression of Black Children* (1975), *Harvesting New Generations: The Positive Development of Black Youth* (1986), and *Explosion of Chicago's Street Gangs, 1900 to the Present* (1987). His writings for youth include *Afrocentric Self Inventory and Discovery Workbook for African American Youth* (1989), and *The Black Fairy and Other Plays* (1993). In 1969, he received the Malcolm X Manhood Award, and in 1970 an award from the Concerned Parents of Lawndale. The poem below from *Silhouette* (1970) rides on the major artistic inspiration of his writing, Black music, but in its antiwar theme and lines about building "humane housing" and "survival schools," his social activism also shines brightly.

A Poem for Jazz Lovers and People Who Hate Wars

> Blow the minds
> of neo colonial imperialists
> with a side from one of BUDDY BOLDEN'S
> excursions in rhythm. Let the NEW ORLEANS
> BRASS BAND play dirges for the pentagon's
> war lords. Change the national anthem into
> a blues sermon accompanied with a solo by
> FATS NAVARO. And let BESSIE SMITH moan
> over the silent grave of the unknown soldier.
> Place jazz organs in all churches so the people
> can pray to real soul. Build monuments for the

DELTA BLUES SINGERS and a tomb
    for JELLY ROLL MORTON
that will ring chimes of joy during phoney peace
treaty talks
    Replace midnight bombing raids with
    jam sessions that will wail until
    the ruins of war torn cities have
    been rebuilt with humane housing.
Abolish the draft system
and let those who crave destruction
enlist as mercenaries in judas' army. Commission
COUNT BASIE to write a peace concerto/with reeds
and percussion blowing sounds from the aboriginal
bush land to the azure mouth of cape horn
    and the music of SUN RA soar
through orbit leaving vibrations of love on the
planets of jupiter, mars, mercury, uranus, venus.
Abandon the space program and begin building
                        survival schools to
                        save the next
                        generation.
Cease the armaments race and join the battle of
tenors with ILLINOIS JACQUET and SONNY STITT
blowing on a stage before a group of
                        army deserters.

SAVE OUR SOULS
SAVE THE JAZZ BANDS that were left dragging
                    their music on ramparts st.
SAVE THE FUNKY BLUES MUSICIANS with beat up
                    instruments who have been denied
            scholarships to downtown
            conservatories.

SAVE THE USA from becoming
a first class whore and
being the world's greatest

USENI EUGENE PERKINS

carrier of VD.
Let AMIRI BARAKA write a symphonic poem
To unite the THIRD WORLD and a requiem for
> gluttonous nations that
> feed on the lives of
> unarmed people
> and JAMES BROWN sing a blues hymn
> for the UN security council.

Appoint OLATUNJI as
ambassador to south africa
> to lead a choir of
> white racists in a
> song of repentance

Let there be no more Armageddons to
honor men with medals for being
hired assassins
> (custer's cracked skull
> can never be memorialized
> under the
> stained bugle
> calls of death)

Ban the battle hymn of the republic
From being sung in nursery schools
and close down factories that make
> atrocious weapons to
> commit genocidal acts
> under the name of/god/

Let the world be a be-bop serenade
a crazy chord/   an intermission
> without a final chorus
> RIFFING/RIFFING/RIFFING

SAVE JAZZ

USENI EUGENE PERKINS

183

DESTROY WAR   Make five star generals
                     take violin lessons from
                     STUFF SMITH
Let the world be a jazz melody
                     and
save it from self destruction.

Dick Gregory (b. 1932)

Besides being one of the funniest men in the history of American showbiz, Richard Claxton Gregory has been an activist in civil rights, in politics, and in food and health issues. An activist vegetarian, he dedicated one of his books to "America's health-food stores, chiropractors, and naturopaths, and all others concerned with purifying the system." Because of his efforts to purify many systems—bodily, social, political—he has been dubbed a "fierce crusader" and a "drum major of justice and equality." In 1968, he campaigned for the presidency and was the write-in candidate of the New Party, of which he was also co-chair. Among his classic comedy records are: *Caught in the Act, The Light Side: The Dark Side, Live at the Village Gate,* and *Dick Gregory at Kent State.* Among his books are: *The Shadow That Scares Me* (1968), *No More Lies: The Myth and Reality of American History* (1972), *Dick Gregory's Political Primer* (1972), and most recently *A Callus on My Soul* (2000). The excerpt below comes from his autobiography *Nigger!* (1964)—which bears the famous dedication: "Dear Momma—Wherever you are, if ever you hear the word 'nigger' again, remember they are advertising my book." It also contains a transcription of one of his classic bits: Informed by a waitress in the South that they don't serve colored people, he says, "That's all right. I don't eat colored people. Bring me a whole fried chicken." Then in walk three cousins—Klu, Kluck, and Klan—who say they're going to do to him anything he does to that chicken. Gregory picks it up and kisses it.

   The excerpt below comes from chapter 4 of the autobiography and details the months just before his big showbiz break and his growing insights into race and comedy. The Apex he refers to is a nightclub he owned for a while.

From *Nigger!*

I lost the Apex Club in the summer of 1959, and the next year and a half was up and down, in and out, hustling and scuffling and pestering people to listen to me, hire me, pay me. But I was moving now, and tasting that thing. The Apex had put the monster back in me for good. In August I got my old job back at the Esquire, at ten dollars a night. I started bugging Herman Roberts, the owner of the biggest Negro night club in America, to come out and catch my act. He wouldn't move. So I brought the mountain to him. The Pan-American Games were in Chicago that year, and I knew a lot of the athletes. I borrowed some money, and rented Roberts Show Club for one night to throw a party for the teams. Naturally, it was a one-man show. Afterwards, Herman Roberts came up to me and asked how much I wanted to be master of ceremonies at his club. I said $125 a week. He nearly slipped and said: "Is that all?"

All the top Negro acts played Roberts in those days—Sarah Vaughan, Count Basie, Sammy Davis, Jr., Billy Eckstine, Nipsey Russell, Dinah Washington. There was Red Saunders' big house band, an eight-girl chorus line, and more than a thousand seats. When I stood on that electrically powered stage and introduced the acts and gave the coming attractions, I felt like a top Negro act, too. I rented a furnished apartment for $25 a week and brought Lil and Michele into Chicago. The kitchen was in the basement, but it was home and we were together. Told everybody I was on my way. Had me a few words with that dumb Esquire management. Too quick. The Roberts job folded a month later; I didn't know he only kept his M.C.'s four weeks at a time.

Lil got her old job back at the University of Chicago, and we bought a ten-year-old Plymouth for fifty dollars. No insurance and no floorboards, but every day, with six-month-old Michele on the front seat, the old car made the rounds. Booking agents, night-club owners, people who knew people. Now and then we'd come up with something, ten dollars here, fifty there, once a $175-a-week gig at a white honky-tonk. I lasted only a week there. Told the management they'd have to stop those B-girls from tricking the tourists so badly if they wanted to retain an artist of my caliber.

So Michele grew a little older in the front seat of that Plymouth. She never cried, never carried on, just lay there all wrapped up in blankets against the wind coming in from underneath. We pestered more people, kept going around to the union, the American Guild of Variety Artists. On Monday nights, AGVA members got a chance to audition in front of an audience of white night-club owners and agents. Every time I asked them to put me on an AGVA night they asked me if I could sing or dance.

"I'm a comedian, sir."

"We'll have an opening for you in about a year and a half."

Whenever things got too tight, I'd pick up a little money washing cars, doing little things here and there. Then Herman Roberts called again. Only ten dollars a night to start during this time, and I'd have to help the waiters seat the customers during the Sammy Davis, Jr., engagement. But I could stay for as long as I was funny. It was at Roberts that I learned one of the greatest lessons in show business.

Sammy Davis, Jr., and Nipsey Russell were appearing on the same bill at Roberts, probably the biggest attraction the club ever had. They were playing to 90-per-cent white audiences, and for many of those customers it was their first trip to the South Side of Chicago. For most, it was the first time they had ever been to the South Side at night. The Club was packed with white executives who were slipping the waiters fifty-dollar tips for ringside tables. Nipsey would open the show, with a lot of racial comedy, and he absolutely slayed that white audience. They couldn't laugh hard enough. Nipsey stole that show, even against Sammy Davis with all his talents. I couldn't believe it. I tried to figure it out.

A few nights after Nipsey had opened at Roberts, he was called down for an AGVA night. The word had gotten out how well he was going over uptown. I went downtown that Monday night to a white club and watched Nipsey work that audience of white night-club owners. It was the same routine he had killed the customers with at Roberts, but that night Nipsey just sat up there and died. He couldn't get the same response he got at Roberts.

And then I began to figure it out. A white man will come to the Negro club, so hung up in this race problem, so nervous and afraid of the neighborhood and the people that anything the comic says to relieve his tension will absolutely knock him out. The harder that white man laughs, the harder he's saying, "I'm all right, boy, it's that Other Man downtown." That white customer in the Negro club is filled with guilt and filled with fear. I've seen a white man in a Negro club jump up and say "Excuse me" to a Negro waitress who just spilled a drink in his lap. If that same thing happened in a white night club, that man would jump up, curse, and call his lawyer. That was the kind of audience that Nipsey slayed in the Roberts Show Club. But when Nipsey went downtown for AGVA night he was in the white man's house, and the white man felt comfortable and secure. He didn't have to laugh at racial material that he really didn't want to hear.

This gave me something to think about, to work with. Some day I'm going to be performing where the bread is, in the big white night clubs. When I step up on that stage, in their neighborhood, some of them are going to feel sorry for me because I'm a Negro, and some of them are going to hate me because I'm a Negro. Those who feel sorry might laugh a little at first. But they can't respect someone they pity, and eventually they'll stop laughing. Those who hate me aren't going to laugh at all.

I've got to hit them fast, before they can think, just the way I hit those kids back in St. Louis who picked on me because I was raggedy and had no Daddy. I've got to go up there as an individual first, a Negro second. I've got to be a colored funny man, not a funny colored man. I've got to act like a star who isn't sorry for himself—that way, they can't feel sorry for me. I've got to make jokes about myself, before I can make jokes about them and their society—that way, they can't hate me. Comedy is friendly relations.

"Just my luck, bought a suit with two pair of pants today—burnt a hole in the jacket."

That's making fun of yourself.

"They asked me to buy a lifetime membership in the NAACP, but I told them I'd pay a week at a time. Hell of a thing to buy a lifetime membership, wake up one morning and find the country's been integrated."

That makes fun of the whole situation.

Now they're listening to you, and you can blow a cloud of smoke at the audience and say:

"Wouldn't it be a hell of a thing if all this was burnt cork and you people were being tolerant for nothing?"

Now you've got them. No bitterness, no Uncle Tomming. We're all aware of what's going on here, aren't we, baby? Now you can settle down and talk about anything you want: Fall-out shelters, taxes, mothers-in-law, sit-ins, freedom riders, the Congo, H-bomb, the President, children. Stay away from sex, that's the big pitfall. If you use blue material only, you slip back into being that Negro stereotype comic. If you mix blue and topical satire that white customer, all hung up with the Negro sex mystique, is going to get uncomfortable.

In and out of Roberts in 1960, I had plenty of time to think. I realized that when I started working the white clubs, one of my big problems was going to be hecklers—especially in the beginning when I'd be in honky-tonk white clubs. Handling a heckler just right is very important to a comic. Unless you're well known as an insulting comedian you can't chop hecklers down too hard or the crowd will turn against you. Most hecklers are half drunk anyway, and you will lose a crowd if you get mean with a drunk. On the other hand, you have to put a heckler down. If a heckler gets the best of you, that crowd will start to feel sorry for you. I had worked it out pretty well in the Negro clubs. I'd put a drunken heckler down gently: "Man, I'd rather be your slave than your liver," and that would go even better in a white club. Whenever I got a vicious heckler, I could say something like: "Now how would you like it if I came to your job and kicked the shovel out of your hand?" That would work fine, too. But some day, somewhere, I'd be in a white club and somebody would get up and call me a nigger.

I worried about that. When that white man calls me nigger, every other white man in that club is going to feel embarrassed. The customers are going to tie in that uncomfortable feeling with that club—even after I'm gone—and the club owner knows this. He would rather keep me out of his club than take a chance on losing customers. It was the same thing when I got kicked in the mouth as a shoeshine boy—the bartender ran me out of the place, even though he felt sorry for me, because he couldn't afford to have the customers fight. But now I'm a man and I have to take care of myself. I need a fast comeback to that word. That split second is all the difference between going on with the show or letting the customers feel pity and a little resentment for the entertainer who got put down.

I used to make Lillian call me a nigger over the dinner table, and I'd practice the fast comeback. Somehow, I couldn't get it right. I'd always come back with something a little bitter, a little evil.

"Nigger."

"Maybe you'd feel more like a man if you lived down South and had a toilet with your name on it."

"No, Greg, that's not right at all"

I was lying around the house one night, watching television and feeling mad at the world. I'd been out of work for three weeks. The snow was so deep I hadn't even been outside the house for four days. Lil was sitting in a corner, so calm and peaceful, reading a book. There was no one else to pick on.

"Hey, Lil."

"Yes, Greg."

"What would you do if from here on in I started referring to you as bitch?"

She jumped out of the chair. "I would simply ignore you."

I fell off the couch and started laughing so hard that old stomach of mine nearly burst. That was it. The quick, sophisticated answer. Cool. No bitterness. The audience would never know I was mad and mean inside. And there would be no time to feel sorry for me. Now I'd get that comeback.

I got my chance a few weeks later, in a run-down neighborhood club on the outskirts of town. The customers were working-class white men, laborers, factory hands, men whose only marks of dignity were the Negroes they bossed on the job and kept away from on weekends. It happened in the middle of the late show on the second night. Loud and clear.

"Nigger."

The audience froze, and I wheeled around without batting an eye. "You hear what that guy just called me? Roy Rogers' horse. He called me Trigger."

I had hit them so quick that they laughed, and they laughed hard because that was what they really wanted to believe the guy had called me. But I had only bought myself a little time. There was an element in the house that really knew what he had called me. I had the crowd locked up with that fast comeback, so I took a few seconds to look them over and blow out some smoke.

"You know, my contract reads that every time I hear that word, I get fifty dollars more a night. I'm only making ten dollars a night, and I'd like to put the owner out of business. Will everybody in the room please stand up and yell nigger?"

They laughed and they clapped and I swung right back into my show. Afterwards, the owner came over and gave me twenty dollars and shook my hand and thanked me. I had made my test.

The weather broke, and Michele and I got back into the Plymouth and made our rounds. Another gig in a white club, a little place in Mishawaka, Indiana, ninety-eight miles from Chicago on the other side of South Bend. I drove the distance every night because at ten dollars I couldn't afford a hotel. That club was a big thing in Mishawaka, and the white folks lined up early to get in. It was on a Saturday night, the place was packed, and I kept noticing a group of white girls sitting on the lounge chairs near the back. They were drinking pretty heavily, and laughing at all the wrong places.

Suddenly, one of the girls shouted: "You're handsome."

Every white man in the place froze. That's that sex angle, thrown right in your face, and the whole room hates you for it. Okay, here we go.

"Honey, what nationality are you?"

"Hungarian."

"Take another drink. You'll think you're Negro. Then you'll run up here and kiss me and we'll both have to leave town in a hurry."

That busted it. The room came all the way down again, and you could hear the relief in that explosion of laughter. If there was any hate left in that room, it was for that girl.

I felt stronger and stronger now, more confident that I could handle anything that came up.

Conrad Kent Rivers (1933–1968)

Conrad Kent Rivers's success with poetry began in high school, when his "Poor Peon" won the Savannah, Georgia, State Poetry Prize in 1951. He went on to publish many poems in such magazines as the *Antioch Review*, the *Kenyon Review, Negro Digest,* and many others. His books of poetry include *Perchance to Dream, Othello* (1959), *These Black Bodies and This Sunburnt Face* (1962), and *Dusk at Selma* (1965). After graduating from Chicago State, he taught in the Gary public schools until his sudden death in 1968, the same year the interesting Heritage series from London's Paul Breman house published his powerful *The Still Voice of Harlem.* Breman also published posthumously his *The Wright Poems* (1972), where he pursues the idea of Richard Wright's returning from Paris to lead a Black cultural revolution. The poems below come from these two volumes. For the 1962 anthology *Sixes and Sevens,* he wrote this:

> ". . . I am not at peace with myself or my world. I cannot divorce my thoughts from the absolute injustice of hate. I cannot reckon with my color. . . . And I shall continue to write about race—in spite of many warnings—until I discover myself, my future, my real race. . . . I agree with Baldwin that 'nobody knows my name.' All the standards for which the western world has lived so long are in the process of breakdown and revision; and beauty, and joy, which was in the world before and has been buried so long, has got to come back."

One of his most famous poems is the short "Watts:" "Must I shoot the / white man dead / to free the nigger / in his head?" The Conrad Kent Rivers Prize has been a coveted award of the Chicago writing community, which he honored many times, including with the poems below to Richard Wright and Hoyt W. Fuller.

Four Sheets to the Wind and a One-Way Ticket to France, 1933

As a Black Child I was a dreamer
I bought a red scarf and women told me how
Beautiful it looked.
Wandering through the heart of France
As France wandered through me.

In the evenings,
I would watch the funny people make love,
My youth allowed me the opportunity to hear
All those strange
Verbs conjugated in erotic affirmations,
I knew love at twelve.

When Selassie went before his peers and
Africa gained dignity
I read in two languages, not really caring
Which one belonged to me.

My mother lit a candle for King George,
My father went broke, we died.
When I felt blue, the champs understood,
And when it was crowded, the alley
Behind Harry's New York bar soothed my
Restless spirit.

I liked to watch the Bohemians gaze at the
Paintings along Gauguin's bewildered paradise.

Braque once passed me in front of the Cafe Musique
I used to watch those sneaky professors examine
The populace,
American never quite fitted in, but they
Tried, so we smiled.

I guess the money was too much for my folks,
Hitler was such a prig and a scare, they caught
The last boat.
        I stayed.

Main street was never the same, I read Gide
And tried to
Translate Proust. (Now nothing is real except
French wine.)
For absurdity is reality, my loneliness unreal,

And I shall die an old Parisian, with much honor.

Underground

(black cat)

Under bright city lights
I swing on rusty water pipes

like a wolf running wacky
across high circus wires.

I frequent basement parlors
where jazz freaks a blonde
drunk on black jazzmen blowing
sartonian melodies.

In air-cooled clean apartments where
dim darkness is defined powerless
by a parted sun patently and
niggardly going berserk, baby,
in the first person singular
I swing through the city full of blues.

A mourning letter from Paris

(for Richard Wright)

All night I walked among your spirits, Richard:
the Paris you adored is most politely dead.

I found French-speaking bigots and some sterile blacks,
bright African boys forgetting their ancestral robes,
a few men of color seeking the same French girl.

Polished Americans watched the stark reality
of mass integration, pretending not to look homeward
where the high ground smelled of their daughters' death.

I searched for the skin of your bones, Richard.
Mississippi called you back to her genuine hard clay,
but here one finds a groove, adapts, then lingers on.

For me, my good dead friend of searing words
and thirsty truth, the road to Paris leads back home:
one gets to miss the stir of Harlem's honeyed voice,
or one forgets the joy to which we were born.

CONRAD KENT RIVERS

In defense of black poets

(for Hoyt)

The critics cry unfair
    yet the poem is born.
Some black emancipated baby
    will scratch his head
wondering why you felt compelled
    to say whatever you said.

A black poet must bear in mind
    the misery.
The color-seekers fear poems
    they can't buy for a ten-dollar
bill or with a clever contract.
    Some black kid is bound to read you.

A black poet must remember the horrors.
    The good jobs can't last forever.
It shall come to pass that the fury
    of a token revolution will fade
into the bank accounts of countless blacks
    and freedom-loving whites.

The brilliant novels shall pass
    into the archives of a 'keep cool
we've done enough for you' generation:
    the movement organizations already
await their monthly checks from Downtown
    and

only the forgotten wails of a few black
    poets and artists
shall survive the then of then,
    the now of now.

CONRAD KENT RIVERS

Johari Amini-Hudson (b. 1935)

Born Jewel Latimore, Johari Amini took a Swahili name meaning "jewel—worthy of trust," which aptly describes her long presence on the Chicago literary scene. She greatly aided Haki Madhubuti in starting Third World Press in 1967 and was a key member of the Organization of Black American Culture (OBAC). She has published many poems in important journals; among her books are *Black Essence* (1968), *Images in Black* (1969), and *Let's Go Somewhere* (1970), which contains the poems reprinted below. Immensely important in forging the new style of the Black Arts Movement, she wrote some of its most beautiful, experimentally vernacular, and hard-edged poems. Gwendolyn Brooks's words about Amini end my introduction to this collection, and I refer the reader there for a testimony of how much she has meant to Black writing in Chicago.

Black Expressions: circa chicago state (& othr state institutions)

the catalogue could have told you
if you had peeped its unreality of values sayin
dont feed the community—eat it

pop crack and snapple pop pop it reads
take this stairway to total blindness
of all the black buds which will settle asphyxiated
anywhere at the bottom of your sunken lovely gut
while you swallow to keep them out of sight
lightly handled smooth to white right
into the noncolor of death

pop pop pop Poppit is the commercial
—say baby, you a poet? i need some culture—

if you serious brother dont keep fallin off the Sphinx
bring me a pigshead and deal with where we are
and why our children still have no land to inherit
thats somebodys joke thats somebodys pale joke
whitewashed like a mask for evil spirits

pop pop pop poppppppp

while we illusion our natural existence for the sister
cuttin her hair to skirt length (14 inches before bendin over)
slippin to liberation like a season goin through changes
unconscious that to liberate is to polarize end from end
not up from up but up from down

pop pop pop crack and snapple
the catalogue could have told you where its comin from

even from the pale pop of coke in your pipe
popped to keep you not hearin the melted corridors in
your mind spread to a pulse of

can you culture can you culture can you culture

you can culture freedom after we liberate us
be actual to deal in solid movements not facsimile raps
turn it over through reality

like Henry Byrd from 43rd
the concentric reflection of what we need
just to survive bein here

turn it over yourself through your self
turn it over past the shorter run of now
turn it over infinity and BE

(Untitled)

(in commemoration of the blk/ family)

we will be no generashuns to cum for blks r
killing r.selves did u hear bros. did u hear the
killings did u hear the sounds of the killing
the raping of the urgency of r soil consuming r
own babies burned n the acid dri configurashuns
of the cycles balancing did u hear. did u hear.
hear the sounds of the balancing & checking off

JOHARI AMINI-HUDSON

checking off erasing r existence from the count
of the cosmos while r mother moans for the loss
of r funkshun & who we will never be did u hear
bros. hear. hear. hear the sounds of r mother of
her moaning as she moans while we allow her to
lie stretch ing herself from Dakar to Dar es
Salaam & she moans & tears her flesh & gushes
did u hear the gushing bros. did u hear. hear. did
u hear the sounds of the gushing oil from her
members wetly spraying the auto mated powers of
a foreign god who ruts in. to her did u hear the
sounds. sounds. bros. sounds of the rutting did u
hear. hear did u hear the rutting of the animal
with the golden hair rutting in. to her urgency
eating the sacrificed & futile fetuses erupted
n the fascinated juices of the cycles of pills
which will control the number of her mouths did
u hear. did u hear the cycles turning bros. did u
hear them we will be no mor. . . .

Clarence Major (b. 1936)

Clarence Major was born in Atlanta but grew up on the South Side where, he says, "the writerly disposition that was then evolving was shaped by my life in Chicago." His wide-ranging styles—often praised for their mixtures of slang, history, avant-garde experimentalism, vigor, and gentleness—are rooted in the fact that while he remains firmly planted in Black culture and its South Side moods, Major has also shaped a truly international, cosmopolitan career and vision. "Paris! Why Paris? Why did I—or any African American artist or writer—go to Paris?" he asks in a recent essay. But he knows that "Even before the end of slavery, free mulattos, some of them artists, were traveling to Paris," thereby establishing a tradition followed by hundreds of artists, dancers, musicians, and writers—including Beauford Delaney, Josephine Baker, James Baldwin, Richard Wright, and Major himself, whose 1985 book of poems, *Inside Diameter: The France Poems,* contains some of his most powerful work. Among his many other books of poetry are *Swallow the Lake* (1970), *Surfaces and Masks* (1988), and the wonderful *Syncopated Cakewalk* (1974), from which the poems below come. He has also published collections of short stories, novels, and a dictionary (the 1994 *Juba to Jive: A Dictionary of African-American Slang*). He is also a noted painter, photographer, editor, and essayist. "Discovering Walt Whitman" comes from *Necessary Distance* and is a wonderful counterpart to the 1981 essay by June Jordan "For the Sake of People's Poetry: Walt Whitman and the Rest of Us," where she refers to Whitman as "the one white father who shares the systemic disadvantages of his heterogeneous offspring."

Discovering Walt Whitman

I first found the work of Walt Whitman when I was seventeen years old, in a bleak Catholic Salvage Store on Forty-first Street near State, in segregated Chicago. The copy of *Leaves of Grass* was very old, very musty, but the price was only twenty-five cents. I bought the book and lived with it for quite a while, despite its odor. (My books, in general, were a weird assortment, many of them having come from such dusty shops on the South Side.)

I often lay in my bed in my small room in our home and fingered the old book. I frequently wondered about it having been published during Whitman's lifetime. How remote was the possibility that his hands had touched it? Whitman had died sixty-two years before that year in the summer of my growing pains, yet the physical reality of that book gave me a sense of him different from the one that came so forcefully through his lines. Witness:

> *I loafe and invite my soul,*
> *I lean and loafe at my ease, observing a spear of summer grass.*
> (from "Song of Myself")

What else, except this, is meant by the attainment of oneness with all that is?

And how well, from my childhood's brief stay in the forest behind my grandmother's home, I knew what Whitman meant in the unrestrained glory concealed in the leanness of lines such as,

> *With delicate-colored blossoms,*
>   *and heart-shaped leaves of rich green*
> *A sprig, with its flower, I*
>   *break.*
> (from "Song of Myself")

But there was never any Whitman in school. There was Shakespeare. Whitman was too revolutionary for South Side high schools.

Still, I was always discovering things on my own. Just as I had discovered, Paul Laurence Dunbar and Phillis Wheatley, I found Whitman, and enjoyed his openness, his emotional outbursts, his long lines measured against short lines, his healthy frankness in matters sexual and racial, his acceptance of his own body without the usual Puritan hang-ups, his natural understanding of who and what human beings are, what they amount to, living together in a society. Whitman fought social restrictions, the Puritanical stifling air. But it is still here to breathe.

Whitman is valuable because he was a good and original poet and because he found his own way to be good at making poems. I remember sitting on the floor in the library on an Air Force base in Cheyenne, Wyoming, for two hours one day when it was below zero outside, reading and rereading *Leaves*. It kept coming back into my life. And even now while describing important events in my life, Whitman has a place again.

William Carlos Williams (who read some of my early poems and wrote to me about them), in *Spring and All,* said: "When in the condition of imaginative suspense only will the writing have reality, as explained partially in what precedes—Not to attempt, at that time, to set values on the word being used, according to pre-supposed measures, but to write down that which happens at that time—"

When I was working on the *Dictionary of Afro-American Slang,* I discovered that Whitman had a message for me: "Language," he wrote, "is not an abstract construction of the learned, or of dictionary-makers, but is something arising out of the work, needs, ties, joys, affections, tastes, of long generations of humanity, and has its basis broad and low, close to the ground."

CLARENCE MAJOR

And the "ground" to Whitman, never forget, was not the symbol of degradation. It stood for all glory.

Read the Signs

I don't want to speak of your sky
and my sea and their land
and our people—or of the cars
the roads the houses.
The sky is a long list of verbs.
The sea is its table of contents.
The landscape is something people move across.
Out of their cars,
people themselves are like bushes near water.
They drink it through their roots.
The background tension you feel
comes on because talking begins from fear.
These roads we use are actually dried-out rivers
that lead us into each other's lives.

A Guy I Know on 47th and Cottage

The day of the strong rap
does not build to a close.

I see it, the heavy plop, climb
from the mouths of twelve-year-olds

in backyards trying to be honey cats
like their fathers. Same

values—big cars giant hearts.
Laying a nickel on somebody

to impress the Lady. Grand
Theft Money. Moving up from lazy

bread to French muffins. Hawking foreign
chicks rather than mellow yella. In the future

CLARENCE MAJOR

I can just see him grown and slick
in a hog on a heavy map he thinks is the end,

the greatest. See him throwing a few dimes
to the Grape Society in the nearby alley.

He'll go to see his mama and sister about
once a month to lay a big buck on them,

knowing Mother's Day will not come
till the end of the month.

The Syncopated Cakewalk

My present life is a Sunday-morning cartoon.
In it, I see Miss Hand and her Five Daughters
rubbing my back and the backs of my legs.
Nat King Cole provides the music and the words.
It's 1949. Finished with them, I take off
on a riverboat, down the Mississippi, looking for work.
On deck they got the Original Dixieland Jazz Band
doing "Big Butter and Egg Man."
A guru has the cabin next to mine and everybody
who visits him whimpers something terrible!
Stood on deck after dinner watching the clouds
form faces and arms. The Shadow went
        by giggling to himself.
An Illinois Central ticket fell from his pocket.
Snake Hips picked it up and ran.
Texas Shuffle, who sat in with the Band last night,
        this morning, dropped his fiddle cases
in the ocean and did the Lindy all the way
to the dinning room.
I got off at Freak Lips Harbor.
Boy from Springfield said he'd talk like Satch for me
        for a dime. I gave him a Bird
and an introductory note to the Duke of Ellington.
Found my way to the Ida B. Wells Youth Center.

Girl named Ella said I'd have to wait to see Mister B.
Everybody else was out to lunch.
In the waiting room got into a conversation.
          with a horse thief from Jump Back. Told him:
My past life is a Saturday-morning cartoon.
In it, I'm jumping Rock Island freight cars, skipping
Peoria with Leadbelly, running from the man,
accused of being too complex to handle.
Sorry. Just trying to prove my innocence.
Meanwhile, Zoot, Sassy, Getz, Prez, Cootie, everybody
          give me a hand.
Finally, Mister B comes in. Asks about my future.
All I can say is, I can do the Cow-Cow Boogie
          on the ocean and hold my own in a chase chorus
          among the best!
Fine, says Mister B, *you start seven in the morning!*

Sterling Plumpp (b. 1940)

Born in rural Mississippi in 1940, Sterling Plumpp has for thirty years taught at the University of Illinois, Chicago, and produced a body of poetry that gives him considerable claim to be one of the country's most distinguished blues-jazz poets. Somber inflections from his Mississippi origins combine with a rougher, more boisterous Chicago voice to create a style that sets him apart from poets like Langston Hughes and Michael Harper, who have also written many jazz-blues poems. The first selection below comes from the haunting collection *Blues Narratives* (1999), which deals in large part with his mother's death, and through that the Black will to survive. The other two pieces are from *Horn Man* (1995), based on the life and music of legendary Chicago saxophonist Von Freeman, whom Plumpp calls "Von. / A / Free / man," thus expanding him into a symbol of various modes and energies of freedom. Among Plumpp's other books are *Black Rituals* (1972), a prose work dealing with psychological oppression in the Black community; and many books of poetry, including *Clinton* (1976, winner of an Illinois Arts Council Literary Award), *The Mojo Hands Call, I Must Go* (1982, winner of the Sandburg Poetry Prize), *Blues: The Story Always Untold* (1989), and *Ornate with Smoke* (1997). Plumpp has said of his poems that they trace "the survival lines of my people in the many ways they did things." His music poems illustrate what Ralph Ellison once said about the blues: that they were "one of the techniques through which Negroes have survived and kept their courage during the long period when many whites assumed, and some still assume, they were afraid."

From *Blues Narratives*

#13

I moan
my song and
I do
not moan it
loud

I moan
my song and
I do
not moan it
loud

Cause
I am just a stranger

whether I am
all alone
or in a crowd

I commit
to memory your agony
and confessions of
the last slave to die
in America

(It is your responsibility
to carry it)

You tell

it to me hours before
you are gone

You pay my fare
wells with a request

The irony
you telling a son
stranded on a bridge
between love and ambivalence how

to assist you on
to the stage of exit

but the morgue
cosmetician thinks
you are going
to a party

I order him
to remove powder
and rouge

so blues
lines can still
reside in this symphony
of night which is
your face

> *When I*
> *ask for bread*
> *ask for medicine*
> *ask for clothes*
> *ask for rent*

> *When I*
> *ask for bread*
> *ask for medicine*
> *ask for clothes*
> *ask for rent*

> *They say*
> *Yesterday*
> *that money was all*
> *ready spent*

From *Horn Man*

BE-BOP

1.

Be-Bop is precise clumsiness.
    Awkward lyricism
    under a feather's control.
A world in a crack.
Seen by ears.
    Von Freeman's
tenor Apocalypses /beginning
skies fussy about air and protective
    of trombones on Jacob's Ladder
    strung from basses
in a corner of handclaps.

Drums praying over evil
    done by trumpets
    and dances in fingertips.
Be-Bop is elusive hammerlocks
a piano accords crescendos
    in blue moanings.
Lingers in beats marching
    across faces of sense.
Harmonic nightmares obeying
    pianissimos of tones
erupting from barks of Powell.
Be-Bop is unexpected
    style punching music
with garlic in tempo.
    Billie's pain
    and a cup of insinuations
    drunk by laughter
    before tears arise.

       7.

All about laughter over pain.
(A hall telephone for sale.

A quartet. This singular tenor's rampages.
Chicago pathfinder strutting on broken glass
and bricks. So much live talk and the advice
of curtains. Pulled over opportunities.
Each a night /a leap year from evolutions
in his speech. Jug's big hits
among my foolishness where tomorrows
climb on bones of nightscarred lynchings.
Ascend heavens where my songs elicit
their metaphors from blood. And, clocks
I teach, affirm time I conjure. Night
after night, landscapes offer pilgrims
a place to dream. (all my wife—in—laws
on parade.

The tall anticipation of oak
spreads over: you can help yourself,
baby, you can rise . . .

Haki R. Madhubuti (b. 1942)

Haki Madhubuti was born in Detroit as Don L. Lee in 1942 and his daring voice, inventive phrasing, and ability to capture the rhythms and sardonic moods of Black speech have made him one of the two or three most imitated Black poets in America. Since 1984, he has been an associate professor of English at Chicago State University, and, with Gwendolyn Brooks and Richard Wright, has had perhaps the most important impact on Black writing from Chicago. His many volumes of poetry include *Don't Cry, Scream* (1969), *Killing Memory, Seeking Ancestors* (1987), and *Groundworks: New and Selected Poems of Don L. Lee/Haki R. Madhubuti, 1966–1996*. He also edited the highly influential 1971 anthology *Dynamite Voices I: Black Poets of the 1960s*, a celebration of the Black Arts Movement of that decade, of which he was a major figure. But Madhubuti's influence has extended far beyond his writing. As editor-publisher of Chicago's Third World Press, director of the Institute of Positive Education, founder of the Gwendolyn Brooks Center, and fierce crusader for independent Black institutions, his impact on the cultural unity and social, psychological, educational, and economic vision of Black people in America and throughout the world has been enormous. Among his books speaking directly to such issues are *Enemies: The Clash of Races* (1978) and *African Centered Education: Its Value, Importance and Necessity in the Development of Black Children* (1994). Even without the help of a major national distributor, Madhubuti's books have sold more than a million copies. In 1990, he published *Black Men: Obsolete, Single, Dangerous?* Here his focus is on the problems with and hopes for "Afrikan American Families in Transition," as part of his subtitle reads. The book is a compendium of analysis, advocacy, and memoir sprinkled with poems—and lists, like "The Five Most Often Used Excuses Black Men Give to Black Women," "200 Books All Black People Should Study," and "Twelve Secrets of Life." There are chapters on food and marriage, and—among much advice directed towards Black men—a chapter called "Before Sorry: Listening to and Feeling the Flow of Black Women." The selections below come from this book. In "Never Without a Book," the prefatory essay to his list of two hundred books, he tells us that from 1961 to 1966 his "study regimen . . . was to read a book a day and write a 150 to 200-word review of the book." Such intensity and determination, matched with a unique personal grace, runs not only through his writing but also through his relationships with others.

From *Black Men: Obsolete, Single, Dangerous?*

The B Network

> brothers bop & pop and be-bop in cities locked up
> and chained insane by crack and other acts
> of desperation computerized in pentagon cellars producing
> boppin brothers boastin of being better, best & beautiful.

if the boppin brothers are beautiful where are the sisters
who seek brotherman with a drugless head unbossed or beaten
by the bodacious West?

in a time of big wind being blown by boastful brothers,
will other brothers beat back backwardness to better & best
without braggart bosses beatin butts,
takin names and diggin graves?

beatin badness into bad may be urban but is it beautiful &
    serious?
or is it betrayal in an era of prepared easy death hangin on
    corners
trappin young brothers before they know the difference between
big death and big life?

brothers bop & pop and be-bop in cities locked up
and chained insane by crack and other acts
of desperation computerized in pentagon cellars producing
boppin brothers boastin of being better, best, beautiful
and definitely not *Black*.

the critical best is that
brothers better be the best if they are to avoid backwardness
brothers better be the best if they are to conquer beautiful
    bigness
Comprehend that bad is only *bad* if it's big, Black and better than
boastful braggarts belittling our best and brightest
with bosses seeking inches when miles are better.
brothers need to bop to being Black & bright & above board
the black train of beautiful wisdom that is bending this bind
towards a new & knowledgeable beginning that is
bountiful & bountiful & beautiful
While be-boppin to be
better than the test,
brotherman.

better yet write the exam.

HAKI R. MADHUBUTI

WHERE IS THE FUTURE?

It was late Friday on a hot July night that the temperature rose to 101 degrees, driving mothers, fathers and children out of projects and tenements to front stoops, parks, bar stools and small back-alley crap games. Anything to deal with the heat. Johnny J., T.C. and Bigfoot were throwing sevens for small change in the back of the Godfather No. 2 lounge on Chicago's west side.

At about 1:00 A.M., lights from two directions hit their game, and they were ordered to "hug the ground" by two white male cops and one Black female cop. One of the white cops told all three to get up and spread eagle against the wall of the Godfather lounge and ordered the Black woman cop to search the Black men. As the woman went up and down Bigfoot's pants legs he moved as she touched his penis and commented "ain't that a bitch." At that moment, the Black woman cop—hearing only the word "bitch" and feeling his movement—fell backwards, pulled her 38 special, and proceeded with surgeon's accuracy to blow the right side of Bigfoot's head off. The Black woman cop was congratulated, promoted, decorated by her superiors and detailed to another Black community. All three Black men had records, and T.C. and Johnny J. were given three years for resisting arrest. What had been described as "justifiable homocide" was in the real world "one less nigger," murdered not by a white or Black male cop, but by a Black woman cop. Few saw the significance of this act.

Bigfoot, at twenty-five, was in the prime of his life and *never* had a chance. To die at such a young age and at the hands of a Black woman remains a mysterious irony that will plague us as we move into the 21st century. What may be the ultimate and most profound reality of our current situation may well be that some of the mothers that bring life may indeed be the mothers or daughters of mothers that aid Black men and white men in the removal of Black men from this part of the earth. It's a perfect situation. No voices of protest will fill the streets because it is well known that "niggers" with criminal records are fair game for anybody, especially if one has a license to carry a weapon.

Much of the current Black studies have focused on either the Black family, Black women, Afrika, the Black homosexual community or Europe's and America's influence on the Black world. Few Black scholars or activists have given serious attention to the condition of Black men. There are many reasons for this: 1) much of the published scholarly work on Black people is by Black men and many of them do not see the importance of public self-analysis; 2) it is easier to get studies on Black women or the Black family published; 3) few Black male scholars wish to "wash dirty clothes" in public—and the other side of that is if the Black male situation is accurately assessed, it also means for the intelligent scholars and activists to "clean up their own acts;" 4) many of the scholars and activists are actually functioning in their personal lives contrary to the best interests of Black people (some outright traitors) and finally; 5) studies that bring clarity and direction to the Black male situation as an integral part of the Black family/community are unpopular, not easy to get publish and very dangerous. Too many Afrikan American scholars have looked at the Black situation in America from a European sociological framework, and in doing so, their work has been instrumental in distorting reality and exists as a body of "negative ammunition" to secure faculty positions and publishing contracts, and is ego grease for their warped worldview and sense of importance.

NOT ALLOWED TO BE LOVERS

The root, as well as the quality, of Black life is in the relationship established between Black men and women in a white supremacist system. Black struggle, that is the liberation of our people, starts in the home. This is not to suggest that the dominant society does not affect what happens in the home, but to a significant degree individual members of the family—regardless of the political system they endure—are still able to define relationships among themselves and the society if they are able to *divest* themselves of *role models imposed from the outside.* Indeed, this is not easy and requires an almost complete negation of present values to those that put people in relationships first and prioritize the development of children. Sound and loving relationships are the core of a sane, happy and fruitful life. This is crucial because all too often our patterns of behavior have nothing to do with the real world but are sincere imitations of white European-American madness.

Black life, especially interaction between Black men and women, is perceived from the outside as being fragmented, unstable, insecure, and woman-dominated. This image is solidified by white and Negro doctoral theses and mass media nonsense. If this view of the Black situation is "the" truth (and yes there are elements of truth here), we are indeed in trouble and possibly headed for complete destruction as a people. However, if our family construction, as I believe, was/is built upon a very positive man-woman relationship, one that has enabled us to weather the most severe form of human bondage, then and only then is there hope.

HAKI R. MADHUBUTI

Yes, there is hope, but in the last twenty-seven years or so there has been serious cultural slippage in the Black community to the point that many Black men and women are becoming antagonists, and the liberating cooperation, respect and single-mindedness of spirit and purpose that existed are being replaced with the most gross forms of competition, decadent individualism and sexual exploitation.

Black men in the United States are virtually powerless, landless and moneyless in a land where white manhood is measured by such acquisitions. Most Afrikan Americans have been unable to look at their lives in a historical-racial-political-economic context. Thereby, without the proper tools to analyze, many Black men have defined their lives as Black duplicates of the white male ethos. The problem (and there are many) is that Black men in relationship to Black women cannot, a great majority of the time, deliver the "American dream." Therefore, the dream is often translated into a Black male/female nightmare where Black men, acting out of frustration and *ignorance*, adopt attitudes that are not productive or progressive in relationship to Black women, i.e., many Black men end up treating (or trying to treat) Black women like white men treat white women. The political and sexual games that exist in most cultures of the world that are largely demeaning and disrespectful to women become, due to a lack of *self definition*, Black men's games also.

From "Never Without a Book"

By 1960, the paperback revolution was changing the entire publishing industry, and books written by Blacks were becoming the "in" thing. By this time, I had discovered the "Chicago" writers Frank London Brown *(Trumbull Park)*, Lerone Bennett, Jr. *(Before the Mayflower)* and Gwendolyn Brooks *(A Street in Bronzeville, Annie Allen* and *Maud Martha)*. The works of Langston Hughes entered my world with his *The Langston Hughes Reader*. The "boy" jobs were unstable and didn't pay enough to meet my major expenses of food and housing, so I decided to leave Chicago.

The year 1960 was to be a pivotal one for a number of reasons. I discovered that the needs and problems of what little family I had were so great that they could not help me. I also learned that life's options for a young Black man ranged from few to almost none. The only value a high school diploma had was that, for one who could read, it would facilitate entrance into the armed forces. However, due to a minor heart problem, I couldn't pass the physical and was rejected by the Air Force.

HAKI R. MADHUBUTI

After being rejected by the military (the poor boy's answer to the future and full employment) I did not see too much of a bright tomorrow. I joined a Black magazine selling caravan that traveled throughout down-state Illinois. We stopped in small towns—going from door to door—hawking the popular magazines of the day. There was little money or enjoyment in this work, but it was a way to get out of Chicago. I traveled with an all Black group of young women and men in a caravan of four cars. My second "skill" came into use because the selling pitch was "We are working our way through college." The interesting thing about this slice of life is that this was the first time college *ever entered my mind at a serious level.* I did not think that a university education was possible for poor Black people in America.

Anyway, my travels with these young "entrepreneurs" ended in St. Louis where they left me in a two-dollar-a-day hotel with a serious virus that would not allow food or liquid to remain in my body. Upon recovery, I did "boy" work to survive and spent my evenings in the public library of St. Louis. By that time I had discovered Carter G. Woodson's *The Negro in Our History*; W. E. B. DuBois' *Souls of Black* Folks, *Black Reconstruction in America*, *Dust of Dawn*, *The Suppression of the African Slave-Trade to the United States*; and *Crisis* magazine. However, the work that was to cause me much conflict and inner searching was the *Philosophy and Opinions of Marcus Garvey.* I was becoming more and more aware of the issue of *color,* and these books gave me the historical and political foundation that would lead me to a realistic and deadly understanding of *white world supremacy.*

In October of 1960, without funds or the possibility of a job in a city that was less friendly than Detroit or Chicago, I tried to join the military again. This time it was to be the U.S. Army. Because of my "heart" condition, I knew that the physical exam could be a repeat of my Air Force experience. Therefore, when I walked into the examining room, which was a large, wide open area, I looked for the youngest doctor. They were all white males. During my examination, he caught an irregular heartbeat and asked if I had a heart problem. I promptly said, "No. This is the first time that I've been away from home. I've never been around this many white people before, and I'm a bit nervous." I got in and was shipped to Fort Leonard Wood, Missouri, for basic training.

On the bus to basic training, I was reading Paul Robeson's *Here I Stand*. The book, according to the drill sergeant that welcomed us to the camp, was written by a Black communist (the word "Black" was just as negative as "communist" in 1960) and would only confuse and corrupt my negro mind.

He took the book, held it high above his head as an example of "forbidden fruit," and—in between gutter room invectives—tore the pages from the book, distributing them to the new male recruits and instructing the "ladies" to use the pages as toilet paper. I will not go into this in any more depth except to say that, for me, the military was a blessing in disguise, even though it was there that I had put my life in the hands of men less intelligent than I.

By this time, I was reading E. Franklin Frazier's *Black Bourgeoisie* and Drake's and Cayton's *Black Metropolis*. Race-politics in the United States was heating up, and upon completion of basic training, I was shipped south to Fort Bliss, Texas, for advanced training in military mediocrity. In Texas, partially because there was little to do, I made a decision that would change my life. I took a speed reading course that enabled me to increase my reading speed greatly. I decided that I would become as knowledgeable as possible about Afrikan and Afrikan American people. I was nineteen, and I consciously stopped apologizing for being Black and went on the offense.

Carolyn M. Rodgers (b. 1945)

One of the great American poets to emerge from Chicago in the 1960s, Carolyn M. Rodgers played a major role in Chicago's vibrant Organization of Black American Culture community and, in 1967, helped Haki Madhubuti and Johari Amini found one of Chicago's most important cultural institutions, the Third World Press. In 1970, she received the Society of Midland Authors Poet Laureate award. Author of a novel and many short stories, she is most noted for her poetry, collected in over a dozen books and broadsides, including *Paper Soul* (1968), *how I got ovah* (1975, for which she received a National Book Award nomination), *The Heart as Evergreen* (1978), and *Finite Forms* (1985). She is remarkable for her continued growth as a poet, and the poems below come from *We're Only Human Poems* (1996) and *A Train Called Judah* (1998), two remarkable chapbooks published at her Eden Press (P.O. Box 804271, Chicago, IL 60680). These contain some of the best poetry of her life and deserve as much recognition as any of her other work. From the beginning, Rodgers achieved a unique fusion of what critic Bettye J. Parker-Smith called a "rough hewn, folk spirited" ethos with deep concern for racial, spiritual, and gender issues. The poems below retain this fusion but also go beyond it—moving with even greater ease and sophistication along an international set of concerns and geographies, and understanding and feeling more deeply the large horrors and small redeeming virtues that issue from our humanity.

Prodigal Objects

    when i lose something,
    i am all out in the streets
    looking for it.
    it doesn't matter if I lost it as home,
    or school, or at church.
    i think maybe I'll see it
    way cross town in impossible places.
    department stores, restrooms, hospital
    lobbys, telephone booths.

        earrings, loves, books, buttons,
    notebooks, pens,

    i'm looking for them all.
    say, maybe i lost whatever it is
    in California, and here I am in Chicago,
    2000 miles away, looking for it.

or maybe i lost it in Africa and one
day I get a certain feeling and I'm
in Chicago and i know i lost it, say
400 years ago in Africa,
but on this particular day, I just know
i'm gong to find it in Chicago.

it doesn't matter what it is.

no, it really doesn't matter what it is,
or where I lost it either
what matters is the feeling of finding
(there is a law of finding),
what matters is finding on lost days.

and I'm finding that somedays
what matters as much, is being found.

Sheep

this is how it could be.
this is how it has been someplace,
i think.

with the one arm that i
have managed to salvage from
the ravishing effects of bursitis,
i have just pushed open one of
the three hatches on the bus
i have boarded.

as i walk back to my seat, i
am awed. all summer long, i
have been boarding buses,
with broken or nonexistent air conditioning
where the passengers sit passively in
the hot and stuffy cars looking
sweaty and faintly ill.
with the hatches open, breezes can cool

CAROLYN M. RODGERS

the entire bus as it speeds through the city
streets or along the expressway to downtown.

as i sit in my seat i wonder—
is this how it happens?
you get on a bus one day, riding into life,

and it is hot and stuffy and all the
sheep are sitting there
looking at the closed compartment holes
gasping through the heat for every
smothering breath.

and nobody moves, nobody moves.
if it were a stickup, everybody has
got the right idea.
you can hear a pin drop it is so quiet
except for the bleated breathing.

finally, someone in those last few rides to
Dachau, say for example, sees an opening
in the side of the boxcar and through the
press, they ease towards it, and when the
train slows down, they kick out an exit
for themselves, they jump off the side
of the slaveship, run through the woods

to the underground railroad; there they
join with others to tear down the walls
with bare berlin hands, and east and west,
someone raises a tightly clenched fist
and cries, amande. amande.

and we can all breathe again.
and we can get air.

yes, we get relief, and we ride off into
the sunset or sunrise

CAROLYN M. RODGERS

(with the music playing softly in the
background)

we ride now, vigilant into life, instead
of obedient,
to death.

In the Shadow of Turning: Throwing Salt

Salt is what
it all becomes.
Salt always did make me crave
sugar. If I could have turned and
looked back, like Lot's wife,
I never would have.
Turning is for other memories.

Memories are actually seasons
of homeless dreams.
The main event in life is something
we think we can plan, but can't.
A nest or fishnet of categories. Of hunger.
A need river, running wild in every
imaginable direction.

It would have all been salt, and me,
craving sugar.

Jazz: Mood Indigo

a thin feeling of purple blue
covers me like a fine silvery

green fishnet mist of water.
and my fingers, my soul and my mouth
are blue like berry—stained.

i wish that i could have been a steel
grey boulder shoulder holding you up,

CAROLYN M. RODGERS

and you, a slick fine highway going
anywhere special, somewhere . . .
but you yourself are broken, you tell me,
your life all in pieces. you have
fallen, fallen down
and my fingers and my soul are blue, blue,
blue like berry stained.

Clarence Page (b. 1947)

One of the country's most distinguished journalists, Clarence Page is currently the Washington-based senior correspondent for the *Chicago Tribune*. He spent many years working in print and TV journalism in Chicago, becoming, in 1984, the first Black on the *Tribune*'s editorial board. He is an essayist and panelist for PBS's *NewsHour* and a frequent guest on *The MacLaughlin Group* and other TV news programs. His writing appears in many newspapers and magazines, including the *Wall Street Journal*, *Washington Monthly*, the *Chicago Reader, New York Newsday*, and the *New Republic*. Besides an Illinois UPI Award, an E. S. Beck Award for overseas reporting, and the 1987 McGuire Award for his columns on constitutional rights, Page won a 1972 Pulitzer Prize as part of a *Tribune* task force on voter fraud, and the 1989 Pulitzer Prize for commentary. The essay below comes from *Showing My Color* (1996), a collection of some of his articles on race.

From *Showing My Color*

From "Politics: The 'Race Card' vs. the 'Class Card'"

I am amused whenever Republicans denounce Democrats for waging "class warfare," for their complaint only acknowledges the power class holds as a strategic issue for Democrats, comparable to the power of race for Republicans. Both are delicate issues. Yet effective appeals to class consciousness, suspicions, and resentments win elections.

It only shows that the GOP knows what the game really is.

For better or worse, effective politics is often nothing more than an effective appeal to the resentments of those who vote in large numbers, directed against a target group that doesn't. A reputation for soaking the poor doomed Republican hopes in elections in which the poor, or those who view themselves as poor, outnumbered those who saw themselves as rich. In fact, polls show 90 percent or more of Americans view themselves as middle class, giving America the largest middle class the world has ever known. Here, as in most issues, politics is a manipulated interplay of perceptions. The realignment that has occurred since the 1960s is attributable, more than anything else, to perceptions that Democratic programs, according to Nixon adviser Kevin Phillips, in *The Emerging Republican Majority*, had moved from "taxing the few for the benefit of the many [the New Deal] to programs taxing the many on behalf of the few [the Great Society]."

If white middle-class voters failed to see Democrats as caring about them anymore, even though the largest share of federal spending continues to go to middle-class entitlements like Social Security and Medicare, it was largely because conservatives persuaded numbers of whites that government spending was generally being wasted, mostly on blacks.

Today it is easy to see more clearly than ever that behind middle-class anger, whether it is directed against blacks or taxes, is a greater problem afflicting the group Secretary of Labor Robert Reich called the "anxious class." They are the vast numbers of Americans who see and feel a growing divide between rich and poor, skilled and unskilled, the secure and the insecure in post-industrial America. They have been feeling increasingly nervous about the trend, which appears to be irreversible, and about the weak responses both major parties were making to it.

This middle-class anxiety explains why party loyalty shrunk to record lows by the mid-1990s and the urge to find alternatives soared. In the midst of it all, three years after Doug Wilder's rebuff in New Hampshire, America had a new great black hope. His name was Colin Powell.

The retired army general, first black chairman of the Joint Chiefs of Staff, high commander of the Persian Gulf conflict two-tour Vietnam veteran, and self-made son of Jamaican immigrants to Harlem and the South Bronx, emerged as the front-runner in all demographic, political, and ideological groups—male, female, white, minority, liberal, conservative, Democrat, and Republican—well ahead of the declared field.

Powell's emergence benefited mightily from a national yearning for heroes and "outsiders," as most pundits put it, but more significantly, he embodied more than any other black hero or celebrity the nation's yearning to transcend its agony over race.

Unlike Jesse Jackson, Powell was introduced to the public eye without mention of race. Media stories played down his race and played up the popular *universals* in his life, images that touched on cherished all-American values: born to an immigrant household in a poor ethnic neighborhood; a poorly motivated high school performer who found himself in ROTC; excelled in the army, served *two tours* in Vietnam; studied a year as a White House Fellow during the Nixon years, and eventually was introduced to the world as a key national security adviser to the Gipper himself, Ronald Reagan.

For years he is seen conferring confidently, authoritatively, and (and this was important) *non-threateningly* in the inner circle of advisers to Presidents Reagan and Bush. Not only did he walk, talk, and behave like one of the boys—no dashikis, confrontational talk, or appeals to white guilt here—but he also looked, in his high-*gravitas* way, like the *smartest* guy in the room.

Then there's Desert Storm, where General Norman Schwarzkopf led the forces in the field but Powell confidently led the nation through press conferences that acted to restore whatever lost confidence the nation had in its military forces and, by subtle connection, in the competence of black Americans to hack it with the opportunities we had, at long last, been given.

Even the fact that Powell came to the public eye, through the army had important cultural significance, since the military is the first and, for many, the last time many white American males can recall making a genuine friendship, *Forrest Gump*–style, across racial lines.

Blacks, women, the disabled, and other oppressed and alienated people yearning to feel *rehumanized* after years of dehumanization could find a lot to like about Powell, too. He embodied the desire all oppressed people have to be seen as people first.

Americans became so invested in the notion of Colin Powell as a black man who had made it on merit and merit alone despite his racial assignment to American society's lowest caste, confirming the durable goodness of the American Dream, that he actually appeared to have turned his race into an *advantage*.

National polling on racial attitudes, conducted by Paul M. Sniderman, a Stanford University political scientist, for the National Science Foundation, supports that point. Sniderman found that Powell's race, in some polls, actually "magnifies his political strength," he said. When whites of all ideological stripes encounter an individual black person whose character refutes negative racial stereotypes, he said, "their response is to respond *even more positively* to him." In other words, white voters will vote for a black who is not *too black* in the sense of their stereotypes about blackness. Powell fit that bill.

But I did not believe for a minute that Powell's popularity showed that Americans suddenly had outgrown their racial hang-ups. On a less sanguine note, the army also plays to another white ideal: It is a place that has a reputation, although somewhat overblown, for whipping rebellious youths, particularly poor youths of color, into line and teaching them *their place*. In some ways, Powell may have benefited from the ancient notion that black people could do a better, more economical job of overseeing other blacks and keeping them in line than white people could.

Few were eager to say Powell was not *qualified for the job* in the way so many blacks had been blocked in the past. Quite the opposite, he offered an image, an icon, an ideal, a *role model* for what so many whites had said they had been looking for in a qualified black all along.

In short, Powell was a beneficiary of the *Bill Cosby effect.* He was so famous and so widely admired that white people quickly forgot he was not white, while black people delighted in remembering that he was black. I first began to experience this firsthand in the early 1980s while working as a television reporter in Chicago. I was astonished to find working-class white ethnics in neighborhoods that once greeted Martin Luther King with rocks, bottles, and bricks treating me like a celebrity. "You're not black anymore, Clarence," said a seasoned white producer back at the studio. "You're on television now."

So it was for Colin Powell. Like Bill Cosby, Oprah Winfrey, or the two Michaels, Jordan and Jackson, he had *crossed over* in the minds of white America to the larger white audience. It was Powell's good fortune to emerge at the right time to capitalize on a little-recognized but deeply felt American yearning for "positive" black role models. Americans by the 1980s might have been too hip, too cynical, too disbelieving of the old verities to accept "Ozzie and Harriet" or "Father Knows Best" as anything better than quaint nostalgia. Yet many of those same cynics eagerly embraced "The Cosby Show," making it the nation's number-one show for several years in a row. Americans, it appeared, would accept "Father Knows Best" or "Ozzie and Harriet" after all, as long as it was played with a black cast in an ostensibly urban neighborhood.

The same may have been true for Powell. Maybe American voters were looking for Oprah Winfreys and Bill Cosbys in politics, too. The age of the Eisenhower-style leader was over, according to the prevailing wisdom. Americans in their post-cold war isolationism were not wildly enthusiastic about scouting out any new ones, until they were offered an Eisenhower who happened to be black. Wilder, with much hard work, filled the bill in Virginia. But he couldn't get out of the starting gate in New Hampshire. Race had something to do with it, but so perhaps was his appearing to be too obviously a *politician.* Powell coyly and cleverly insisted that he was not, even while he clearly was politicking.

Wilder also was black and a Democrat, a combination that Republicans had cleverly and thoroughly demonized in the minds of many voters since the 1960s when Lyndon B. Johnson's strong support of civil rights and Richard M. Nixon's racially coded conservatism sent whites scurrying away from the Democratic Party like rabbits from a prairie fire.

All of this worked in Powell's favor as the right man at the right time. For many Americans, he helped confirm that America's fabled meritocracy still works. After all, had Powell's Jamaica-born parents decided to go to England under British Commonwealth laws instead of to Harlem, he might have risen to sergeant-major, at best. Instead, he had risen to this country's top military post and might become the nation's commander-in-chief, a full confirmation of the American ideal and a signal to all those other promising young men and women out there that all you have to do is to work hard, dress well, speak good English, play by the rules, and *fit in* with the standards of the mainstream, which is to say the white world, and you will get your reward. If he had benefited from affirmative action at any point along the way, it was by no means obvious, which is just how such programs should work. The prospect of a Colin Powell presidential campaign offered the prospect of blessed relief, a welcome oasis on a political landscape that had turned into a dust bowl of racial rancor and competing resentment. Inasmuch as whites once held blacks down to feel good about themselves, today's whites could feel good about themselves by lifting up at least this one black.

Americans deeply value such good feelings, deeply enough to award bonus points to a likable black candidate whose race can help them feel good about how open-minded they have always imagined themselves. Many of the white suburban Republicans who crossed over to make Carol Moseley-Braun the Senate's first black woman member told pollsters the wish to "make history" figured strongly in their decision, which is another way of saying they felt good about voting for a black woman. Voters like to help make history in ways that move America forward. As long as his sparkling image remained pristine clean, America needed to know that Colin Powell could succeed. Or, to put it another way, if he could not succeed, could any person of color? Would his failure not be unwanted confirmation of a terrible truth, that there really truly is something fundamentally wrong with America's sense of fairness? America needed Colin Powell to assuage white guilt. He made it possible for white Americans to say confidently, *No, I am not opposed* to *all black candidates;* I *am only opposed* to *those black candidates who are not like Colin Powell.* He became a Rorschach inkblot test of whatever or whomever we wanted him to be, a direct reflection of our best vision of ourselves.

There was a lesson here for crossover candidates everywhere. White people are more open to voting for a black candidate than ever before. But, to win white votes, it still is necessary, first of all, to ease white guilt.

It is not essential to be so conservative that you alienate much of the black mainstream, but it doesn't hurt. It is not insignificant that the only two black Republicans in Congress, Connecticut's Gary Franks and Oklahoma's J. C. Watts, both came from districts that were predominantly white. (It also did not hurt Watts's popularity that he was a former University of Oklahoma football hero. If anything counts as much as military heroism in our culture, it is athletic "heroism.") It is a telling development of this, the age of the crossover black candidate, that they win by first becoming a perceived ally to the interests of their white constituents.

Can a black candidate who has been elected by whites effectively represent blacks? Lani Guinier was criticized as a "quota queen" for bringing up such questions for discussion in her scholarly papers on voting rights. In writing the Supreme Court's five-to-four decision to ban race as a "pre-dominant factor" in drawing congressional districts, Justice Anthony Kennedy denounced the "racial stereotyping" that expects blacks to vote differently from whites. Yet blacks do tend to vote for blacks and whites for whites, and the gulf between their political attitudes as groups is wide and deep. For example, one 1986 poll found that 74 percent of blacks thought federal spending on programs to assist blacks should be increased, compared to 17 percent for whites. Kennedy would have blacks and whites work harder to campaign for each other's votes, which is a noble goal and one that conservative critics of Voting Rights Act enforcement have called for. Ironically, it may result in the restoration of substantial black populations to the districts of staunchly conservative white Republicans like Newt Gingrich, forcing a moderation in their racial messages. That already happened with black representative Gus Savage, a virulently anti-Israel firebrand whose far South Side Chicago district was extended after the 1990 census into the suburbs, picking up more suburban white voters. . . .

As long as race remains an American dilemma, as Gunnar Myrdal famously declared it to be in the early 1940s, it will play a salient role in American politics. Americans of all races need to learn who their real enemies are. It is not the members of other races. It is those who use race as a smokescreen to hide the nation's deeper agonies over class and a dream of upward mobility that for too many members of all races appears to be rapidly slipping away.

CLARENCE PAGE

Charles Johnson (b. 1948)

Born in Evanston, Illinois, Charles Johnson first created books that were collections of cartoons—*Black Humor* in 1970 and *Half-Past Nation Time* in 1972. He also writes screenplays. *The Sorcerer's Apprentice* (1986) is a collection of stories, and his highly regarded novels include *Faith and the Good Thing* (1974), *Oxherding Tale* (1982), and *Middle Passage* (1990), a brilliant portrayal of the sea voyages that brought slaves to the Americas. It won the National Book Award, and in 1998 Johnson received a MacArthur Fellowship. After graduating from Southern Illinois University, Johnson did Ph.D. work in philosophy at SUNY-Stony Brook. His style—which combines folk elements, a sure ear for the vernacular, and an exploration of Black history—is closely related to the neo-realism of Toni Morrison and Alice Walker, though Johnson has stirred controversy by strongly urging Black writers to move beyond these writers. For Johnson, a large part of what he advocates has to do with a more free-wheeling mixing of genres, time frames, and histories, and especially with his philosophical bent. "I am committed," Johnson has said, "to the development of what one might call a genuinely systematic philosophical black American literature, a body of work that explores classical problems and metaphysical questions against the background of black American life." Besides phenomenology à la Husserl, Johnson is also a devotee of Asian philosophy and the martial arts, and in some of his work—the story "China," for example, which along with the story below comes from *Sorcerer's Apprentice*—Johnson can be seen, as he says, "attempting to interface Eastern and Western philosophical traditions, always with the hope that some new perception of experience—especially 'black experience'—will emerge . . ."

The Education of Mingo

Once, when Moses Green took his one-horse rig into town on auction day, he returned to his farm with a bondsman named Mingo. He came early in a homespun suit, stayed through the sale of fifteen slaves, and paid for Mingo in Mexican coin. A monkeylike old man, never married, with tangled hair, ginger-colored whiskers like broomstraw, and a narrow knot of a face, Moses, without children, without kinfolk, who seldom washed because he lived alone on sixty acres in southern Illinois, felt the need for a field hand and helpmate—a friend, to speak the truth plainly.

Riding home over sumps and mudholes into backcountry imprecise yet startlingly vivid in spots, as though he were hurtling headlong into a rigid New Testament parable, Moses chewed tobacco on that side of his mouth that still had good teeth and kept his eyes on the road and ears of the Appaloosa in front of his rig; he chattered mechanically to the boy, who wore tow-linen trousers a size too small, a straw hat, no shirt, and shoes repaired with wire. Moses judged him to be twenty. He was the youngest son of the reigning king of the Allmuseri, a tribe of wizards, according to the auctioneer, but they lied anyways, or so thought Moses, like abolitionists and Red Indians; in fact, for Moses Green's money nearly everybody in the New World from Anabaptists to Whigs was an outrageous liar and twisted the truth (as Moses saw it) until nothing was clear anymore. He was a dark boy. A wild, marshy-looking boy. His breastbone was broad as a barrel; he had thick hands that fell away from his wrists like weights and, on his sharp cheeks, a crescent motif. "Mingo," Moses said in a voice like gravel scrunching under a shoe, "you like rabbit? That's what I fixed for tonight. Fresh rabbit, sweet taters, and cornbread. Got hominy made from Indian corn on the fire, too. Good eatings, eh?" Then he remembered that Mingo spoke no English, and he gave the boy a friendly thump on his thigh. "'S all right. I'm going to school you myself. Teach you everything I know, son, which ain't so joe-fired much—just common sense—but it's better 'n not knowing nothing, ain't it?" Moses laughed till he shook; he liked to laugh and let his hair down whenever he could. Mingo, seeing his strangely unfiled teeth, laughed, too, but his sounded like barking. It made Moses jump a foot. He swung 'round his head and squinted. "Reckon I'd better teach you how to laugh, too. That half grunt, half whinny you just made'll give a body heart failure, son." He screwed up his lips. "You sure got a lot to learn."

Now Moses Green was not a man for doing things halfway. Education, as he dimly understood it, was as serious as a heart attack. You had to have a model, a good Christian gentleman like Moses himself, to wash a Moor white in a single generation. As he taught Mingo farming and table etiquette, ciphering with knotted string, and how to cook ashcakes, Moses constantly revised himself. He tried not to cuss, although any mention of Martin Van Buren or Free-Soilers made his stomach chew itself; or sop cornbread in his coffee; or pick his nose at public market. Moses, policing all his gestures, standing the boy behind his eyes, even took to drinking gin from a paper sack so Mingo couldn't see it. He felt, late at night when he looked down at Mingo snoring loudly on his corn-shuck mattress, now like a father; now like an artist fingering something fine and noble from a rude chump of foreign clay. It was like aiming a shotgun at the whole world through the African, blasting away all that Moses, according to his lights, tagged evil, and cultivating the good; like standing, you might say, on the sixth day, feet planted wide, trousers hitched, and remaking the world so

CHARLES JOHNSON

it looked more familiar. But sometimes it scared him. He had to make sense of things for Mingo's sake. Suppose there was lightning dithering in dark clouds overhead? Did that mean rain? Or the Devil whaling his wife? Or—you couldn't waffle on a thing like that. "Rain," said Moses, solemn, scratching his neck. "For sure, it's a storm. Electricity, Mingo." He made it a point to despoil meanings with care, choosing the ones that made the most common sense.

Slowly, Mingo got the hang of farm life, as Moses saw it—patience, grit, hard work, and prayerful silence, which wasn't easy, Moses knew, because everything about him and the African was as different as night and day, even what idealistic philosophers of his time called structures of intentional consciousness (not that Moses Green called it that, being a man for whom nothing was more absolute than an ax handle, or the weight of a plow in his hands, but he knew sure enough they didn't see things quite the same way). Mingo's education, to put it plainly, involved the evaporation of one coherent, consistent, complete universe and the embracing of another one alien, contradictory, strange.

Slowly, Mingo conquered knife and spoon, then language. He picked up the old man's family name. Gradually, he learned—soaking them up like a sponge—Moses's gestures and idiosyncratic body language. (Maybe too well, for Moses Green had a milk leg that needed lancing and hobbled, favoring his right knee; so did Mingo, though he was strong as an ox. His *t*'s had a reedy twang like the quiver of a ukulele string; so did Mingo's.) That African, Moses saw inside a year, was exactly the product of his own way of seeing, as much one of his products and judgments as his choice of tobacco; was, in a sense that both pleased and bum-squabbled the crusty old man, himself: a homunculus, or a distorted shadow, or—as Moses put it to his lady friend Harriet Bridgewater—his own spitting image.

"How you talk, Moses Green!" Harriet sat in a Sleepy Hollow chair on the Sunday afternoons Moses, in his one-button sack coat and Mackinaw hat, visited her after church services. She had two chins, wore a blue dress with a flounce of gauze and an apron of buff satin, above which her bosom slogged back and forth as she chattered and knitted. There were cracks in old Harriet Bridgewater's once well-stocked mind (she had been a teacher, had traveled to places Moses knew he'd never see), into which she fell during conversations, and from which she crawled with memories and facts that, Moses suspected, Harriet had spun from thin air. She was the sort of woman who, if you told her of a beautiful sunset you'd just seen, would, like as not, laugh—a squashing sound in her nose—and say, "Why, Moses, that's not beautiful at all !" And then she'd sing a sunset more beautiful—like the good Lord coming in a cloud—in some faraway place like Crete or Brazil, which you'd probably never see. That sort of woman: haughty, worldly, so clever at times he couldn't stand it. Why Moses Green visited her . . .

Even he didn't rightly know why. She wasn't exactly pretty, what with her gull's nose, great heaps of red-gold hair, and frizzy down on her arms, but she had a certain silvery beauty intangible, elusive, inside. It was comforting after Reverend Raleigh Liverspoon's orbicular sermons to sit a spell with Harriet in her religiously quiet, plank-roofed common room. He put one hand in his pocket and scratched. She knew things, that shrewd Harriet Bridgewater, like the meaning of Liverspoon's gnomic sermon on property, which Moses couldn't untangle to save his life until Harriet spelled out how being and having were sorta the same thing: "You kick a man's mule, for example, and isn't it just like ramming a boot heel in that man's belly? Or suppose," she said, wagging a knitting needle at him, "you don't fix those chancy steps of yours and somebody breaks his head—his relatives have a right to sue you into the poor-house, Moses Green." This was said in a speech he understood, but usually she spoke properly in a light, musical voice, such that her language, as Moses listened, was like song. Her dog, Ruben—a dog so small he couldn't mount the bitches during rutting season and, crazed, jumped Harriet's chickens instead—ran like a fleck of light around her chair. Then there was Harriet's three-decked stove, its sheet-iron stovepipe turned at a right angle, and her large wooden cupboard—all this, in comparison to his own rude, whitewashed cabin, and Harriet's endless chatter, now that her husband, Henry, was dead (when eating fish, he had breathed when he should have swallowed, then swallowed when he should have breathed), gave Moses, as he sat in his Go-to-meeting clothes nibbling egg bread (his palm under his chin to catch crumbs), a lazy feeling of warmth, well-being, and wonder. Was he sweet on Harriet Bridgewater? His mind weather-vaned—yes, no; yes, no—when he thought about it. She was awesome to him. But he didn't exactly like her opinions about his education of young Mingo. Example: "There's only so much he can learn, being a salt-water African and all, don't-chooknow?"

"So?"

"You know he'll never completely adjust."

"So?" he said.

"You know everything here's strange to him."

"So?" he said again.

"And it'll *always* be a little strange—like seeing the world through a fun house mirror?"

Moses knocked dottle from his churchwarden pipe, banging the bowl on the hard wooden arm of his chair until Harriet, annoyed, gave him a tight look. "You oughtasee him, though. I mean, he's right smart—r'ally. It's like I just shot out another arm and that's Mingo. Can do anything I do, like today—he's gonna he'p Isaiah Jenson fix some windows and watchermer-callems"—he scratched his head—"fences, over at his place." Chuckling, Moses struck a friction match on his boot heel. "Only thing Mingo won't do is kill chicken hawks; he feeds 'em like they was his best friends, even calls 'em Sir." Lightly, the old man laughed again. He put his left ankle on his right knee and cradled it. "But otherwise, Mingo says just what I says. Feels what I feels."

"Well!" Harriet said with violence. Her nose wrinkled—she rather hated his raw-smelling pipe tobacco—and testily laid down a general principle. "Slaves are tools with life in them, Moses, and tools are lifeless slaves."

The old man asked, "Says who?"

"Says Aristotle." She said this arrogantly, the way some people quote Scripture. "He owned thirteen slaves (they were then called *banausos*), sage Plato, fifteen, and neither felt the need to elevate their bondsmen. The institution is old, Moses, old, and you're asking for a peck of trouble if you keep playing God and get too close to that wild African. If he turns turtle on you, what then?" Quotations followed from David Hume, who, Harriet said, once called a preposterous liar one New World friend who informed him of a bondsman who could play any piece on the piano after hearing it only once.

"P'raps," hemmed Moses, rocking his head. "I reckon you're right."

"I know I'm right, Moses Green." She smiled.

"Harriet—"

The old woman answered, "Yes?"

"You gets me confused sometimes. Abaht my feelings. Half the time I can't rightly hear what you say 'cause I'm all taken in by the way you say it." He struggled, shaking saliva from the stem of his pipe. "Harriet, your Henry, d'ya miss him much? I mean, abaht now you should be getting married again, don't you think? You get along okay by yourself, but . . . I been thinking I . . . Sometimes you make me feel—"

"Yes?" She brightened. "Go on."

He didn't explain how he felt.

Moses, later on the narrow, root-covered road leading to Isaiah Jenson's cabin, thought Harriet Bridgewater wrong about Mingo and, strange to say, felt closer to the black African than to Harriet. So close, in fact, that when he pulled his rig up to Isaiah's house, he considered giving Mingo his farm when he died, God willing, as well as his knowledge, beliefs, and prejudices. Then again, maybe that was overdoing things. The boy was all Moses wanted him to be, his own emanation, but still, he thought, himself. Different enough from Moses so that he could step back and admire him.

Swinging his feet off the buckboard, he called, "Isaiah!" and, hearing no reply, hobbled, bent forward at his hips, toward the front door—"H'lo?"—which was halfway open. Why could he see no one? "Jehoshaphat!" blurted Moses. From his lower stomach a loamy feeling crawled up to his throat. "Y'all heah? Hey!" The door opened with a burst at his fingertips. Snatching off his hat, ducking his head, he stepped inside. It was dark as a poor man's pocket in there. Air within had the smell of boiled potatoes and cornbread. He saw the boy seated big as life at Isaiah's table, struggling with a big lead-colored spoon and a bowl of hominy. "You two finished al-raid-y, eh?" Moses laughed, throwing his jaw forward, full of pride, as Mingo fought mightily, his head hung over his bowl, to get food to his mouth. "Whar's that fool Isaiah?" The African pointed over his shoulder, and Moses's eyes, squinting in the weak light, followed his wagging finger to a stream of sticky black fluid like the gelatinous trail of a snail flowing from where Isaiah Jenson, cold as stone, lay crumpled next to his stove, the image of Mingo imprisoned on the retina of his eyes. Frail moonlight funneled through cracks in the roof. The whole cabin was unreal. Simply unreal. The old man's knees knocked together. His stomach jerked. Buried deep in Isaiah's forehead was a meat cleaver that exactly split his face and disconnected his features.

"Oh, my Lord!" croaked Moses. He did a little dance, half juba, half jig, on his good leg toward Isaiah, whooped, "Mingo, what'd you do?" Then, knowing full well what he'd done, he boxed the boy behind his ears, and shook all six feet of him until Moses's teeth, not Mingo's, rattled. The old man sat down at the table; his knees felt rubbery, and he groaned: "Lord, Lord, Lord!" He blew out breath, blenched, his lips skinned back over his tobacco-browned teeth, and looked square at the African. "Isaiah's daid! You understand that?"

Mingo understood that; he said so.

"And you're responsible!" He stood up, but sat down again, coughing, then pulled out his handkerchief and spit into it. "Daid! You know what daid means?" Again, he hawked and spit. "Responsible—you know what that means?"

He did not; he said, "Nossuh, don't know as I know that one, suh. Not Mingo, boss. *Nossuh!*"

Moses sprang up suddenly like a steel spring going off and slapped the boy till his palm stung. Briefly, the old man went bananas, pounding the boy's chest with his fists. He sat down again. Jumping up so quick made his head spin and legs wobble. Mingo protested his innocence, and it did not dawn on Moses why he seemed so indifferent until he thought back to what he'd told him about chicken hawks. Months ago, maybe five, he'd taught Mingo to kill chicken hawks and be courteous to strangers, but it got all turned around in the African's mind (how was he to know New World customs?), so he was courteous to chicken hawks (Moses groaned, full of gloom) and killed strangers. "You idjet!" hooted Moses. His jaw clamped shut. He wept hoarsely for a few minutes like a steer with the strangles. "Isaiah Jenson and me was friends, and—" He checked himself; what'd he said was a lie. They weren't friends at all. In fact, he thought Isaiah Jenson was a pigheaded fool and only tolerated the little yimp in a neighborly way. Into his eye a fly bounded. Moses shook his head wildly. He'd even sworn to Harriet, weeks earlier, that Jenson was so troublesome, always borrowing tools and keeping them, he hoped he'd go to Ballyhack on a red-hot rail. In his throat a knot tightened. One of his eyelids jittered up, still itchy from the fly; he forced it down with his finger, then gave a slow look at the African. "Great Peter," he mumbled. "You couldn'ta known that."

"Go home now?" Mingo stretched out the stiffness in his spine. "Powerful tired, boss."

Not because he wanted to go home did Moses leave, but because he was afraid of Isaiah's body and needed time to think things through. Dry the air, dry the evening down the road that led them home. As if to himself, the old man grumped, "I gave you thought and tongue, and looka what you done with it—they gonna catch and kill you, boy, just as sure as I'm sitting heah."

"Mingo?" The African shook his long head, sly; he touched his chest with one finger. "Me? Nossuh."

"Why the hell you keep saying that?" Moses threw his jaw forward so violently muscles in his neck stood out. "You kilt a man, and they gonna burn you crisper than an ear of corn. Ay, God, Mingo," moaned the old man, "you gotta act responsible, son!" At the thought of what they'd do to Mingo, Moses scrooched the stalk of his head into his stiff collar. He drilled his gaze at the smooth-faced African, careful not to look him in the eye, and barked, "What're you thinking *now*?"

"What Mingo know, Massa Green know. Bees like what Mingo sees or don't see is only what Massa Green taught him to see or don't see. Like Mingo lives through Massa Green, right?"

Moses waited, suspicious, smelling a trap. "Yeah, all that's true."

"Massa Green, he owns Mingo, right?"

"Right," snorted Moses. He rubbed the knob of his red, porous nose. "Paid good money—"

"So when Mingo works, it bees Massa Green workin', right? Bees Massa Green workin', thinkin', doin' through Mingo—ain't that so?"

Nobody's fool, Moses Green could latch onto a notion with no trouble at all; he turned violently off the road leading to his cabin, and plowed on toward Harriet's, pouring sweat, remembering two night visions he'd had, recurrent, where he and Mingo were wired together like say two ventriloquist's dummies, one black, one white, and there was somebody—who he didn't know, yanking their arm and leg strings simultaneously—how he couldn't figure, but he and Mingo said the same thing together until his liver-spotted hands, the knuckles tight and shriveled like old carrot skin, flew up to his face and, shrieking, he started hauling hips across a cold black countryside. But so did Mingo, his hands on his face, pumping his knees right alongside Moses, shrieking, their voice inflections identical; and then the hazy dream doorwayed luxuriously into another where he was greaved on one half of a thrip—a coin halfway between a nickel and a dime—and on the reverse side was Mingo. Shaking, Moses pulled his rig into Harriet Bridgewater's yard. His bowels, burning, felt like boiling tar. She was standing on her porch in a checkered Indian shawl, staring at them, her book still open, when Moses scrambled, tripping, skinning his knees, up her steps. He shouted, "Harriet, this boy done kilt Isaiah Jenson in cold blood." She lost color and wilted back into her doorway. Her hair was swinging in her eyes. Hands flying, he stammered in a flurry of anxiety, "But it wasn't altogether Mingo's fault—he didn't know what he was doin'."

"Isaiah? You mean Izay-yah? He didn't kill Izay-yah?"

"Yeah, aw no! Not really—" His mind stuttered to a stop.

"Whose fault is it then?" Harriet gawked at the African picking his nose in the wagon (Moses had, it's true, not policed himself as well as he'd wanted). A shiver quaked slowly up her left side. She sloughed off her confusion, and flashed, "I can tell you whose fault it is, Moses. Yours! Didn't I say not to bring that wild African here? Huh? Huh? Huh? You both should be—put to sleep."

"Aw, woman! Hesh up!" Moses threw down his hat and stomped it out of shape. "You just all upsetted." Truth to tell, he was not the portrait of composure himself. There were rims of dirt in his nails. His trouser legs had blood splattered on them. Moses stamped his feet to shake road powder off his boots. "You got any spirits in the house? I need your he'p to untangle this thing, but I ain't hardly touched a drop since I bought Mingo, and my throat's pretty dr—".

"You'll just have to get it yourself—on the top shelf of the cupboard." She touched her face, fingers spread, with a dazed gesture. There was suddenly in her features the intensity found in the look of people who have a year, a month, a minute only to live. "I think I'd better sit down." Lowering herself onto her rocker, she cradled on her lap a volume by one M. Shelley, a recent tale of monstrosity and existential horror, then she demurely settled her breasts. "It's just like you, Moses Green, to bring all your bewilderments to me."

The old man's face splashed into a huge, foamy smile. He kissed her gently on both eyes, and Harriet, in return, rubbed her cheek like a cat against his gristly jaw. Moses felt lighter than a feather. "Got to have somebody, don't I?"

In the common room, Moses rifled through the cupboard, came up with a bottle of luke-warm bourbon and, hands trembling, poured himself three fingers' worth in a glass. Then, because he figured he deserved it, he refilled his glass and, draining it slowly, sloshing it around in his mouth, considered his options. He could turn Mingo over to the law and let it go at that, but damned if he couldn't shake loose the idea that killing the boy somehow wouldn't put things to rights; it would be like they were killing Moses himself, destroying a part of his soul. Besides, whatever the African'd done it was what he'd learned through Moses, who was not the most reliable lens for looking at things. You couldn't rightly call a man responsible if, in some utterly alien place, he was without power, without privilege, without property—was, in fact, property—if he had no position, had nothing, or virtually next to nothing, and nothing was his product or judgment. "Be damned!" Moses spit. It was a bitter thing to siphon your being from someone else. He knew that now. It was like, on another level, what Liverspoon had once tried to deny about God and man: *If* God was (and now Moses wasn't all that sure), and if He made the world, then a man didn't have to answer for anything. Rape or murder, it all referred back to who-or-whatever was responsible for that world's make-up. Crest fallen, he tossed away his glass, lifted the bottle to his lips, then nervously lit his pipe. Maybe. maybe they could run, if it came to that, and start all over again in Missouri, where he'd teach Mingo the difference between chicken hawks and strangers. But, sure as day, he'd do it again. He couldn't change. What was *was*. They'd be running forever, across all space, all time so he imagined—like fugitives with no fingers, no toes, like two thieves or yokefellows, each with some God-awful secret that could annihilate the other. Naw! Moses thought. His blood beat up. The deep powerful stroke of his heart made him wince. His tobacco maybe. Too strong. He sent more whiskey crashing down his throat. Naw! You couldn't have nothing and just go as you pleased. How strange that owner and owned magically dissolved into each other like two crossing shafts of light (or, if he'd known this, which he did not, particles, subatomic, interconnected in a complex skein of relatedness). Shoot him maybe, reabsorb Mingo, was that more merciful? Naw! He was fast; fast. Then manumit the African? Noble gesture, that. But how in blazes could he disengage himself when Mingo shored up, sustained, let be Moses's world with all its sores and blemishes every time he opened his oily black eyes?

Thanks to the trouble he took cementing Mingo to his own mind, he could not, by thunder, do without him now. Giving him his freedom, handing it to him like a rasher of bacon, would shackle Mingo to him even more. There seemed, just then, no solution.

Undecided, but mercifully drunk now, his pipebowl too hot to hold any longer, Moses, who could not speak his mind to Harriet Bridgewater unless he'd tied one on, called out: "I come to a decision. Not about Mingo, but you'n' me." It was then seven o'clock. He shambled, feet shuffling, toward the door. "Y'know, I was gonna ask you to marry me this morning"—he laughed; whiskey made his scalp tingle—"but I figured living alone was better when I thoughta how married folks—and sometimes wimmin with dogs—got to favoring each other . . . like they was wax candles flowing tergether. Hee-hee." He stepped gingerly, holding the bottle high, his ears brick red, face streaky from wind-dried sweat, back onto the quiet porch. He heard a moan. It was distinctly a moan. "Harriet? Harriet, I ain't put it too well, but I'm asking you now." On the porch her rocker slid back, forth, squeaking on the floorboards. Moses's bottle fell—bip!—down the stairs, bounced out into the yard, rolled, and bumped into Harriet Bridgewater. Naw, he thought. Aw, naw. By the wagon, by a chopping block near a pile of split faggots, by the ruin of an old handpump caked with rust, she lay on her side, the back fastenings of her dress burst open, her mouth a perfect O. The sight so wounded him he wept like a child. It was then seven-fifteen.

October 7 of the year of grace 1855.

Midnight found Moses Green still staring down at her. He felt sick and crippled and dead inside. Every shadowed object thinging in the yard beyond, wrenched up from its roots, hazed like shapes in a hallucination, was a sermon on vanity; every time he moved his eyes he stared into a grim homily on the deadly upas of race and relatedness. Now he had no place to stand. Now he was undone. "Mingo . . . come ovah heah." He was very quiet.

"Suh?" The lanky African jumped down from the wagon, faintly innocent, faintly diabolical. Removed from the setting of Moses's farm, the boy looked strangely elemental; his skin had the texture of plant life, the stones of his eyes an odd, glossy quality like those of a spider, which cannot be read. "Talky old hen daid now, boss."

The old man's face shattered. "I was gonna marry that woman!"

"Naw." Mingo frowned. From out of his frown a huge grin flowered. "You say—I'm quoting you now, suh—a man needs a quiet, patient, uncomplaining woman, right?"

Moses croaked, "When did I say that?"

"Yesstiday." Mingo yawned. He looked sleepy. "Go home now, boss?"

"Not just 'yet." Moses Green, making an effort to pull himself to his full height, failed. "You lie face down—heah me?—with your hands ovah your head till I come back." With Mingo hugging the front steps, Moses took the stairs back inside, found the flintlock Harriet kept in her cupboard on account of slaves who swore to die in the skin of freemen, primed it, and stepped back, so slowly, to the yard. Outside, the air seemed thinner. Bending forward, perspiring at his upper lip, Moses tucked the cold barrel into the back of Mingo's neck, cushioning it in a small socket of flesh above the African's broad shoulders. With his thumb he pulled the hammer back. Springs in the flintlock whined. Deep inside his throat, as if he were speaking through his stomach, he talked to the dark poll of the boy's back-slanting head.

"You ain't never gonna understand why I gotta do this. You a saddle across my neck, always will be, even though it ain't rightly all your fault. Mingo, you more me than I am myself. Me planed away to the bone! Ya understand?" He coughed and went on miserably: "All the wrong, all the good you do, now or tomorrow—it's me indirectly doing it, but without the lies and excuses, without the feeling what's its foundation, with all the polite make-up and apologies removed. It's an empty gesture, like the swing of a shadow's arm. You can't never see things exactly the way I do. I'm guilty. It was me set the gears in motion. Me . . ." Away in the octopoid darkness a wild bird—a nighthawk maybe—screeched. It shot noisily away with blurred wings askirring when the sound of hoofs and wagons rumbled closer. Eyes narrowed to slits, Moses said—a dry whisper—"Get up, you damned fool." He let his round shoulders slump. Mingo let his broad shoulders slump. "Take the horses," Moses said; he pulled himself up to his rig, then sat, his knees together beside the boy. Mingo's knees drew together. Moses's voice changed. It began to rasp and wheeze; so did Mingo's. "Missouri," said the old man, not to Mingo but to the dusty floor of the buckboard, "if I don't misremember, is off thataway somewheres in the west."

Fred Hampton Sr. (1948–1969)

One of the most infamous incidents in Chicago history occurred at 4:45 A.M. on December 4, 1969. At that moment, Chicago police entered Black Panther headquarters at 2337 West Monroe, starting a one-sided gun battle that killed Panther leaders Mark Clark and Fred Hampton. Indeed, "assassinated" or "murdered" are now the terms more commonly used. That year saw eleven South Side youths killed in police skirmishes, a dozen Panthers killed or wounded, and over one hundred Panthers arrested. Subsequent research has shown that much of this was under the direction of the FBI, which tracked and harassed Panther leaders and carried out a concerted effort to beat down the Panthers militarily. Five thousand people attended Hampton's funeral, where he was eulogized by such Black leaders as Ralph Abernathy and Jesse Jackson, who said: "when Fred was shot in Chicago, black people in particular, and decent people in general, bled everywhere." Hampton's assassination has been commemorated in much literature, notably in Haki Madhubuti's "One-Sided Shoot-out," which ends: "our enemies scope the ways of blackness in three bad / shifts a day. / in the A.M. their music becomes deadlier. / this is a game of dirt. / only blackpeople play it fair." Hampton, who started as a Youth Council leader for the NAACP before founding and chairing the Illinois Black Panther Party, had been known as a restrained, articulate organizer. However, the following excerpts from his most important speech, as well as several interviews he gave to Chicago papers in the late 1960s, show that his frustration with obstacles to reform—as well as everyday brutality against Blacks—drove him to accept violence as often necessary, especially for self-defense. The speech is titled with the phrase now most associated with Hampton. In 1990, a "Fred Hampton Day" was declared in Chicago. His son, Fred Hampton Jr., also gained notoriety as a political prisoner. He was released in September 2001 after nearly ten years in jail and intense protest by the International Campaign to Free Fred Hampton Jr. and the Democratic Uhuru Movement.

From "You Can Murder a Liberator, but You Can't Murder Liberation"

ALL POWER TO THE PEOPLE.

What we are basically going to be talking about today is what the pig is doing to the Panthers all around the country. We are going to have to talk about what we are going to have to do about the repression that they are putting on the Black Panther Party. We are not worried about getting off it—let's try to deal with it.

We got to talk first of all about the main man. The main man in the Black Panther Party, the main man in the struggle today—in the United States, in Chicago, in Cuba and anywhere else—the main man in the liberation struggle is our Minister of Defense, and yours too, Huey P. Newton. He's the main man because the head of the imperialist octopus lies right in this country and whoever is dealing with the head of the octopus in this country is the main man. He's in jail now. We must tell the world that Huey P. Newton was tried by the pigs and they found him guilty. He was tried by the people, who found him not guilty, and we say let him go, let him free, because we find him not guilty. This is our relentless demand. We will not let up one day, we will not give up the struggle to liberate our Minister of Defense, Huey P. Newton, and we will continue to exert pressure on the power structure and constantly bombard them with the people's demand that Huey P. Newton be set free.

It was Huey P. Newton who taught us how the people learn. You learn by participation. When Huey P. Newton started out what did he do? He got a gun and he got Bobby and Bobby got a gun. They had a problem in the community because people was being run over—kids were being run over—at a certain intersection. What did the people do? The people went down to the government to redress their grievances and the government told them to go to hell: "We are not going to put no stoplights down there UNTIL WE SEE FIT." What did Huey P. Newton do? Did he go out and tell the people about the laws and write letters and try to propagandize 'em all the time? NO! . . . He got him a shotgun, he got Bobby and he got him a hammer and went down to the corner. He gave Bobby the shotgun and told him if any pig motherfuckers come by blow his motherfuckin brains out. What did he do? He went to the corner and nailed up a stop sign. No more accidents, no more trouble . . . What'd the people do? They looked at it, they observed; they didn't get a chance to participate in it. Next time what'd they do? Same kind of problem came up. The PEOPLE got THEIR shotguns, got THEIR nine millimeters, got THEIR hammers. How'd they learn? They learned by observation and participation. They learned one thing. When there is a fire you gather round the fire. Huey got a shotgun and everybody gathered round him and Bobby. . . . As the vanguard leader he taught the people about the power structure; he led the people down the correct road of revolution. What are we doing?

Our Breakfast for Children program is feeding a lot of children and the people understand our Breakfast for Children program. We sayin' something like this—we saying that theory's cool, but theory with no practice ain't shit. . . . We have a theory about feeding kids free. What'd we do? We put it into practice. That's how people learn. A lot of people don't know how serious the thing is. They think the children we feed ain't really hungry. I don't know five year old kids that can act well, but I know that if they not hungry we sure got some actors. We got five year old actors that could take the academy award. Last week they had a whole week dedicated to the hungry in Chicago. Talking 'bout the starvation rate here that went up 15%. Over here where everybody should be eating. Why? Because of capitalism.

What are we doing? The Breakfast for Children program. We are running it in a socialistic manner. People came and took our program, saw it in a socialistic fashion not even knowing it was socialism . . . What'd the pig say? He say, "Nigger—you like communism?" "No sir, I'm scared of it." "You like socialism?" "No Sir, I'm scared of it," "You like the breakfast for children program?" "Yes sir, I'd die for it." Pig said, "Nigger, that program is a socialistic program." "I don't give a fuck if it's Communism. You put your hands on that program motherfucker and I'll blow your motherfucking brains out." And he knew it. We been educating him, not by reading matter, but through observation and participation. By letting him come in and work our program. Not theory and theory alone, but theory and practice. The two go together. We not only thought about the Marxist-Leninist theory—we put it into practice. This is what the Black Panther Party is about.

Some people talk a lot about communism, but the people can't understand and progress to the stage of communism right away or because of abstract arguments. They say you got to crawl before you can walk. And the Black Panther Party, as the vanguard party, thought that the Breakfast for Children Program was the best technique of crawling that any vanguard party could follow. And we got a whole lot of folks that's going to be walking. And then a whole lot of folks that's gonna be running. And when you got that, what you got? You got a whole lot of PIGS that's gonna be running. That's what our program's about.

The Black Panther Party is about the complete revolution. We not gonna go out there and half do a thing. And you can let the pigs know it. They come here and hide—they so uncomfortable they sitting on a tape recorder. . . . All they got to do is come up to 2350 West Madison any day of the week and anybody up there'll let them know, let the motherfucker know: Yes, we subversive. Yes, we subversive with the bullshit we are confronted with today. Just as subversive as anybody can be subversive. And we think them motherfuckers is the criminals. They the ones always hiding. We the ones up in front. We're out in the open, these motherfuckers should start wearing uniforms. They want to know if the Panthers are goin' underground—these motherfuckers IS underground. You can't find 'em. People calls the pigs but nobody knows where they at. They're out chasing us. They hiding—can't nobody even see 'em.

When people got a problem they come to the Black Panther Party for help and that's good. Because, like Mao says, we are supposed to be ridden by the people and Huey says we're going to be ridden down the path of social revolution and that's for the people. . . .

We in the Black Panther Party have another brother I want to take some time to rap about. This brother is constantly on our mind. This brother's name is Michael White—Mickey White. . . . He's being held now in jail for $100,000 bail. . . .

Mickey White is a proven revolutionary. He's not nobody we THINK is going to be a revolutionary. He's not nobody we trying to make a revolutionary. He's a proven revolutionary. All of you have to understand that Mickey White is a Panther in ideology, he's a Panther in word and he's a Panther in deed. He's a Panther that understands it's a class struggle—not a race question. You have to understand the pressures the Black Panther Party goes through saying this. You can see the pressures the Black Panther Party goes through by making a coalition with whites.

When the Black Panther Party stood up and said we not going to fight racism with racism US said "NO, we can't do that because it's a race question and if you make it a class question then the revolution might come sooner. We in US ain't prepared for no revolution because we think that power grows from the sleeve of a Dashiki." They are armed with rhetoric and rhetoric alone. And we found that when you're armed with rhetoric and rhetoric alone a lot of times you get yourself hurt. Eldridge Cleaver told them, even though you say you fight fire with fire best, we think you fight fire with water. . . . He said, we're not going to fight racism with racism, we're going to fight racism with solidarity. Even though you think you ought to fight capitalism with black capitalism, we're going to fight capitalism with socialism.

***

We used to run around yellin 'bout Panther Power—the Panthers run it. We admit we made mistakes. Our ten point program is in the midst of being changed right now, because we used the word "white" when we should have used the word "capitalist." We're the first to admit our mistakes. We no longer say Panther Power because we don't believe the Panthers should have all the power. We are not for the dictatorship of the Panthers. We are not for the dictatorship of Black people. We are for the dictatorship of the people.

***

So what do we say? Don't get the pigs offa us cause we can stand em. We jail Mickey White, we should let em murder Bobby Hutton, we should let em run Eldridge Cleaver out of the country. Why? Because you can jail a revolutionary, but you can't jail the revolution. You can run a freedom fighter around the country but you can't run freedom fighting around the country. You can murder a liberator, but you can't murder liberation.

Kill a few and get a little satisfaction. Kill some more and you get some more satisfaction. Kill 'em all and you get complete satisfaction. We say All Power to the People—Black Power to Black People and Brown Power to Brown People, Red Power to Red People and Yellow Power to Yellow People. We say White Power to White People EVEN. And we say Panther Power to the vanguard Party and we say don't kill a few and don't kill some more. As a matter of fact we rather you didn't move until you see we ready to move, and when you see we ready to move you know we not dealing with a few, we not dealing with some more. You know that when we get ready to move we dealing from complete—that's what we're after—total, everything, everybody—complete satisfaction.

***

POWER TO THE PEOPLE

Warren Foulks (d. 1980)

The poem below is one of only three pieces I have used from the Organization of Black American Culture's *NOMMO* anthology, the marvelous volume published to celebrate twenty years of its Writer's Workshop. The brief note about Foulks identifies him only as a member of the workshop from 1973 to 1976. He died in 1980, survived then by a daughter, Serene.

#5 The Courts

I was raised on the courts with nothing but my
attitude for protection taking funerals to the
hoop cause I didn't want to end up
                                        shoppin storefront images.
I've been a cigarette smoke dance blown through
a storm of cities. Like I say I was raised on the courts
with a clash by night following a death of
                                        dust storms.
You couldn't call us weak for chanting fate
at our mothers on the way to the night lite
downtown rhythms of whispering
                                        cause hell everybodys coming home.
You couldn't call us weak if we cried or
eased ourselves in the sexrites of dance
cause I was raised on the courts starving
on environmental chilli and watching my family
                                        become falling voices.
That's why I can understand romantic violence
in your eyes. That's why I can accept a gift of
sounds and wrapped touches, knowing we may have blues for
    dinner
and still offer you a gift for tides.

I was raised on the courts and since my
        dialogue was singing and the sister raps
            we often shared caste kisses,
                    but why couldn't we launch a rescue of suffering?

Cause after all the trading of gifts and everybody coming home, the courts are a cologne image, the climax has swept by and I'm still taking funerals to the hoop, prayin that somebody don't pin my shit.

Michael Warr (dates unavailable)

One of Chicago's most important institutions is the Guild Complex, a cross-cultural literary arts center, which Michael Warr helped found, and which he directed from 1989 to 1999. Warr's brilliant directorship built his reputation as an arts administrator and entrepreneur, and he has gone on to establish a remarkably wide-ranging career in arts consulting and directing, making major contributions to projects for the Lila Wallace Reader's Digest Fund, the Ford Foundation, and the MacArthur Foundation, among others. In 2003, he took on the program directorship of Dance Africa Chicago at Columbia College, which had named him Arts Entrepreneur of the year in 1998. An acclaimed journalist who still works with Chicago public radio WBEZ, his Poetic Aperture project combines his writing and photo-journalism about Africa, where for many years he worked as a correspondent based in Ethiopia for the BBC, the *Manchester Guardian*, and the *Economist*. He has performed poetry and lectured on topics ranging from the arts, to U.S.–African relations, to technology in places as distinct as the Sorbonne, the John F. Kennedy School of Government at Harvard, and Chicago's famed jazz and poetry club the Green Mill. He is also a fine poet in his own right. The poems below come from 1991's *We Are All the Black Boy*.

Not Black Enough

He ain't
'posed to know nothing.
Words like Africanus Afarensis,
Xanthochroi or hope,
Are not to grace his
Jig vocabulary.
He to stay in his place
Be the token jiving Negro
His Negritude set by
Suburban rejects knowledgeable
In the ways of black folk.
His world too global.
He ain't never written 'bout using
Crack and a straightening comb.
Where are the bitches in his poems?
Why ain't he holding his dick?
Why he walking upright?
Where his jheri curls?

What he doing with that
White girl? Oh, I did not
Know she was Mexicana.
He need more roaches and
Chittlings in his imagery.
More hubcap allusions.
Need a ghettoization of
His metropole mind.
Need Guns n' Roses
To teach him black.

>Chicago
>February 1990

Something's Got to Go

Each time I see that hunched-back
Polish lady at the Division-Ashland el,
Her life wrapped in an empty Jewel bag.
Her carcass reeking of no place to wash.
Her skin cracked like desperate parts
Of the waterless Eritrean desert.
Her ankles swollen like a dead
Drought-stricken cow.

When I see her partially erect,
On her varicose-mapped legs.
Pissing outside the North and Damen
Currency Exchange.
Teetering on the edge
Of an excuse for existence
In transmogrified Wicker Park.

When I see her staring at Arandas
With that starved look in her eyes.
Lying on that ad bench quoting Joel 2:32.
I want to impale the system
On a diamond-studded stake.
I want to hammer an infected thorn

Into its unholy temple
Reinterpreting the Bible.

I want to make a big mistake
With Chase Manhattan Bank.
Claiming it is an Iranian airliner
In a seemingly illegal space.
Every time the boys in blue
Blow another Mrs. Bumpers down.
I want to do a Rambo on the State.
Dismantling its decrepit body politic.
Mastering the possibilities
Of what is possible with power.

Chicago
July 1988

Angela Jackson (b. 1951)

Born in Greenville, Mississippi, and raised on Chicago's South Side, Angela Jackson has long been a central, if mysterious, presence on the Chicago poetry scene. Her poems have appeared in numerous publications, and she has won several major prizes, including the 1985 National Book Award, for *Solo in the Boxcar Third Floor E;* an NEA Creative Writing Fellowship; the 1993 Chicago Sun-Times Book of the Year Award; and the 1994 Carl Sandburg poetry prize, for *Dark Legs and Silk Kisses: The Beatitudes of the Spinners,* a book of poems using spiders and their silk as central metaphors. Jackson's strange, penetrating visions range from the apocalyptic to the everyday, from the heaviness of injustice to the lightness of being carried away by love. The last phrase in the following tribute to Hoyt W. Fuller not only describes central qualities of her poetry but also provides the title to her recent collection of selected and new poems *And All These Roads Be Luminous.*

Journey to Africa

Hoyt W. Fuller, 1923–1981

The streets turn to dust where you grew up
  wind over quiet hills to a red brick church
     white steeple a star.
The world you knew ends here:
    a swath if ash swaddling a dispirited flesh
    swollen, misshapen with embalmer's mishandling.
 Not like you, not like you at all.

The holy man said you were Africa. All your
meanings flew up on his great voice. (When you
    walked so briskly, you caught the wind
    around the bend of your elbows, gusts
    gathered around swift-body and fell
    away.)
    You were fire-quick. Furious.
    No one saw the ash.
    This is how I remember.

The streets turn to dust where once white
hoods marched while you watched the devilment down

slanting roads like destiny.
The slow slopes would not give you up
before dusk.

       You were a sudden sunset: colors
       that crashed into earth. Our squinting eyes
       seek the grave, definite horizon on the quiet
       hills,
       in a wild nostalgia for flesh,
       and sweet sense.
It was the Darkland that stirred you out of the sleepy
dust of dreams and denial. The clamorous
skin, undying cloth that dared buried bones
to walk. Oh, you swore by sunrise.
Even when weariness robbed you of fire
and took it to caves to warm the
ravenous soil. Squinting still, we sift for meanings

       If there were more
       to say, you would say
                   even the dust shall
                       rise,
             and all these roads be
                       luminous.

ANGELA JACKSON

Leanita McClain (1952–1984)

The first Black member of the *Chicago Tribune*'s editorial board and only its second Black columnist, Leanita McClain was propelled up the ranks of journalism by her talent and perfectionism, and into the national spotlight by the first piece below, a "My Turn" opinion column printed by *Newsweek* in October 1980. Her former husband, Clarence Page, the first Black *Tribune* columnist, said in his introduction to *A Foot in Each World,* a collection of McClain's work: "The emerging class of black professional baby boomers needed a voice, and Leanita McClain was becoming that voice." But such stardom proved costly, and McClain took her own life on May 29, 1984. The *Time* magazine obituary of June 11 said that her death came "after bouts of depression brought on at least in part, friends said, by the strain of being a role model and by the furor resulting from an article she wrote for the Washington Post ... which prompted the [Chicago] city council to consider demanding an apology." That article is also included below. McClain's elegant, but also blunt and passionate writing brought into focus the intersection of race, politics, justice, and family life. She also often probed the very construction of racial categories, as in an April 1, 1984, column on James Baldwin entitled "There Are No White People." Summarizing Baldwin, she writes that whiteness "is a fraud ethnics who arrived on these shores perpetrated against themselves out of the necessity to deny the humanity of blacks. . . . no one was 'white' before they came here, were, in fact, proud to be hyphenated Americans, with strong ties to their mother country. But then their fear of people of color led them to fade into a generic whiteness to better ensure and exert their collective power." But her writing also shows that fear often drives Blacks into a generic Blackness, and these contending fears and generic outlooks seem almost certainly to have been other large factors in her death.

The Middle-class Black's Burden

Newsweek, 13 October 1980

I am a member of the black middle class who has had it with being patted on the head by white hands and slapped in the face by black hands for my success.

Here's a discovery that too many people still find startling: when given equal opportunities at white-collar pencil pushing, blacks want the same things from life that everyone else wants. These include the proverbial dream house, two cars, an above-average school and a vacation for the kids at Disneyland. We may, in fact, want these things more than other Americans because most of us have been denied them so long.

Meanwhile, a considerable number of the folks we left behind in the "old country," commonly called the ghetto, and the militants we left behind in their antiquated ideology can't berate middle-class blacks enough for "forgetting where we came from." We have forsaken the revolution, we are told, we have sold out. We are Oreos. . . .

The truth is, we have not forgotten; we would not dare. We are simply fighting on different fronts and are no less war weary, and possibly more heartbroken, for we know the black and white worlds can meld, that there can be a better world.

It is impossible for me to forget where I came from as long as I am prey to the jive hustler who does not hesitate to exploit my childhood friendship. I am reminded, too, when I go back to the old neighborhood in fear—and have my purse snatched—and when I sit down to a business lunch and have an old classmate wait on my table. I recall the girl I played dolls with who now rears five children on welfare, the boy from church who is in prison for murder, the pal found dead of a drug overdose in the alley where we once played tag.

My life abounds in incongruities. Fresh from a vacation in Paris, I may, a week later, be on the milk-run Trailways bus in Deep South backcountry attending the funeral of an ancient uncle whose world stretched only 50 miles and who never learned to read. Sometimes when I wait at the bus stop with my attache case, I meet my aunt getting off the bus with other cleaning ladies on their way to do my neighbors' floors.

But I am not ashamed. Black progress has surpassed our greatest expectations; we never even saw much hope for it, and the achievement has taken us by surprise.

In my heart, however, there is no safe distance from the wretched past of my ancestors or the purposeless present of some of my contemporaries; I fear such a fate can reclaim me. I am not comfortably middle class; I am uncomfortably middle class.

I have made it, but where? Racism still dogs my people. There are still communities in which crosses are burned on the lawns of black families who have the money and grit to move in.

What a hollow victory we have won when my sister, dressed in her designer everything, is driven to the rear door of the luxury high rise in which she lives because the cab driver, noting only her skin color, assumes she is the maid, or the nanny, or the cook, but certainly not the lady of any house at this address.

I have heard the immigrants' bootstrap tales, the simplistic reproach of "why can't you people be like us." I have fulfilled the entry requirements of the American middle class, yet I am left, at times, feeling unwelcome and stereotyped. I have overcome the problems of food, clothing and shelter, but I have not overcome my old nemesis, prejudice. Life is easier, being black is not.

I am burdened daily with showing whites that blacks are people. I am, in the old vernacular, a credit to my race. I am my brothers' keeper, and my sisters', though many of them have abandoned me because they think that I have abandoned them.

I run a gauntlet between two worlds, and I am cursed and blessed by both . . . I can also be used by both. I am a rope in a tug of war. If I am a token in my downtown office, so am I at my cousin's church tea. I assuage white guilt. I disprove black inadequacy and prove to my parents' generation that their patience was indeed a virtue.

I have a foot in each world, but I cannot fool myself about either. I can see the transparent deceptions of some whites and the bitter hopelessness of some blacks. I know how tenuous my grip on one way of life is, and how strangling the grip of the other way of life can be.

Many whites have lulled themselves into thinking that race relations are just grand because they were the first on their block to discuss crab grass with the new black family. Yet too few blacks and whites in this country send their children to school together, entertain each other or call each other friend. Blacks and whites dining out together draw stares. . . .

Some of my "liberal" white acquaintances pat me on the head, hinting that I am a freak, that my success is less a matter of talent than of luck and affirmative action. I may live among them, but it is difficult to live with them. How can they be sincere about respecting me, yet hold my fellows in contempt? And if I am silent when they attempt to sever me from my own, how can I live with myself?

Whites won't believe I remain culturally different; blacks won't believe I remain culturally the same.

I need only look in a mirror to know my true allegiance, and I am painfully aware that, even with my off-white trappings, I am prejudged by my color.

As for the envy of my own people, am I to give up my career, my standard of living, to pacify them and set my conscience at ease? No. I have worked for these amenities and deserve them, though I can never enjoy them without feeling guilty.

These comforts do not make me less black, nor oblivious to the woe in which many of my people are drowning. As long as we are denigrated as a group, no one of us has made it. Inasmuch as we all suffer for everyone left behind, we all gain for everyone who conquers the hurdle.

How Chicago Taught Me to Hate Whites

Washington Post, 24 July 1983

Chicago—I'd be a liar if I did not admit to my own hellish confusion. How has a purebred moderate like me—the first black editorial writer for the *Chicago Tribune*—turned into a hate-filled spewer of invective in such little time?

Even today, the vicious, psychotic events leading up to and following Harold Washington's election as the first black mayor of Chicago leave me torn as never before. I've become a two-headed, two-hearted creature. . . .

In one day my mind has sped from the naive thought that everything would be all right in the world if people would just intermarry, to the naive thought that we should establish a black homeland where we would never have to see a white face again.

The campaign was a race war. So is the continuing feud between Harold Washington and the white aldermen usurping his authority. Even black and white secretaries in City Hall are not speaking to each other. But why am *I* so readily doubting and shutting out whites I thought of as friends?

I am not one of those, despite a comfortable life, who have forgotten my origins. It is just that I had not been so rudely reminded of them in so long.

Through 10 years working my way to my present position at the *Tribune,* I have resided in a "gentrified," predominantly white, North Side lakefront liberal neighborhood where high rents are the chief social measure. In neither place have I forgotten the understood but unspoken fact of my "difference"—my blackness.

Yet I have been unprepared for the silence with which my white colleagues greeted Washington's nomination. I've been crushed by their inability to share the excitement of one of "us" making it into power. I've built walls against whites who I once thought of as my lunch and vacation friends. And I've wrapped myself in rage as this sick, twisted city besieged the newspaper with letters wishing acts of filth by "black baboons" on the daughters of its employees. Just because it endorsed this black man.

An evilness still possesses this town and it continues to weigh down my heart. During my morning ritual in the bathroom mirror, my radio tuned

LEANITA MCCLAIN

253

to the news-talk station that is as much a part of my routine as shaping my eyebrows, I've heard the voice of this evil. In what would become a standard "bigot-on-the-street" interview, the voice was going on about "the blacks." "The blacks" this, "the blacks" that, "the blacks, the blacks, the blacks." My eyes fogged, but not from the bathroom steam.

"The blacks." It is the article that offends. The words are held out like a foul-smelling sock transported two-fingered at the end of an outstretched arm to the hamper while the nose is pinched shut.

"The blacks." It would make me feel like machine-gunning every white face on the bus. Why couldn't these people just say "blacks," letting it roll from the tongue?

"The blacks." These people were talking about me, as I stood in my bathroom mirror neatly outlining my lips, about to put on a dress-for-success suit and silk blouse. These were the people who dislike welfare recipients for fitting their stereotypes and who despise me because I do not. The users of "the blacks" make no distinction, unlike the liberals who in their weaker moments will say: "Well, I wouldn't mind having you next door. You're different, you know." Leanita McClain. "The black." Just another nigger.

The tears returned when Jane Byrne, soundly defeated in the primary, announced a write-in campaign to save the city from the brash black man and his opponent, the avuncular Jew. My editorial-writer colleagues were probably left in as much disbelief by the obscenity I spat at the television as by anything that little snow queen had just said. With my back to the closed door of my office, seemingly focused on my word processor, I cried in anger. My God, I implored. What do these white people want of us?

My transformation began the morning after Washington's primary victory. Everyone in Chicago stayed up until 2 A.M. when Washington claimed victory. Horrified white Chicago turned in for a fitful night. But no one black slept either, though there were never so many bright black eyes as there were the next morning. That morning black people had a step and a beat that was more than the old joked-about "natural rhythm." Smiles shown as brilliant as the blue Washington buttons that a white political editor astutely interpreted as "blue buttons of hope." Those buttons would become a badge of courage, of oneness. Even now many blacks continue to wear them.

Black strangers exchanged sly smiles on the streets. . . . The black man won! We did it! It rose to the stratosphere, crystallized and sprinkled every one of us like sugared rain. We had a feeling, and above all we had power.

LEANITA McCLAIN

No one in this town had talked about anything but the election for weeks. But suddenly the morning after the primary, whites could not find enough other things to talk about if they talked at all. Not just the most bigoted of bigots, but all whites, even the more open-minded of my fellow journalists. Even the standard niceties took on a different quality. Their "good mornings" had the tenor of death rattles, not just the usual pre-coffee hoarseness. There was that forced quality, an awkwardness, an end to spontaneity, even fear in the eyes of people who had never thought about me one way or the other before.

So many whites unconsciously had never considered that blacks could do much of anything, least of all get a black candidate this close to being mayor of Chicago. My colleagues looked up and realized, perhaps for the first time, that I was one of "them." I was suddenly threatening. The difference that everybody had tried to cover up was there in the open. . . . Happy black people can only mean unhappy white people in this town. (I never realized how far I had strayed.)

I would begin that morning to build my defenses brick by brick, to shut out people I had cried with, people I had never felt more akin to than when we traveled to foreign lands, touting our shared Americanism. I would begin to discern the full frontal view of the evil. It is the evil that caused white coworkers to stop talking when blacks strolled by. It is the evil that led blacks to caucus and revert to the old days of talking about "whitey." It is the evil of protesters, their faces red hot with hate, at a Catholic church where former Vice President Walter Mondale and Washington were jeered.

The theme of these ensuing months was set and hardening. So intense and oppressive was the atmosphere here that black and white *Tribune* colleagues sought refuge in my office from the foulness. A white colleague came in to explain away why he could not vote for Harold Washington. . . . One black female on the staff was thrown into a fit of anxiety one day, troubled by suddenly not even wanting to go to lunch with one of the white women on the staff with whom she is close.

The lone black Tribune reporter on the campaign trail, Monroe Anderson, was so beaten down by what he was seeing in the streets that he came into my office-turned-retreat, enfolded himself in a chair and just stared at the floor. Anderson is indisputably one of the most devil-may-care persons on the staff. . . . His exceptional sense of humor keeps everyone going. But during this election it failed even him. As the hate campaign against Washington got meaner, I began to realize I had not been overreacting. . . .

LEANITA MCCLAIN

The *Chicago Tribune* endorsed Harold Washington in a long and eloquent Sunday editorial. It was intended to persuade the bigots. It would have caused any sensible person at least to think. It failed. The mail and calls besieged the staff. The middle range of letters had the words "LIES" and "NIGGER LOVERS" scratched across the editorial.

Hoping to shame these people, make them look at themselves, the newspaper printed a full page of these rantings. But when the mirror was presented to them, the bigots reveled before it. The page only gave them aid and comfort in knowing their numbers. That is what is wrong with this town; being a racist is as respectable and expected as going to church.

Filthy literature littered the city streets like the propaganda air blitzes of World War II. The subway would be renamed "Soul Train." The elevators in City Hall would be removed because blacks would prefer to change floors by swinging from the cables. (Anderson, temporarily regaining his jocularity, plastered the flyers like art posters allover his work cubicle. Most black staffers knew it was laughing to keep from crying. Whites grew more silent.) In the police stations, reports were whispered about fights between longtime black and white squad-car partners. Flyers proclaiming the new city of "Chicongo," with crossed drumsticks as the city seal, were tacked to police station bulletin boards. The schools actually formulated plans to deal with racial violence, just in case.

I brought the madness from the streets into work with me.

I dissected why some people had cultivated my friendship, why I was so quick to offer it unconditionally, straining as hard as they to prove a point—to say, see how easy it is if we all just smile and pretend?

I had put so much effort into belonging, and the whites in my professional and social circles had put so much effort into making me feel as if I belonged, that we all deceived ourselves. There is always joking about "it"—those matchings of suntans against black skin, or the exchange of dialect or finding common ground on the evils of racism. But none of us had ever dealt with "the deeper inhibitions, myths and misperceptions that this society has force-fed us. . . .

Now I know solving the racial problem will take more than living, marrying and going to school together and all of those other laudable but naive goals I defend. This episode made even these first steps so far from reach.

What is there, then, to believe in? Who was I to trust? How was I to know which whites were good and which were bad? How many of my co-workers wouldn't even want *me* next door? After all of these years of lunch dates and the familial togetherness that comes naturally from working next to someone 40 hours a week, how could I know who was on the level? If I was feeling this way, what were my brothers and sisters in the street feeling? Could this town be razed in a deranged moment?

What litmus test could I devise? I distanced myself from everyone white, watching, listening, for hints of latent prejudice. But there were no formulas to follow. Even an expression of support for Washington would not convince me, so certain was I of everyone's dissemblance. I drew up a mental list of those whites who could and could not be trusted. Revelation after revelation, doubt after doubt assaulted me.

First on the list was Kay—bouncy, smiley Kay. (No real names are used.) How she had used me all of these years, like a black pet, to prove her liberalism. I was safe; she could show me off without ever having to deal with the real issue. The next time she came skipping in to show me the "neat" pair of shoes she had found during her lunch hour or to talk about the "neat" movie she had seen or the "neat" restaurant we should try, I would throw my dictionary at her and advise her that having one black person—me—on her Christmas card list did not make her socially aware.

What about Clark? He always said the right things about race, viewed injustice with the proper alarm. But suddenly I questioned his sincerity . . . What did he know? He had not lived in this skin.

What about Ken, kind-eyed, sensitive, cultured, thoughtful, cerebral Ken? No, he couldn't be a racist. Or could he?

What about Nan, with whom I had traveled? She headed the boards of church agencies in the poorest black neighborhoods. Now there was an exception. We had talked about race matters, about matters of the heart, about the differences that somehow did not alter those things that made us the same.

What about Lydia in Michigan, who had shared all my life's secrets? She too, passed.

It would be so easy just to dismiss everyone white. Why was it so easy for whites to classify me—"the blacks," or you exceptional blacks and the rest of "the blacks"—but not so easy for me to classify them?

. . . Everyone was suspect.

Bitter am I? That is mild. This affair has cemented my journalist's acquired cynicism, robbing me of most of my innate black hope for true integration.

LEANITA MCCLAIN

257

It has made me sparkle as I reveled in the comradeship of blackness. It has banished me to nightmarish bouts of sullenness. It has made me weld on a mask, censor every word, rethink every thought. It has put a face on the evil that no one wants to acknowledge is within them. It has made me mistrust people, white and black. This battle has made me hate. And that hate does not discriminate.

I've abhorred the gaggles of smug, giggly little white kids, out spending daddy's money, who start life a thousand yards ahead of black kids. I've detested my colleagues at the *Chicago Tribune*, whose antiseptic suburban worlds are just as narrow. . . .

I've been repulsed by the scruffy black kids with their shoeshine kits on glitzy Michigan Avenue, all too real a reminder of the station to which some would like to remand blacks and the limits that I've tried to overcome. I've detested the pin-striped white junior executives who make their contribution to race relations in the quarters they flick to these kids. (Fortunately, I've noticed no rubs of the kids' heads for good luck.)

And of course, I've despised the bigots, the only group toward whom I do not continually have to re-examine my emotions.

The election has come and gone. Washington won, but to look at the battlefield, the rebuilding that must be done is defeating.

I have resumed lunching with some of the white colleagues I avoided for weeks, though the conversation will stay forever circumscribed. Some have fallen away, failures of my litmus test. New ones have been found. But no white will ever be trusted so readily again with the innermost me. It is difficult to have the same confidence in my judgment about whites that I used to have. It is difficult to say "friend."

Is that saying I have become a bigot? Let's just say I have returned to the fold, have become "integration shy." At least I tried once to extend my hand, which is more than most whites can say; they do not encounter enough blacks in their lifetime to try.

Why is Chicago this way? Why my beloved city, so vital, so prosperous, so exhilarating? I do not have an answer. I wish I did.

So here I am, blacker than I've ever been. But above all, human—a condition I share with everyone of every hue. I feel. I mistrust. I cry. And I now know that I can hate.

Sandra Jackson-Opoku (b. 1953)

An award-winning poet and novelist, Sandra Jackson-Opoku has been a strong presence in Chicago's writing community since the early 1970s. Active in the educational and cultural affairs of Chicago's Black community, she teaches at Columbia College and at Chicago State University and is also a dramatist and freelance script writer and journalist, her non-fiction having appeared in the *Chicago Daily Defender, Essence,* and many other periodicals. Her interest in African heritage began in earnest in 1974 when she was an exchange student in Nigeria, and her growing passion for it and its manifestations in African American folklore infuse her work. The ancestors poem below, taken from the important *NOMMO* anthology, is one of her most famous works, and early on she was known mostly as a poet—her first book of poems, *My East Is in My Limbs,* appearing in 1978. In 1997, her play *Affirming Traditions, Transcending Conditions* was produced, and the NEA Fellowship she had won largely on the merit of her first novel, *The Tender Mending* (1982), cowritten with a friend, bore fruit with *The River Where Blood Is Born* (1997). This expansive novel traces two centuries of a family from eighteenth-century Africa, through the Middle Passage to Barbados, and into Illinois and the wider United States. It received extensive praise and placed her in the front ranks of African American novelists writing today in the folk-tinged, magical- and neo-realist styles used variously and importantly by Toni Morrison, Richard Perry, Charles Johnson, and others. Below is also the prologue to her most recent novel, 2001's *Hot Johnny and the Women Who Loved Him.* A necessarily short sample, it nonetheless shows how the fluid poetry of her prose style creates a living, magical sense of Black folklore, its strength, and its hard-won perceptions of life's longings.

From *Hot Johnny and the Women Who Loved Him*

PROLOGUE
STONE SOUP

> He knew just how to feed them

You see all our hungry faces in the photo album of his life. And you wonder. Who is he and what is he to you? You would never understand unless you know our story. So I'm going to tell you a fairy tale. Maybe you haven't heard this version.

Once upon hard times Little Grandma Gracita planned a potluck picnic. We reached into cupboards and took out what we had. Every woman thought the other might bring something better to the table. Oh, it was sad. No fried chicken, no potato salad, no watermelon. Nothing but scrap bones, carrot tops; a pitiful spread. The mushy potatoes could hardly believe their eyes. I was the last to arrive, the one who brought pearl onions.

Into this all steps a man named John, too good-looking to be good. Or so they say. If you didn't know different, you would cast him as the snake. Don Juan, con man, rogue. He said he knew just how to feed them.

He brought out a pot and made a big fire. Into it went all their offerings, along with something special: a stone from his pocket, glowing with his own warmth. Bubbling in the broth of magic, stone soup was made. It was a miracle, and it was good! Each one ate until she was full. And they all lived happily ever after?

Hardly. Real stories never end like the fairy tales do. Hot Johnny would stay so long as the soup simmered, dishing miracles into everyone's bowl. When the pot boiled over or turned cold, he would leave with his soup stone. Have you ever wondered where he went? He with all his hidden fires. We with all our hungers.

Yes, we have our hungers. Don't be tempted to cast us as the victims. We take him in, hoping to touch his magic, and we ourselves are remade.

I remember Hot Johnny like a ray of sun that touches your skin. It warms you for a moment, but you can't keep it with you. I remember him in tomorrow's dream, the bright one that dashes across your eyes right before you awaken. I remember him like John the Baptist. A chanted blessing and a splash of water, and those he touches are forever changed.

But God's gift to women is not easy to be. He has never been sure of his power, you see. He doubts our intentions, questions our devotion. Those closest to him have even seen his scars.

Cooks don't always get to enjoy what they create. What's the use of having cake unless you eat it, too? What's the sense in making stone soup unless you have a taste? Dishing up miracles for everyone else, what happens to Hot Johnny's own hungers?

The beginning of the story starts at the end.

SANDRA JACKSON-OPOKU

260

Much more than just one woman,
there are endless spirits
roaming inside me
River Mothers
moving, and
memory much
older
I
And
who but we
fall heir to such
memory, such dream?

River Mothers moving,
History wrapped around my tongue

There are spirits, stirring inside me

SANDRA JACKSON-OPOKU

D. L. Crockett Smith (b. 1954)

A professor of English at Williams College, David L. Smith's articles have appeared in numerous periodicals, including *Ebony,* the *Georgia Review,* and the *Chicago Review.* With Jack Salzman and Cornel West, he edited the five-volume *Encyclopedia of African-American Culture and History.* Writing under the pen name D. L. Crockett Smith, he has published many poems and was active in Chicago's OBAC (Organization of Black American Culture) Workshops from 1976 to 1980, the year he received his Ph.D. in English from the University of Chicago. His latest collection of poetry is *Civil Rights.* A previous collection, *Cowboy Amok,* is built on his uses of imagery from the mythic West—and "Western." The poem below was a precursor to *Cowboy Amok,* first appearing in *Open Places,* and again in *NOMMO: A Literary Legacy of Black Chicago (1967–1987),* OBAC's wonderful twentieth anniversary anthology.

Cowboy Eating His Children

Goya said it best
in a song without words:
Saturn devouring his son.

mad god with blood
on his lips and raw flesh
stuck beneath his fingernails.

weaver of words and illusions:
you command F-15s and television.
you try to bewitch us with your smile.

you try to twist back the arms
on the clock of history
just by flicking your tongue.

your unreal image
haunts us in our bedrooms.
we shiver at your voice
slithering through the air.

we hear you chanting:
"this bomb is a PEACE bomb."

"these dead children were TERRORISTS."
"we must fight the COMMUNISTS at all costs."
but someone's foot keeps sticking in your teeth.

Goya, they say, lived
in a darkened mansion.
his nightmare visions
hung on every wall.

you have the mansions, Cowboy.
you have the magic voice.
you spin these tales and visions.
we sit before our tvs watching you.

we listen as you croon
the words of war.
East against West, North against South.
we see the pieces of your children
dangling from your mouth.

D. L. CROCKETT SMITH

Marvin Tate (b. 1959)

The flamboyant Marvin Tate often seems both clown and prophet—obsessed, as one reviewer put it, with the "holy and perverse." Born and raised in Chicago's South Lawndale community, Tate has worked with preschoolers and taught writing and poetry in the public schools. He is famous for his spoken-word performances, both solo and with his band, the eclectic and highly regarded Marvin Tate's D-Settlement. Both poems below are from his *Schoolyard of Broken Dreams* (1994), the first miraculously capturing much of his wild soulfulness. Though the poem's speaker knows there's a sell-out quality in trying to escape the burden of Blackness, he is also willing to offer the services of his space shuttle, a move inspired by the space-travel fantasies of Chicago-born music genius Sun Ra. The second poem, much quieter, though still fanciful, questions whether escape is possible at all.

Soulville Revisited

Greg Williams had changes
he had decided one day that he wasn't
going to be black no mo'
said that he was tired of seeing black
tired of eating
                        dreaming
talking
            walking·
freaking
            fucking
thinking
            worrying
b l a c k

burned his 100% rayon dashiki and swapped
it for a Dead Kennedy jacket complete
with Sid and Nancy buttons and a pair of
construction orange combat boots

told me that revolution was just a bunch of
poor folks stuck in reverse, talking that
race rhetoric and that the only revolution

that he was going to be down for was getting
his glass dick back from his boy Lonnie
who was using it all last week
gone is his once bushy

                                  erratic

Jupiter

                    Sugarfoot/Hendrix shaped
afro faded and now he's digging a government
cheese colored mohawk

yeah, Greg was known for changing, sometimes
for the worse, he'd be talking like somebody
had poured some 7UP into his funk; the last
I heard, he was hanging with his phat freak
named Wanda, they were talking about flying
to Pluto to check and see if Sun Ra had any
of that space pot for sale. I told them to
give me a few dollars and I'd take them
anywhere they wanted to go in my space shuttle . . .

The Ebony Mannequin in the Marshall Fields State Street Store Window

To remain anonymous
her bent fedora tilted slightly
over her right eye

embarrassed? perhaps,
you know most nude women are
when strangers stop and stare

I noticed how she reached
sadly towards me, as if I were her knight
in black jeans and beat up cowboy boots
to rescue her away from the glazed-eyed
audience, but I too stared

at the paint peeling from her nipples
as the window displayer hurriedly
undressed her from winter to spring fashions.

MARVIN TATE

Rohan Preston (dates unavailable)

Winner of the inaugural Henry Blakely award given by Gwendolyn Brooks, Rohan Preston also won major Illinois Arts Council poetry fellowships in 1996 and 1998. The poems below come from *Dreams in Soy Sauce,* published by Tia Chucha Press in 1992. In 1996, he coedited (with Daniel J. Wideman) the highly regarded *Soulfires: Young Black Men on Love and Violence,* published by Penguin. Active for many years at the Guild Complex and on the Chicago poetry scene, he has been an arts critic for the *Chicago Tribune* and is the current theater critic for the *Minneapolis Star Tribune.* The first poem below alludes to the suicide of *Tribune* colleague Leanita McClain, also represented in this anthology. Rohan Preston's poems brilliantly transform a world of personal allusions and fantasy dreaming into social metaphor.

This One

This one I dedicate to Chairman Flax
Grand Wizard, Grand Dragon of white fire
this one is for you, Buckra,
for your melanin fears and thin skin
for your film transparency, flimsy negatives—
I can see clear through you.

You wish that I would have desires
to twist and bend inside your sister
till she spoke in some primal twang,
or to approach your mother in some garage—
a tall, tall shadow gliding, sliding along—
but that's not my program, Scruffy.
You wish that I would circumcise you
and ram ram ram—till you bleed some more—
but I have too many things to do.
I know—I know. It's a density thing.
You command me to make me understand
what Leanita meant when she wanted
to blow up every wan face on the bus
(put some ruddiness into these northern winds);
you dare me to pump an Uzi and perforate
my insignia through your pallid chest,
initial a jacket that's never to be worn—

keep drooling those nightmares on your pillow, Buddy.
Oh, yea, you want me to bark at you
when you say bow-wow; to grunt with you
when you scratch your balls; to fart with you
when you open your mouth—that I do do.
You got into Leanita's head and made her
take herself out—that's the hard way, you know.

I work my own schedule, HannibalOverTime
and do things with effective minimal effort.
The knowledge that you think I lack
I already know. The next time I meet
you on some cross-burning lawn, you
will have a lot to learn, once and for all.

June 12, 1990: Chicago, Illinois

Dreams in Soy Sauce

1.

Mum, my dearest grand mamaa, slumps
over a pail bleaching clothes, the bubbles
pop beneath her fingers (squish-squish,
squish-squish like a croaking lizard).
Her back is turned towards me and as I
approach her left side she says, "The floor,
the floor. I've cleaned and waxed the floor—
it shines beautifully!" Mum's neck ripples
like a turkey's. She ordinarily does not
say anything with such force. I have not seen
or written to her for a year or so. Her head still
bowed, she squints softly, "I'm pissed at you."

2.

At the nightclub, they stab people who dance
on the staggered steps of the stage, stab them
in the legs. A Eurasian singer, smothered
with ashen foundation, flings his hair and beats
his head against a patient steel pole in a cage—

ROHAN PRESTON

his teeth bared and bloody. I have only come to dance.
A dire deconstructionist from New Haven,
(black lipstick, cigarette black) plants a ratchet
into my left calf, leaving a too-anxious gush
in its wake. I kick him in the face, grab the knife,
and take off.

3.

Then find myself on a train through
Greenwich, behind a day school with a cricket pitch,
blazoned copper. The carillon chimes us to dinner.
A young bowler in starched white reddens
his trousers while shining the ball on his pocket.
I ask him, googly or leg-breaker? Spin ball or pace?
He does not answer; but a pasted spectator,
the one from that same nightclub, offers something
to drink. I run away from her to find myself
in a West Side disco on the Hudson where
it is always night. Some guards, fingers dangling,
question my pass and ask each other if I had a right
to keep the knife. (I did not realize it was in my hand.)
They examine my gash, skin up their faces half-
smelling something, half-pleasured, and nod.
I may come in.

4.

In Provincetown, another cut-out paste-up (white face,
all-black eyes) streams up and spills out of a Spider,
a play-car really. She is squired by a linebacker
who dashes into a carpet store. They must want
their knife back. I panic. I have lost it. The lineman
comes out of the shop and hails a cop-car
as if it were a cab. They wave to me with
hands that spin in board games.

November 11, 1990: Chicago, Illinois

ROHAN PRESTON
268

Barack Obama (b. 1961)

Born in Hawaii to a Kenyan father and a white mother from Kansas, Barack Obama also spent many of his earlier years in Indonesia with his mother and stepfather, Lolo. After graduating from Columbia University, he became a community organizer in Chicago, working in some of the poorest neighborhoods on the South Side. He left Chicago for three years to obtain a law degree at Harvard, where he became the first Black person to be elected president of the *Harvard Law Review*. In 1992, he married Michelle Robinson, a life-long resident of the South Side and another Harvard Law School graduate, and directed Illinois Project VOTE, registering 150,000 new voters. He practiced civil rights law, became a senior lecturer in law at the University of Chicago, and served three terms in the state senate before winning a landslide victory for the U.S. Senate in November 2004. Earlier that year, he gave the keynote address at the Democratic National Convention and is considered the party's brightest rising star. Even before he arrived in Washington to take his Senate seat, talk of an eventual run for the presidency swirled and has only increased. Thus he has had to spend some time in his early Senate career lowering expectations. At a town meeting in Naperville, Illinois, in early February 2005, he joked that a Senate colleague had said to him, "Barack, you've been here a week already, and we still have poverty and unemployment. You're not living up to the hype!" In 1995, long before he was such a luminous national figure, he wrote *Dreams from My Father: A Story of Race and Inheritance*, a wonderfully articulate, probing memoir. Sandwiched between details of his origins and his trip to Kenya to trace his father's roots is the story of his coming to Chicago, where he first fully worked out his desire to be a community organizer. Today he makes his home on the South Side and attends Trinity Church. At the center of the excerpt below is his first meeting with Trinity's pastor, Rev. Jeremiah Wright.

From *Dreams from My Father: A Story of Race and Inheritance*

[A]s segregated as Chicago was, as strained as race relations were, the success of the civil rights movement had at least created some overlap between communities, more room to maneuver for people like me. I could work in the black community as an organizer or a lawyer and still live in a high rise downtown. Or the other way around: I could work in a blue-chip law firm but live in the South Side and buy a big house, drive a nice car, make my donations to the NAACP and Harold's campaign, speak at local high schools. A role model, they'd call me, an example of black male success.

Was there anything wrong with that? . . . That was one of the lessons I'd learned these past two and a half years, wasn't it?—that most black folks weren't like the father of my dreams, the man in my mother's stories, full of high-blown ideals and quick to pass judgment. They were more like my stepfather, Lolo, practical people who knew life was too hard to judge each other's choices, too messy to live according to abstract ideals. No one expected self-sacrifice from me . . . As far as they were concerned, my color had always been a sufficient criterion for community membership, enough of a cross to bear.

Was that all that had brought me to Chicago, I wondered—the desire for such simple acceptance? That had been part of it, certainly, one meaning to community. But there had been another meaning, too, a more demanding impulse. Sure, you could be black and still not give a damn about what happened in Altgeld or Roseland. You didn't have to care about boys like Kyle, young mothers like Bernadette or Sadie. But to be right with yourself, to do right by others, to lend meaning to a community's suffering and take part in its healing—that required something more. . . .

It required faith. I glanced up now at the small, second-story window of the church, imagining the old pastor inside, drafting his sermon for the week. Where did your faith come from? he had asked. It suddenly occurred to me that I didn't have an answer. Perhaps, still, I had faith in myself. But faith in one's self was never enough. . . .

. . . I met with more black ministers in the area, hoping to convince them to join the organization. It was a slow process, for unlike their Catholic counterparts, most black pastors were fiercely independent, secure in their congregations and with little obvious need for outside assistance. Whenever I first reached them on the phone, they would often be suspicious or evasive, uncertain as to why this Muslim—or worse yet, this Irishman, O'Bama—wanted a few minutes of their time. And a handful I met with conformed to the prototypes found in Richard Wright novels or Malcolm X speeches: sanctimonious gray- beards preaching pie-in-the-sky, or slick Holy Rollers with flashy cars and a constant eye on the collection plate.

For the most part, though, once I'd had a chance to meet these men face-to-face, I would come away impressed. As a group, they turned out to be thoughtful, hardworking men, with a confidence, a certainty of purpose that made them by far the best organizers in the neighborhood. They were generous with their time, interested in the issues, surprisingly willing to open themselves to my scrutiny. One minister talked about a former gambling addiction. Another told me about his years as a successful executive and a secret drunk. They all mentioned periods of religious doubt; the corruption of the world and their own hearts; the striking bottom and shattering of pride; and then finally the resurrection of self, a self alloyed to something larger. That was the source of their confidence, they insisted: their personal fall, their subsequent redemption. It was what gave them the authority to preach the Good News.

Had I heard the Good News? some of them would ask me.

Do you know where it is that *your* faith is coming from?

When I asked for other pastors to talk to, several gave me the name of Reverend Wright. . . . Younger ministers seemed to regard Reverend Wright as a mentor of sorts. . . . Older pastors were more cautious with their praise, impressed with the rapid growth of Trinity's congregation but somewhat scornful of its popularity among young black professionals. ("A buppie church," one pastor would tell me.)

Toward the end of October I finally got a chance to pay Reverend Wright a visit and see the church for myself. It sat flush on Ninety-fifth Street in a mostly residential neighborhood a few blocks down from the Louden Home projects. I had expected something imposing, but it turned out to be a low, modest structure of red brick and angular windows, landscaped with ever-greens and sculpted shrubs and a small sign spiked into the grass—FREE SOUTH AFRICA in simple block letters. Inside, the church was cool and murmured with activity. . . .

Eventually a pretty woman with a brisk, cheerful manner came up and introduced herself as Tracy, one of Reverend Wright's assistants. . . . As I followed her back into a kitchen toward the rear of the church, we began to chat, about the church mostly, but also a little about her. It had been a difficult year, she said: Her husband had recently died, and in just a few weeks she'd be moving out to the suburbs. She had wrestled long and hard with the decision, for she had lived most of her life in the city. But she had decided the move would be best for her teenage son. She began to explain how there were a lot more black families in the suburbs these days; how her son would be free to walk down the street without getting harassed; how the school he'd be attending had music courses, a full band, free instruments and uniforms. . . .

As we were talking, I noticed a man in his late forties walking toward us. He had silver hair, a silver mustache and goatee; he was dressed in a gray three-piece suit. He moved slowly, methodically, as if conserving energy, sorting through his mail as he walked, humming a simple tune to himself.

"Barack," he said as if we were old friends, "let's see if Tracy here will let me have a minute of your time."

"Don't pay him no mind, Barack," Tracy said, standing up and straightening out her skirt. "I should have warned you that Rev likes to act silly sometimes."

. . . He had grown up in Philadelphia, the son of a Baptist minister. He had resisted his father's vocation at first, joining the Marines out of college, dabbling with liquor, Islam, and black nationalism in the sixties. But the call of his faith had apparently remained, a steady tug on his heart, and eventually he'd entered Howard, then the University of Chicago, where he spent six years studying for a Ph.D. in the history of religion. He learned Hebrew and Greek, read the literature of Tillich and Niebuhr and the black liberation theologians. The anger and humor of the streets, the book learning and occasional twenty-five-cent word, all this he had brought with him to Trinity almost two decades ago . . . [I]t became clear in that very first meeting that, despite the reverend's frequent disclaimers, it was this capacious talent of his—this ability to hold together, if not reconcile, the conflicting strains of black experience—upon which Trinity's success had ultimately been built.

His approach had obviously worked: the church had grown from two hundred to four thousand members during his tenure; there were organizations for every taste; from yoga classes to Caribbean clubs. He was especially pleased with the church's progress in getting more men involved, although he admitted that they still had a way to go.

"Nothing's harder than reaching young brothers like yourself," he said. "They worry about looking soft . . ."

The reverend looked up at me then, a look that made me nervous. I decided to shift the conversation to more familiar ground, telling him about DCP and the issues we were working on, explaining the need for involvement from larger churches like his. He sat patiently and listened to my pitch, and when I was finished he gave a small nod.

"I'll try to help you if I can," he said. "But you should know that having us involved in your effort isn't necessarily a feather in your cap."

"Why's that?"

Reverend Wright shrugged. "Some of my fellow clergy don't appreciate what we're about. They feel like we're too radical. Others, we ain't radical enough. Too emotional. Not emotional enough. Our emphasis on African history, on scholarship—"

"Some people say," I interrupted, "that the church is too upwardly mobile."

The reverend's smile faded. "That's a lot of bull," he said sharply. "People who talk that mess reflect their own confusion. They've bought into the whole business of class that keeps us from working together. Half of 'em think that the former gang banger or the former Muslim got no business in a Christian church. Other half think any black man with an education or a job, or any church that respects scholarship, is somehow suspect.

"We don't buy into these false divisions here. It's not about income, Barack. Cops don't check my bank account when they pull me over and make me spread-eagle against the car. These miseducated brothers, like that sociologist at the University of Chicago, talking about 'the declining significance of race.' Now, what country is he living in?"

But wasn't there a reality to the class divisions, I wondered? I mentioned the conversation I'd had with his assistant, the tendency of those with means to move out of the line of fire. He took off his glasses and rubbed what I now saw to be a pair of tired eyes.

"I've given Tracy my opinion about moving out of the city," he said quietly. "That boy of hers is gonna get out there and won't have a clue about where, or who, he is."

"It's tough to take chances with your child's safety."

"Life's not safe for a black man in this country, Barack. Never has been. Probably never will be."

A secretary buzzed, reminding Reverend Wright of his next appointment. We shook hands; and he agreed to have Tracy prepare a list of members for me to meet. Afterward, in the parking lot, I sat in my car and thumbed through a silver brochure that I'd picked up in the reception area. It contained a set of guiding principles—a "Black Value System"—that the congregation had adopted in 1979. At the top of the list was a commitment to God, "who will give us the strength to give up prayerful passivism and become Black Christian activists, soldiers for Black freedom and the dignity of all humankind." Then a commitment to the black community and black family, education, the work ethic, discipline, and self-respect.

A sensible, heartfelt list. . . . There was one particular passage in Trinity's brochure that stood out, though, a commandment more self-conscious in its tone, requiring greater elaboration. "A Disavowal of the Pursuit of Middleclassness," the heading read. "While it is permissible to chase 'middleincomeness' with all our might," the text stated, those blessed with the talent or good fortune to achieve success in the American mainstream must avoid the "psychological entrapment of Black 'middleclassness' that hypnotizes the successful brother or sister into believing they are better than the rest and teaches them to think in terms of 'we' and 'they' instead of 'US'!"

My thoughts would often return to that declaration in the weeks that followed as I met with various members of Trinity. I decided that Reverend Wright was at least partly justified in dismissing the church's critics, for the bulk of its membership was solidly working class, the same teachers and secretaries and government workers one found in other big black churches throughout the city. Residents from the nearby housing project had been actively recruited, and programs designed to meet the needs of the poor. . . .

Still, there was no denying that the church had a disproportionate number of black professionals in its ranks: engineers, doctors, accountants, and corporate managers. Some of them had been raised in Trinity; others had transferred in from other denominations. Many confessed to a long absence from any religious practice—a conscious choice for some, part of a political or intellectual awakening, but more often because church had seemed irrelevant to them as they'd pursued their careers in largely white institutions.

At some point, though, they all told me of having reached a spiritual dead end—a feeling, at once inchoate and oppressive, that they'd been cut off from themselves. Intermittently, then more regularly, they had returned to the church, finding in Trinity some of the same things every religion hopes to offer its converts: a spiritual harbor and the chance to see one's gifts appreciated and acknowledged in a way that a paycheck never can; an assurance, as bones stiffened and hair began to gray, that they belonged to something that would outlast their own lives—and that, when their time finally came, a community would be there to remember.

But not all of what these people sought was strictly religious, I thought; it wasn't just Jesus they were coming home to. It occurred to me that Trinity, with its African themes, its emphasis on black history, continued the role that Reverend Philips had described earlier as a redistributor of values and circulator of ideas. Only now the redistribution didn't run in just a single direction from the schoolteacher or the physician who saw it as a Christian duty to help the sharecropper or the young man fresh from the South adapt to big city life. The flow of culture now ran in reverse as well; the former gang banger, the teenage mother, had their own forms of validation—claims of greater deprivation and hence authenticity, their presence in the church providing the lawyer or doctor with an education from the streets. By widening its doors to allow all who would enter, a church like

Trinity assured its members that their fates remained inseparably bound, that an intelligible "us" still remained.

It was a powerful program, this cultural community, one more pliant than simple nationalism, more sustaining than my own brand of organizing. Still, I couldn't help wondering whether it would be enough to keep more people from leaving the city or young men out of jail. Would the Christian fellowship between a black school administrator, say, and a black school parent change the way the schools were run? . . . Sometimes I would put such questions to the people I met with. They would respond with the same bemused look Reverend Philips and Reverend Wright had given me. For them, the principles in Trinity's brochure were articles of faith no less than belief in the Resurrection. You have some good ideas, they would tell me. Maybe if you joined the church you could help us start a community program. Why don't you come by on Sunday?

And I would shrug and play the question off, unable to confess that I could no longer distinguish between faith and mere folly, between faith and simple endurance; that while I believed in the sincerity I heard in their voices, I remained a reluctant skeptic, doubtful of my own motives, wary of expedient conversion, having too many quarrels with God to accept a salvation too easily won.

The day before Thanksgiving, Harold Washington died.

It occurred without warning. Only a few months earlier, Harold had won reelection, handily beating Vrdolyak and Byrne, breaking the deadlock that had prevailed in the city for the previous four years. . . .

. . . He said he'd be mayor for the next twenty years.

And then death: sudden, simple, final, almost ridiculous in its ordinariness, the heart of an overweight man giving way.

By the time of the funeral, Washington loyalists had worked through the initial shock. They began to meet, regroup, trying to decide on a strategy for maintaining control, trying to select Harold's rightful heir. But it was too late for that. . . .

The loyalists squabbled. Factions emerged. Rumors flew. By Monday, the day the city council was to select a new mayor to serve until the special election, the coalition that had first put Harold in office was all but extinguished. I went down to City Hall that evening to watch this second death. People, mostly black, had been gathering outside the city council's chambers since late afternoon—old people, curiosity seekers, men and women with banners and signs. They shouted at the black aldermen who had cut deals with the white bloc. . . .

But power . . . could outwait slogans and prayers and candlelight vigils. Around midnight, just before the council got around to taking a vote, the door to the chambers opened briefly and I saw two of the aldermen off in a huddle. One, black, had been Harold's man; the other, white, Vrdolyak's. They were whispering now, smiling briefly, then looking out at the still-chanting crowd and quickly suppressing their smiles. . . . I left after that. I pushed through the crowds that overflowed into the street and began walking across Daley Plaza toward my car. The wind whipped up cold and sharp as a blade, and I watched a hand-made sign tumble past me. HIS SPIRIT LIVES ON, the sign read in heavy block letters. And beneath the words that picture I had seen so many times while waiting for a chair in Smitty's Barbershop: the handsome, grizzled face; the indulgent smile; the twinkling eyes; now blowing across the empty space, as easily as an autumn leaf.

Elizabeth Alexander (b. 1962)

Born in New York City and raised in Washington, D.C., Elizabeth Alexander taught at the University of Chicago, winning the Quantrell Prize for excellence in undergraduate teaching. She has published poetry, fiction, and critical essays and reviews in the *Paris Review,* the *American Poetry Review,* the *Washington Post,* the *Village Voice,* and other important periodicals. Her poetry collections include *The Venus Hottentot* (1990), *Antebellum Dream Book* (2001), and *Body of Life,* published in Chicago by Tia Chucha Press in 1996. A collection of essays, *The Black Interior,* was published in 2004, and a fourth collection of poems, *American Sublime,* in 2005. She has won NEA and Guggenheim fellowships, among many other awards, and currently teaches at Yale. The poems below come from the Tia Chucha book and exhibit what she has often been praised for: an intense lyricism and eroticism coupled with a deep sense of history and race/gender consciousness. All these qualities converge naturally around Josephine Baker, and in her "elegy" on Wrigley Field she looks off to the South Side and to Detroit and Detroit's great Black poet Robert Hayden.

The Josephine Baker Museum

1. *EAST ST. LOUIS* (1918)

Mama, danced
a glass
of water balanced
on her head.

"Someone raped
a white woman!"
We ran
at night,
next day
heard tell

of eyes
plucked out,
of scalps
pulled clean,
a bloody sky.

That day
God showed

his face,
grey and shaggy,
in the rain clouds.

2. *Costumes*

The black and white checked overalls
I wore off the boat at Le Havre. Wired skirts
whose trains weigh fifty pounds. Furling,
curling headpieces, and hourglass-
shaped gowns.

Schiaparellis and Poirets! The green suede
Pilgrim shoes and orange jacket,
Harlem-made. The lime chiffon!
the one with egrets
painted on.

I'm sick of *touts le bananes.* Ici,
my uniform: French Air Force, fray-spots
blackened back with ink. And here,
the diamond necklace,
for my glorious Chiquita.

3. *The Wig Room*

A gleaming black sputnik of hair.
A solid figure-eight of hair, glazed black.
Crows' wings of hair, a waist-length switch.

Black profiteroles of mounded hair.
Hair like an Eiffel Tower, painted black.
A ziggurat of patent leather hair.

Black crowns to be taken on and off, that live
in the room when the lights go out, a roomful
of whispering Josephines, a roomful
of wigs in the dark.

4. ABLUTIONS

In the cinema Mammy hands Scarlett
white underthings to cover her white skin.
I am both of them and neither, tall,
tan, terrific, soaking in my tub of milk.

What would it mean to be me on stage
in a bathtub soaping, singing my French
chansons with one pointed foot with painted toes
suggesting what is underneath, suggesting

dusky, houri dreams and is she really
naked? Do they really want to see
the nappy pussy underneath that sweats
and stinks and grinds beneath bananas,

turns to seaweed in the tub? What if
I let my hair go back, or dressed
more often as a man? What if I let myself
get fat? What would it mean to step out

of the bathtub onto the stage and touch
myself, do to myself what I do to myself
in the bedroom when only my animals
watch? What would I be to my audience then?

(Sigh) Come here, baby. Dry me off.

5. DIVA STUDIES

What is original, what
is facsimile? The boys
in the dressing room are showing
me how to skin my hair down flat
like patent leather, black as that.
I show them how to paint eyeballs
on their eyelids to look bright

from the last row, how I line
my eyes like the Egyptian cat.
We carry on, in that dingy,
musky, dusty room overhung
with fraying costumes, peeling
sequins, shedding feathers, mules
with broken heels, mending glue, eye-
lash glue, charcoal sticks and matches,
brushes and unguents and bottles of oil.
The dressing room is my schoolhouse.
My teachers are men more woman
than actual women, and I
am the skinny sixteen-year-old
whose hair is slicked flat because
Congoleum burned it off.
I cross my eyes and knock my knees,
am somehow still a diva.
The boys swoop past and are rare.
The beauty is how this strange
trade works. The truth of it is,
we are fabulous.

Blues

Wrigley illuminates
the night sky violet,

indigo city tonight,
Chicago, city

surrounded by Magikist lips,
baci baci baci

benedicting the expressways.
"Sixty-watt gloom" suffused

Hayden's Detroit, the South
Side's similar neon face.

I elegize cities
and leave them, cities

my imagined Atlantises.
Tonight, all Chicago

is singing the blues.
Autumn came today,

winter next, always.
Elegy, indigo, blues.

ELIZABETH ALEXANDER

Quarysh Ali Lansana (b. 1965)

Quarysh Ali Lansana was born in Enid, Oklahoma, in 1965 but now lives in Chicago, where his long and deep involvement in the arts began as artistic director and board member of the Guild Complex, one of the most important literary arts centers in Chicago. He also directs nappyhead press and currently teaches at Columbia College and Chicago State University. A literary teaching artist and curriculum developer, he has taught workshops in prisons, public schools, and universities in thirty-three states. As a performer, he has collaborated with jazz, blues, reggae, and traditional African musicians and was a founding member of the legendary Black poetry-music ensemble the Funky Wordsmyths. He has received Gwendolyn Brooks's Henry Blakely Award and the Wallace W. Douglas Distinguished Service Award (both in 1999), and the first ever Bob Award from WTTW-TV, for his poetry video *Passage* (with Kurt Heintz). Among his poetry collections are *southside rain* (1999), from which the poems below come, and *The Big World*. He has edited such books as *Illinois Voices* and *Pearl and Powerlines: A Decade of Poetry from Chicago's Guild Complex*. Two other anthologies, *I Represent* and *dream in yourself,* collect works from Chicago's award-winning youth arts employment program Gallery 37. Though often celebrating Black life, even more often his poems combine sharp social commentary with a nostalgic lyricism that results in what I would call "sad sermons," a phrase the poet uses to end "tracks," one of his *southside rain* poems.

hyphen

take the hyphen out
the middle
of my identity
and stick it
to the whole

half and half in half
doesn't even make three-fifths
but a fraction of bad multiplication
ruins the formula

homogenized culture
high in fats
high in saccharin
low in truth and
ready for the tasteless test:
clarence thomas

unorganic
antiseptic takes
on the hyphen
in the middle

this hyphen a clever trickster
providing certain unalienable rights
to brand names and
a false sense of security:

God, the father
God, the son
God, the dollar

america, america
the bastard stepchild
is afraid of her children

we are
afrikans, we
raise afrikans, we
rise afrikans.

and knock the hyphen unconscious.

seventy-first & king drive

night smells catfish crispness
while sista girl works them curls
s's lounge buzz and slam
as brothas basehead
brothas boomin
basshead brothas boomin
base boomin
boomin bass
blowin the plastic in the used-to-be back window
a baby boppin in the backseat

QUARYSH ALI LANSANA

jackie's restaurant is always open
well, in july, until 11:30 pm
urban queens with newport lips
hardened softness serving biscuits of like texture

leo's flowers, a fading pastel
succumbs to evening's wings
chicken wings

wild irish the bouquet of the 'hood

rogers park

at times like now
when words seem a chore
and 71st street a city away
images roll by yawning september days
to dance against lakeside dusk.

poetry is hard to find here
save that wizened oak
crying seasonal tears.

ambivalent leaves ride the air
the avenue a sea of autumn.
i rake words into piles
and dive into a welcome blanket.

fat-free

"The next time you hear 'smooth jazz,' ask yourself what's been
smoothed over."
—Fareed Mahluli Abdul-Wahhab

pacific northwest caucasian cats
purr suburban tones
from ivory mountaintops.
the valley grows restless.

on the backsides of bechet, 'trane,
kenny g slides down mt. rainier.
asks us to help him up.
holds notes beyond his memory

Tyehimba Jess (b. 1965)

Detroit native Tyehimba Jess has been a key presence on the contemporary Chicago arts and poetry scene as a writer and performer for nearly twenty years. He has hosted the "Power of the Word" reading series and is a member of the performance ensemble drapetomania. He published a book of poems, *when niggas love Revolution like they love the bulls: ransom notes from tyehimba jess* and coauthored the play *Blakk Love.* His poem "election day u.s. of a.—u. of s.a." won the Sister City/Chicago Poetry Festival "Poem for Accra" Award. He is currently working on a poem sequence about Leadbelly.

Magic

us.
staring
stupid eyed
at your prestidigitation.
we watch you floating, mid air
like peace
and fire
and power
and grace
as we ask
what did that nigga god do to make him so bad?

and with a 360 swish you answered
i'm never comin down
i own this air
and all in it

we believed and we believed

but now heroman, you fly the courts no more
now you be walkin mortalized with mortal steps
crushin naive dreams we had of livin carefree forevers
and things are a little more solemn now.
no more that *shit don't affect me!*
no more *i clean, i ain't like that*
and *only faggots get that shit!*

and the face of genocide has become just a little clearer since
you brought it home to every basketball court in the hood.

you, smilin giant
you, sleek-footed move master
you, once slidin, pushin, leapin, dribblin, weavin down a court
through forests of flashin arms and legs takin it to the hole
you now serve up in yo face images of

syphilitic tuskegee graves,
smallpox blankets,
disappearing hospital beds in the hood,
needle-spread sickness,
and a horror called doctor bills
all a part of the game played on these asphalt streets.

and now, on all the networks,
the tv smile,
the brave words
as you remind us the magic is still here
we only thinking of the day we last saw you floating, mid air
thinking of peace, grace and power.

how all the rules have been broken at our feet.
magically.

We Live

We live.
a million sun-blackened soul-minds
dynamited from
    rocks
    plains
    hills
    savannahs
    middle passages away.

    burned into buffalo heartland
    searching for red, white, and blue consciousness

TYEHIMBA JESS

We found nothing but echoes coming off the walls,
silently
silently
silently.

We live.
We be your drug taken to forget.
blown into your midnight hour with the cry of nighttime blues
                              shifting choruses
                              motown whispers
                              slowly spitting in your ear.

We live.
not shadows of big lips and tall struts bleedin down your
gone-with-the-wind tiara staircase.
not al jolson charade followed by tv dinner of
the jeffersons
good times
and cosby show kente-clothed niggas.

We live.
AIN'T I A WOMAN she said, and
I AM THE MAN YOU THINK YOU ARE he declared before the
    last bullets rained
on ballroom stage steps.

We live.
and not just the visible ones.
others go unnoticed
    undetected
    unseen
    unheard
    unthought of
until the next prisoner is freed in the middle of the night. (assata!!)
                                                              (assata!!)
                                                              (assata!!)
                                                              (assata!!)

Regie Gibson (b. 1966)

Perhaps the most electric slam poet in America, Regie Gibson has, among many honors, won the 1997 money slam and the 1998 individual slam title. He and his work have been featured in the movie *love jones,* and he has lectured and performed at venues ranging from universities to clubs across the United States and on two other continents. His performance style has often been called "rhythmistical," signifying his weaving together of song, mysticism, the African *griot* tradition, and the hard funk of Black American experience—a combination naturally leading to his other lives as actor, percussionist, and activist. He published *Storms Beneath the Skins* in 1999 (reissued in 2001). "blooz man," his signature piece, was featured in the 2000 Steppenwolf Theater production *Words on Fire,* a celebration of Chicago poetry. Below is the second of the poem's three parts—the first moving from God as blooz man to the poet as blooz man, the third centering on blooz in the parent-child chain of survival.

prayer

for the drummers hands
severed before they could strike skin

for the seventh string of unplayed guitars
gone suicidal with longing

for the fifth tendon of the hobbled upright

the fourth key of discarded trumpets
tortured into silent confession

for the ghostly grey keys of murdered pianos
condemned *to* inhabit the cadavers of their killers

prayer for every dancers legs
stolen and pawned

for all poets made to eat their tongues

the artists eyes

painted shut by the color blind

the singers throat made mausoleum
of infant hymns

this elegy is for your aborted souls

your mahabarata suffocated while dreaming of birth

your music massacred while praying

your song assassinated in flight

for you whose flames
could have scorched

open pathways between us
and ourselves

and for us
condemned to never know it

From "blooz man"

II. REALIZATION

i is whine of all things terrible
scream of all things tremblin

seraph whose wings beat hatred
demon who smiles redemption

i is whisper cushioning
broken bodies in this sepulcher
of tumultuous existence

i is the blooz ma
the blooz man is i

i is blushin flesh of quiverin virgin
i is ho who blows dawns

REGIE GIBSON

i is throbbin eye of battered wife
wonderin where her husbands gone

i is song of fatherless generations
sired by loins of war

i is comin of bedouin soldier
bringin smashin to heads and culture

i is white sail blown by winds of profit
sailin on seas of severed black hands

i is the blooz man
the blooz man is i

i is ornament forged from all shackled human freedoms
an eagles feather trampled neath hooves of final solution

i is shamed thighs of all raped women
demandin the rapists death as retribution

blooz man

black boot steppin
goose steppin/stompin
down the doors of scapegoats

blooz man

screamin stream of ash
blackenin skies over bergen-belsen
dachau and auschwitz

blooz man

i is cuttin *edge:*
of rusted blades

and mouth
of gapin wounds

the angry innocence
of questionin blood
demandin to be answered soon

baptism inside exorcism

missin eye of collective myopia

elegy of praise buried within
fecundity of all anathema

i is fingers of dead
lovers still ticklin one another
cross mine fields
of war torn lands

i is the blooz man
the blooz man is i

Angela Shannon (dates unavailable)

Widely published in such journals as *Ploughshares, TriQuarterly,* and *Crab Orchard Review,* Angela Shannon has also won an Illinois Arts Council poetry award (1996) and the Willow Review Poetry Prize (1997). The poem below illustrates well the wonderful singing quality of her work, a quality that translates well into performance, has made her a key member of Chicago's Blues Ellipsis Collective, and is reflected in the title of her first book of poems, *Singing the Bones Together,* from which "Doris" comes.

Doris

"Slavery is a living wound under a patchwork of scars."
—Kwadwo Opoku-Agyemang

She draped naked buildings with daydreams,
stepped over shattered glass that once
held liquor and flashing fantasy,
painted whole families on boarded windows,
a portrait of mama, papa, cousins and grands,
renamed the made-up children, gave them
spirituals and kente filling the puzzle with song.

"Weren't we captives not submitting slaves?
Weren't we captives not submitting slaves?
Remember we resisted, we resisted."

She still saw the wounds from the Passage,
when Dahomey, Ebo and Asanti were stuffed
in the bowels of boats and the spines of grown
men and women were chained to curve like embryos,
light blocked from eyes, tongues struck silent,
so many days in darkness, we forgot our names.

"I keep a picture of the sun
tucked in the corner of my mind.
I said, I keep a picture of the sun,

the way it rises at home,
tucked in the corner of my mind.
When they tell me, I must be born again,
I say, I never died."

Audrey Petty (b. 1967)

"I had to get away from Chicago to be able to really understand its hold on me," says Petty, who spent her undergraduate years at Knox College in the largely white, far-western Illinois town of Galesburg. Her stories have appeared in *Gumbo: An Anthology of African American Writing, StoryQuarterly, African-American Review,* and *Painted Bride,* with more to appear is such publications as the *Harvard Literary Advocate.* Her poetry has appeared in *Crab Orchard Review* and will be included in *New Sister Voices,* an anthology forthcoming from Southern Illinois University Press, edited by Allison Joseph. Petty is a recent winner of the Tennessee Williams Fellowship from the Sewanee Writers Conference and has won fellowships and grants from the Ford and Mellon Foundations and the Illinois Arts Council. In a special issue of *Callaloo* devoted to emerging Black writers, Trudier Harris wrote that Petty "makes language accessible" but keeps "meaning complex and at times elusive." At the time this anthology was assembled, "Gettysburg" was one of Petty's recent, unpublished stories.

Gettysburg

To . . . my . . . architect. Sharon formulated the same toast whenever the waiter filled and refilled their flutes with Veuve Clicquot. She made the sweetest drunk, slurping her oysters, giggling at the lobster tools, kicking her pinky high each time she took the tiniest sip of champagne. When they woke the next morning, she and Liam sniffed and murmured toward each other until their lips met and sealed.

Back home in Chicago, the rhythm of their routines set apart their time together as visits, as dates. Sharon's parents were old-fashioned, so she devised snug excuses to spend the occasional night at his place. Initially, Sharon's secrecy made those evenings tryst-like, dramatic, and a little bit kinky; more recently, it kept Liam feeling like some frantic, teenaged boy.

Here, they had hours to talk, hours to be quiet. Here, he could touch her whenever he liked. They shared a king-sized bed with a plain, cedar headboard, Shaker nightstands flanking each side. *I will marry you. You will marry me.*

Almost soon. Almost soon.

Liam was ready for soon, though he well understood that Sharon had loose ends to tie. She intended to help her seniors at Lindblom graduate; she had college applications to see through (three more students to convince) and rec letters to write. She had a rent-free spot with her family, so she could pay off student loans and the dental and medical bills she'd suffered between college graduation and Board of Ed insurance. There was a right way to do things.

I will marry you. You will marry me. Sharon pressed her eyelids shut and tried to see it. A kindergartener's crayon outline of an A-frame: their happy life inside. What was hardest to imagine was how she'd break that news to her father. Sharon's mother agreed to gradually prepare him, though she herself had gasped and stammered at the first sight of Liam in a wrinkled snapshot.

A sun's out there somewhere, Sharon said, now opening her eyes wide. Liam leaned in and covered her face with kisses. He made nasal, whinnying noises as he finished with smooches around her mouth. He made her laugh. *Are you a horse or a witch?* she asked, stopping to breathe. He moaned into her neck and rested there.

Liam made her horny. He made her come. She itched to rock on top of him, to fit hips in their inevitable grooves, to draw him shuddering toward her. It was startling—wanting something so badly, something that you could actually have. He'd crave sleep afterwards, and she'd let herself drift. Eventually they'd roll over for room service; eventually they'd lose their morning. Sharon was content to loll and luxuriate in their oversized bed, but she knew that Liam wanted to sightsee. He'd begun to think of Boston as something to share. He hadn't typed an itinerary, but Liam always had a plan.

Sharon stretched out her free arm for the remote on his nightstand and flipped on CNN to officially begin their day. 9:22 already. The President was nominating a new black man for the Court. The chosen one stood dark and alone before the cameras. He wore the insecure smile of a definite Tom.

They rode the T to Harvard Square and Sharon refused Liam's offer to buy her a sweatshirt. She'd kept her response to *nope*, but the flatness of her voice caught Liam unawares. He stopped smiling; he stopped examining the jogging suit display. He'd already missed the look on her face. (She was darting toward magazines and newspapers.) He'd struck a nerve. He didn't know how or why. Liam meandered to stationery and selected half a dozen scenic postcards. He'd outpace his greetings back to Illinois, but that didn't matter. It didn't matter at all. When they strolled through the quad, on their way to falafel, Sharon held his hand again. It was a warm blue day.

They unpacked their shopping bags at the Middle Eastern café, and sucked down large lemonades by the glass. Fattoush, falafel, hummus, olives and feta were on the way. Liam chose a Fenway postcard for his parents and penciled a crude likeness of a three-flat in the high right hand corner of the front image, amidst the gray and green backdrop. His newly leased one-bedroom was just about there, his neighborhood library and Y, his Bay Bank, his grocer, his T stop too. *We're in Beantown!* he began writing on the blank side, and then he summarized his return visit to Hageman and Associates, how enthusiastic the partners there had been. He was an architect. He now belonged to a firm, a leading firm. From Hageman's 17th floor view, Liam had pored over the city: dignified by steeples, gauged arches, gambrel roofs. He didn't need to strain to find the fingerprints of Henry Hobson Richardson. Liam's pen could not keep up with his pulse. *You're both going to love it!* he finished. *Cheers, Liam.*

He paused before starting the skyline card for his sister. Something caught his eye: a peripheral flash. He'd thought it was a spider, spinning its way down to their countertop, but it was his spoon, holding the reflection of the ceiling fan at work above their heads. When he looked across at Sharon she was watching it too, pulling back her tiny braids and resting her face in the opened shell of her brown hands.

Sharon loved ordering food—the contemplation, the possibilities—as much as she loved eating it. But there, in that tight room fragrant with olive oil and spices she couldn't name, Sharon let the spinning in Liam's spoon slow her spinning mind. *Ooh,* she said. *Cool,* she said. And Liam agreed. She adored Liam's boyish, open face. How his gaping revealed the evenness of his teeth. She followed him, returning to the spoon's ecstatic flower; its measured rotation made waiting not waiting. She felt sure that if she watched it long enough—if she watched it closely—she would know what was really important and what was not.

This trip moved her heart in all directions. The day of apartment hunting had gotten under her skin. She was ready for scrutiny, but she was never prepared. One long, pink landlady gawked the whole time they roamed across her hardwood floors. It wasn't until they'd walked down to her own roomy kitchen that she mentioned how someone had *actually come late the night before.* A credit report was being checked. She couldn't say for sure, *but the place might actually be taken.* Her thick accent was serrated: all cartoon.

Liam stood over her ocean-blue Formica table, finishing his application, just in case. He scribbled his social security number, signed his name, and Sharon hugged him from behind with both of her arms. She squeezed him tight, shut her eyes and heard the landlady watching. Sharon knew Liam was ready to move on to the next circled location in the day's classifieds.

Preparing to join him, she straightened and ignored the landlady's reorganizing face. Sharon led the way back to the door, lifting her voice, calling Liam *honey,* though she never ever called him *honey.*

Sometimes Sharon admired him for not seeing the reactions. Back in Chicago, there were often white glances on the El, downtown, in his Northside neighborhood, but it was the brothers who gave disapproval with flair. There was no room not to know what they were saying, no room not to know (without doubt) that they were saying it to you. Black kids were vocal, but not as dedicated in their disapproval. Their mean teasing seemed casual, aimless. She could find the way to look into their eyes. Grown men were something else.

The worst had been weeks and weeks ago. A walk on the beach, right across from the museum in Hyde Park: Liam's idea after an early Saturday breakfast at Salonica. She was half-groggy and full of pancakes, but Liam had gotten her to jog with him in the sand. She held her flip flops in one hand and trotted beside him. He was pumping his arms above his head, in the middle of singing the theme song from Rocky. *Dadaduh, dadaduh.* Approaching on the right, retreating from the lake, a high-yellow man, wiry and mustached. Maybe thirty-five and dressed for running. Buppyish. A moon-shaped, regal face. He took them in with one blank glance: Liam clowning, Sharon waking, about to laugh or sprint. *Black bitch,* he growled and continued his stride.

Liam was too shocked to completely stop smiling, but he lowered his arms and turned to start an impossible argument. Sharon seized his hand, pulling him forward. *Leave it alone, just leave it alone.* Liam felt no anger, no threat; his face was soon normal, placid and mild. Liam could not help his kindness. Sharon pivoted, maneuvering them back towards the lot and his car. Tears had sprung to her eyes and she busied herself with blinking them away. *Wait,* Liam said, extending his arm abruptly, as if she were wandering into traffic. When she turned to him, he kissed her: mouth opened, mouth seeking. And a current zigzagged the back of her neck. *Don't let him hurt us,* he said. *We're fine. We're right.* Sharon nodded, hugged Liam, and felt the tears rise again. The beach was deserted over his shoulder.

Spring had been her favorite season. They'd met and courted one season earlier, when snow was everywhere, when a new year was about to begin, when they were unexposed, layered with wool, fleece and down. When no one with common sense wanted the Lake or the air. Sharon had come to regret the strong sunshine, the overdue thaw.

AUDREY PETTY

As their summer began, "Jungle Fever" became the weapon of choice, a spontaneous serenade that she could almost predict. Again and again, the first line of the chorus sprang at them: sprightly, catchy, and slowed only by bitter laughter. Walking down the sidewalk, creeping down the Drive in his shiny Rabbit (the convertible top down), on the way out of an elevator at Water Tower Place. She could not look at Liam then. She froze as she moved, her gaze fixed on the Lake, the lampposts, the empty entrance of a chichi boutique. Was it shame or rage that kept her neck so stiff? She could never be sure. Once the moment passed, Liam would shrug and they'd recover each other's hands again. They'd try to remember what they'd been saying. No topic would do.

Still, now, in this strange and future city, Sharon kept looking for black people wherever they went. It made her feel lost: they were so hard to find. Liam watched as Sharon walked to the back of the restaurant. He was sure she'd worn those same jeans the first time they'd met, at his sister's Christmas party, months and months ago. Simple, faded, tight just so around her butt. She moved with confidence—she strode—like there was only high dust behind her, but no matter, he willed her to look back at him and she did. She gave a quiet smile and he felt himself beaming. They were lucky.

He was so lucky. Life without her had been simpler but smaller, the neat size and clean image of a postage stamp. Now he couldn't wait for everything to come true—for her to make her home with him in this new place. He'd picked out a ring. More than anything, he wanted to know her and to know her more. She knocked twice then opened the bathroom door.

Liam swung out his chair to the narrowed aisle, unfolding the sports section. Lendl choked at Wimbledon. Done in only round three. The Cubs had squeaked by the Pirates. And the White Sox split a doubleheader with the Royals. The Cubs were his team. The Sox had been hers, fiercely hers. Now she swore that nothing good would come of them in the new, plastic park she refused to call Comiskey. She said there was nothing Comiskey about the place. Said that even the crowds were completely different than before. She'd gone twice with her father and her brother, Michael. She wouldn't return to see the Sox again, not until they blew up that park and started all over with a brain in their head. That's what she'd declare, wrinkling her nose, pouting until she almost snarled. It impressed him, how she cared so much about one single building.

The waiter arrived at the table just as Sharon did. She bounced on her heels, applauding, as he lowered the tray.

Liam had gauged the distance with the atlas. It was out of the way, but it wasn't unreasonable. They could dip into New York City for lunch and arrive at Miss Cameron's B&B by suppertime. Slow down on the way home. Spend the 4th where the war turned, where the new nation began to seal. They could do the whole tour, make love after dinner, in a quaint, clapboard house, and not hurry awake the next day. Be on the road after a hearty breakfast, back in Chicago by dark. He proposed the plan when they returned from their outing to Cambridge, while he changed clothes for a workout in the hotel's gym. Mentioning it just like that, untying his walking shoes, unzipping his chinos—as if the idea were simply a lark, a spontaneous something to wrap up their first getaway.

But the idea wasn't impromptu. He'd made arrangements with a B&B (highly recommended by the Gettysburg Chamber of Commerce, half an hour from the actual fields) one month before, after getting the amazing news and scheduling his Personnel visit with the secretary at Hageman and Associates, after contacting AAA and studying maps for routes and options for their drive. Turned out he'd nabbed the last room available at Miss Cameron's. Someone had just canceled a long weekend stay. The nightly rate was expensive, but Liam didn't hesitate with yes. Miss Cameron's phone voice was almost his Aunt Moira's, raw and uneven as a cat's meow. *Lucky you*, she said. *Lucky, lucky you.*

Gettysburg awaited them. He'd kept the idea in his front pocket, like a small piece of beach glass: opaque and solid, without any edge. *What do you say?* His chipper voice was odd to himself. He pulled on his tank top and sat beside her on their bed. She turned off the TV, dropped the remote on her nightstand and scooted onto Liam's lap. *Gettysburg? Was that on the way? How much longer was the drive? Where would we sleep?* Even after he told her about lunch in New York and accommodations at Miss Cameron's, nothing seemed resolved. *Gettysburg?* she asked again, unclasping her hands. He wondered if he should have made a bigger deal of it, if he should have told her how clearly he'd seen it in his mind.

She seemed to appreciate the idea, but she was unprepared to go. *I went to public school*, she said, smoothing his brows with her fingertips. *I never learned much about that battle, about that place. Not even in college.* He wrapped his arms around her waist and considered her suggestion: they'd watch the PBS tapes together before he left for good, for Boston. (His father had given him *The Civil War* as a gift for his birthday. The set was still wrapped in plastic on his bedroom desk, beside the biographies of Lloyd

Wright, DiMaggio, Lincoln, FDR.) Sharon said they'd watch them all in Chicago, and then—*then* they'd stop in Gettysburg on their next drive out East. Of course she'd ride back with him when he made the move. There was a right way to do things.

Of course. Of course. With their faces so close, they breathed each other's breathing. They were leaving first thing in the morning. Liam felt sluggish, cracked open by a bolt of grief. *Of course? Of course.* Nuzzling, she licked his whiskers, parted his lips, dotted his tongue with her own.

Sharon could tell right away. This one really cared: this one was going to be a bitch. No greeting. No words at all. Just one-sided menus and iceless water in short, scratched glasses plunked in front of them.

This one stayed away a long time. And there they sat, in dead-center Pennsylvania, in a half-empty restaurant, with old men and women who seemed to have exhausted each other, exhausted themselves. One pair here and there actually conversed while they ate, their voices blotted by the clatter of silverware and durable china. One denimmed couple in the rear corner, near the kitchen and payphone, patiently observed Sharon and Liam like they were the guaranteed entertainment, captured on television by Wild Kingdom for Mutual of Omaha. All that was missing was the Marlin Perkins' narration.

Their choices were one page on green xerox paper. At least they had shakes. Cookies n' cream. Chocolate. Banana. Liam was the one who first turned from the table and tried to hail the waitress, but she refused to be seen, standing near the register, looking through the both of them, her mouth a tight fist. *Hello. Hello?* Liam offered, as if there were only a bad connection to overcome. Finally he groaned and left the table to approach her. Hands out of his pockets, he presented her with a few words. He was annoyed, animated. There was color in his cheeks. Sharon couldn't help from rocking at the edge of her seat. The waitress folded her arms, said *sure, sure,* and trailed him to their table. *Chocolate shake, grilled cheese, large fries. A bowl of vegetable soup and a tuna melt with swiss. And water. Water, water, yes.* The waitress capped her pen and hightailed it back to the kitchen. Sharon's bare knees flirted with Liam's underneath the wobbly table. And before too long, she rested her palms on top of his.

Soon they were running out of daylight. Sharon kept reading aloud. Liam had exhausted his requests, so she leafed through their book of reviews and stopped where she pleased. "Blue Velvet," "The Color Purple," "Street Smart," something French about a hunchbacked farmer. They'd made a dozen new plans about what they'd rent back at home. Liam tried to listen closely, occasionally adding his two cents, but he wished she'd put the book aside and be quiet.

He was sick, beginning to sweat as the night cooled. His stomach had twisted past ache to a terrible cramp. He'd lost track of where they were.

Liam grabbed Sharon's arm as she began the first sentence about "Little Shop of Horrors." *I've got to pull over,* he said, checking the rearview then threading the Rabbit to the highway's far shoulder.

Outside, he rounded the bumper as the passing traffic built wind. It wouldn't take much; it wouldn't take long. There was no need to panic. No need at all. He stooped at the ditch, watching his feet and the tangle of weeds beyond gravel. Night was falling in its uneven way. Vomit rose and shot through him. His eyes teared. His nose stung. He hocked and spat and he spat again. He didn't trust that he was emptied.

Sharon handed him a Wet-Wipe and rubbed wide moons on his back.

One.

Two.

Three. A parade of semis came from nowhere. If he couldn't take a normal breath, the sound would knock him down.

Sharon bought bottled water at the next rest stop and raced with them back to the car. She told him how she remembered vomiting long ago, when she was a kid. That awful tang that clung to the back of her throat. *Drink what you can,* Sharon told him, leaning in close, and he drank without pausing until the trace went away. *We'll stop as often as we need to.* They sat with their doors ajar: Liam gulping fluids and poised to bolt; Sharon—unblinking and hands clasped—waiting for his signal.

After Liam threw up near the garbage can, he tugged off his socks and threw them away. He walked to the car at varying speeds, testing how well he knew his body. Rinsed of jitters and pain, he approached something like a massive hangover.

Sharon purchased the last Canada Dry in the vending machine, and then stopped by the john and made compresses with brown, scratchy paper towels. She gave him notice of her every step, her voice as gentle as a mother's. Liam had never seen her like this—so focused, so definite. She laid the towels on his forehead and lightly kissed his lips. This made him happy.

Compresses warmed on his fever and Sharon replaced them before re-taking the wheel. They kept the windows down, fireflies bursting crossfire on all sides as they gathered speed. Sharon was breaking the law for him and the rushing air was a kind of grace. When she mentioned stopping for a hotel, Liam reclined and closed his eyes. *Let's at least make Ohio.*

Sharon kept the radio low. People were talking and that was enough company to keep her alert. Liam shifted, re-shifted from his back to his side. It scared her, how his skin was so pallid. When he turned to face his door, she allowed her guilt to settle and she tried to name it. She was the one who'd wanted to quit the interstate to eat. No tired fast food for such a serious drive. She'd hoped for a real and nourishing meal in a particular location. She'd almost been optimistic. Now she couldn't shake the notion that nothing happened by accident—not meeting Liam, not loving him, not the taint of something wrong in his tuna sandwich either. The next trip she'd take care, pack Gatorade and Pepto, crackers, peanuts, raisins—provisions that would keep.

But what if they had gone to Gettysburg? By now, they'd be safe and sound in some postcard B&B. Sharon had felt certain that Gettysburg would be a pain in the ass, full of tourists with cameras, who thought of the Civil War as simply theirs, the tragic business of white folks. She glanced at doz-ing Liam and hummed a lullaby she knew, the one about quietness and a coach of horses.

Sharon wasn't a soloist, but she'd find herself singing for Liam, culling the best pieces she'd learned in school and church choirs, taking the soprano line instead of the alto one she'd been assigned. He thought she was good. *Your voice is a bell*, he'd say, stroking her belly. The lyrics came back, often arriving right as she needed them. *When you wake, you shall have all the pretty little horses.*

She gunned the gas, never letting it fall below eighty. Well into Ohio, well past eleven, road kill and traffic had thinned, and Sharon began searching for somewhere to crash. She spent more than an hour trying to stop, but every place was filled.

Finally, nearing Cleveland, she followed an exit and traced the frontage road. She saw the sign first. RITE REST LODGE in neon green script. The lodge was unlodge-like: worn white wooden, meager, a single column wide. The lot was nearly vacant. Sharon raised the windows and cut the engine. Liam dozed while she rang for entry. The manager's face appeared, Indian and kind. One night's stay for seventy-two bucks. *Holiday price. Checkout at 11. VISA, Master, AmEx. Discover will do.* His desk clock burned the time in hazy, red numbers. She'd already driven into the next day.

Sharon liked the feel of the key in her hand. The thing was huge and toyish as if it might unlock someplace pretend. Back in the car, she clutched it and sat there for a while, studying Liam. She soon gave herself over to watching, every cell of her humming to stir him awake. When someone stared outright, how could you not feel it? But he wouldn't surface. His features were peaceful. She outlined his jawbone with her index finger. Back and forth, skimming. Back and forth again. *Liam,* she whispered. *Honey. Liam. We're here.*

Tara Betts (b. 1974)

Tara Betts's poems have appeared in publications such as *Obsidian III, Mosaic, Rhapsody in Black, Dialogue,* and the Tia Chucha Press twentieth anniversary anthology *Power Lines.* "Two Brothers," below, was featured in the marvelous Steppenwolf Theatre production *Words on Fire,* a celebration through performance of Chicago poetry, staged in 2000. The second poem shows that while Betts is grounded in an African American identity, her vision is truly pan-ethnic, born of a feeling for the "amalgamation improvisation / within Black," the criss-crossing of Blackness with whiteness, with Mexican, Filipino, Puerto Rican, with North and South and the international that reaches to Egypt and beyond. Such a "collaborationist" ethic shows not only in her writing, but in the way she has become one of the most involved artists in Chicago—teaching, conducting workshops, and performing for the Guild Complex, Gallery 37, Young Chicago Authors, Columbia College, Northwestern School of Law, and primary and secondary schools throughout the area. A fixture in Chicago performance poetry, Betts is also involved in the "Women Out Loud" series at Chicago's Mad Bar and has been part of the Mad Bar's teams in the National Poetry Slam competitions. She has published two chapbooks, *Can I Hang?* and *Switch,* and runs a website at www.tarabetts.net, which features not only her work, but notices of the readings of many Chicago poets.

Two Brothers on 35th Street

The barber's clippers completed a pirouette
And left a trail in Big Brother's fine hair
Resting like soft breaths on his head
Freshly greased to be sweet as sun kisses
His hair cut as precisely as
His lackadaisical laces lacing through his high tops
As exact as the puff & swell of
His black & white plaid shirt
Hanging mid-thigh
A shirttail catches Chicago's March wind

He shivers, while
Baby Brother hovers like a satellite
Baby is a little darker in his black down-filled jacket
Even though he's five
His knit cap blares out
With the curvy, capital W in yellow on his forehead

He could step to the mic
Posture each word like lunging
Kung fu kicks
Flying during Saturday matinees
Baby Brother grins
Showing each square tooth
With a space in between.

Baby Brother turns away
As if he's playing hard to get.
He laughs when Big Brother asks
Gotta boyfriend

Both of them stand in Comiskey Park's shadow
Big Brother bounces to keep warm
And a young girl could smell
Weekends of hard kisses
Nervous touches & cocoa butter
Baby Brother coyly covers
Half his Cherry Now & Later mouth
With one tiny palm
Sayin What's Up? to a female timber song
He ain't in school! He don't go to no Julian!

A woman tells him to tell his Big Brother to stay in school
Like the sisters
Leaving him a heap of sepia butterflies
Dripping deliberate dew sweat
Dropping like ice cubes out of trays
Steel heated into malleable liquid
Big Brother & Baby Brother
Become black silk and amber velvet
Under weight of woman smile

A Mixed Message

What makes me so damned tragic?
not a fragmented exotic mystery

jezebel born from the blood of rape
nor child of the so called integration experiment

I heard folks tell my momma
How can parents put children through that
It makes life so much harder,

I have seen my mind
build bridges within blood
my biology connects with ovaries & melanin
with no capital to spare

I explode from Nella Larsen novels
yet somehow, I am invisible woman
descendant of Invisible Man
niece of an Ex-Colored Man
I balance proud weight & independent discipline
on scales of identity
swinging precarious images of Pinky & Pecola
Decades before my birth

when certificates denied
evident possibility
plain as brown freckles
across my face
when some enjoyed the milk
but avoided sunlight honey
so no secrets would break
into shards of life on racial concrete
where I stand whole/deconstructing
past nicknames
like zebra, mutt or half-n-half
while remembering my father
held me through 11-year-old
tears calling me by name
calling me beautiful

Now, some say
must be Black
could be white
maybe she's pinay
Add Mexican to the list
Puerto Rican
tan white girl
Are you from the South?
Or the best one yet
Are you Egyptian?

At least when I wandered
a continent where textbooks concealed
land anchoring the Sphinx

I rekindle links as I touch
brown hands with palms
the same shade as mine
I find myself within
amalgamation improvisation
within Black
contradicting the bubbling brew of
unidentifiable, indecipherable
ethnic glamor girls
What was she anyway?

No Concubine mistress
nor color caste breeding
rippin paper bag tests into confetti
Ready to dissolve with steam rising
from a glass of other

I defy categories
fill in all the gaps
where miscegenation laws
blotted my birth

TARA BETTS

My voice smatters blood in the face
of Aryan Nations
I am what they feared
Never passed in the world
but passed salves over broken flesh
reclaiming nationhood I lost generations ago
retracing veins from history's corpse
resounding with speech
extending beyond
now

Ken Green (b. 1964)

A graphic artist for the Department of Children and Family Services in Chicago, Ken Green is also perhaps the funniest slam poet on the Chicago scene, and—though he is not the youngest writer in this collection—I end with him because few can follow him on stage. "I have," Green says, "written serious stuff that I am saving for a special occasion, like my anticipated posthumous best-seller." A member of three National Poetry Slam teams (for the Green Mill in 1999 and 2003, and Wicker Park in 2002), he performs at many venues around the Chicago area and, he says, has "even been permitted to transport . . . poetry across state lines." In 2002, he placed second in the Austin International Poetry Festival. Though humor is the hallmark of his writing and performing, audiences also know the seriousness of Green's commentary, whether his subject is heavy—the gunning down of Amadu Diallo by New York police, for example—or lighter, like "cure-all pills with side effects . . . worse than the original ailment." He has published a chapbook entitled *I'm Just Saying . . .*, which does little to dispel the rumor that he does, indeed, own Kiss albums.

Debate

When debating the existence of God
with a grizzly bear,
whatever you do
do NOT mention Nietzsche.
Instead stand perfectly still
and steer the conversation
toward the separation of church and state
and the role of religion
in a free and democratic society,
while you bang on pots and pans to drive home your point.
and be sure to hang your beliefs
high in a tree out of his reach

When discussing the effects of industry on world politics
with a Florida alligator,
try not to mention the connection
between Henry Ford
and the development of the German auto industry.
Instead slowly slip your hand under his lower jaw
and yank upward sharply while shouting

"The workers control the means of production!"
"The workers control the means of production!"
while stroking his soft underbelly to lull him
into a state of false paralysis
and his eventual rejection of an agrarian society

When discussing man's significance in the universe with
lowland silverback gorilla,
whatever you do:
do not laugh when he mentions Area 51
as evidence of life in other sectors of the universe.
Instead, feign agreement and offer the supporting argument of
ancient Egyptian pyramid drawings that suggest
the possibility of intergalactic visitors
before raising the paralyzing dart gun
and quickly shooting him squarely in the chest.

When discussing anything with a human being,
keep your arms inside the vehicle at all times

One Man Parade

I held my own parade today.

I held my own parade today
and took my agenda
up and down the streets of Chicago

I held my own parade today

You probably saw me,
marching up and down the streets of Chicago,
past throngs of onlookers
cheering and shouting their support for my cause.

Or maybe you didn't

But no matter.
I held my own parade today

KEN GREEN

I held a parade for African American
men over 30 named Ken Green who work at DCFS
and like ketchup on eggs

It was a small turnout,
but I more or less carried on,
waving my banner high and shouting:

I'M HERE, I DRINK BEER, GET USED TO IT!

I held my own parade today

Behind the blue-clad wall of a police escort,
(that for some reason stopped for coffee at Dunkin' Donuts)
I strolled through the streets
Under a confetti sky
and promoted my agenda

I'M HERE, I DRINK BEER, GET USED TO IT!

I held my own parade today

I invited all of my factions to join in,
to share in the vindicating spotlight of my cause
Children cheered
Grown men wept
Women yawned
As float after float
Of joyous me
Passed by

"Look, here come the African American men named Ken Green
who are reluctant to admit they own more than four Kiss albums."

"Look, here come the African American men named Ken Green
who are former altar boys but don't know what to think when
their mother unexpectedly takes them to a Baptist church."

"And look, here come the African American men named Ken
Green who wonder if the waitress charged them for the orange
juice they never received."

I held my own parade today.

Of course, there were those among the throng
who opposed my lifestyle,
whose very looks hissed
and saw my presence
as undermining the thinning moral fabric of society.

"We don't want Ken Green in our schools
teaching our children"

"Ken Green should not be allowed to adopt
under any circumstances"

"The Bible clearly states that Ken Green
is an abomination in the eyes of the Lord."

But I press on
Undaunted by my detractors,
I fly my banner high,
a plain black flag
(because I couldn't think of anything else)

I held my own parade today

And like the Italians,
and the Irish
and African Americans
and the Polish
and gays
and the disabled,
I march to tell the world
I exist,

KEN GREEN

I am unique
I demand recognition

I held my own parade today

And next year's will be even bigger.

AFTERWORD

CREDITS

Afterword

This afterword attempts to suggest the greater scope of Black writing in Chicago, but an early reviewer of the manuscript of this book said it sounded too much like an apology. He was right. This afterword began as a string of regrets, a string that gets longer every time I think about it. I am humbled by the depth of the Black writing community in Chicago, and I know for lack of space and knowledge I have left out so many, many names. I can only apologize and beg forgiveness.

Of course, this book is only the proverbial tip of the iceberg even for those included. A few hundred words to represent the tens of thousands of words in *Black Metropolis,* for example, or four poems to represent the astonishing output of someone like Carolyn M. Rodgers. Gwendolyn Brooks didn't get much space either, though I content myself knowing that because of her widespread fame a mere nod in her direction is enough to connect most people to easily available works and the memory of her power. But others left out for one reason or another—mainly the limited pages allowed by the economics of publishing, or permission fees beyond our means to pay—these are deep, unsolvable regrets indeed.

First and foremost, I will immediately agree with anyone who believes omitting Leon Forrest is unforgivable. Chair of African American Studies at Northwestern from 1985 to 1992, he authored four celebrated novels: *There Is a Tree More Ancient than Eden* (1973), *The Bloodworth Orphans* (1977), *Two Wings to Veil My Face* (1984), and the monumental, 1132-page *Divine Days* (1992). I tried to create a montage of passages centered on the mythic Sugar Grove character in *Divine Days,* finally admitting to myself that even thirty pages could not adequately convey the deep, quickly flowing multiple levels of a style so thick with myth and allusion. Critic John Cawelti, quoted on the book's jacket, accurately dubs *Divine Days* a "*Ulysses* of the South Side," and, indeed, the novel opens with quotes from Homer, the Gospel of John, Joyce, and Dostoevsky. A 1993 issue of *Callaloo* was devoted to essays on Forrest's four novels. I also recommend *Relocations of the Spirit* (1994), a collection of his essays, mostly on life in Chicago. From this collection, I included "Souls in Motion" in my previous book, *Smokestacks and Skyscrapers: An Anthology of Chicago Writing* (coedited with David Starkey).

Among other worthy novelists that could not be included is Willard Motley. The opening pages of his *We Fished All Night* is one of the finest evocations of Chicago's Loop, and his most successful novel, *Knock on Any Door,* likewise contains brilliant passages rendering Chicago atmospherics as well as any writer ever has, including Nelson Algren, with whom Motley is often compared. Percy Spurlark Parker comes to mind as a fitting representative of the mystery novels written by Chicago Blacks. More recently, Hugh Holton, while a Chicago cop for more than twenty years, published crime novels such as *Chicago Blues* (1997), *The Left Hand of God* (a 1999 work combining crime and fantasy genres), *Time of the Assassins* (2001), and *The Devil's Shadow* (2001). More attention also needs to be paid someday to writers published by Herman Cromwell Gilbert's Path Press, and to Path Press' cofounder, Bennett J. Johnson.

Of Chicago's many fine short story writers, I would highlight here Marita Bonner, whose work has been collected by Joyce Flynn and daughter Joyce Occomy Stricklin in *Frye Street & Environs.* Though her vision of the possibilities Chicago offered Blacks had turned quite pessimistic by 1940, her 1926 story "Nothing New" introduced her mythical Frye Street as a vision of the multi-ethnic neighborhood that was home to hardship, certainly, but also to promise. Bonner's work set tones and themes that deeply influenced writers like Alice Browning and Era Bell Thompson, and echoes of her work can be heard in younger writers like Audrey Petty.

Bonner also wrote plays, perhaps most famously the reader's play *The Pot Maker.* Though *A Raisin in the Sun* continues to define Black drama in Chicago, the city has been important to many other Black dramatists in America, including August Wilson. Indeed, I can easily imagine a companion volume to this one focused just on Black plays from Chicago. Among the most beloved figures in Chicago theater is Theodore (Ted) Ward. In the Richard Wright selection included here, we learn of Wright's work with the WPA Writers Workshop. When Ward's one-act play *Sick and Tiahd* came in second to a Richard Wright piece in a 1936 Chicago writing contest, the two met and worked together on WPA projects. Ward's major works were *Big White Fog,* about Garveyism, and *Our Lan,* which ran on Broadway in 1947. In 1949, Ward became the first Black playwright to win a Guggenheim fellowship. But he is equally revered as a community arts leader. With Langston Hughes, Paul Robeson, and others, he helped found the Negro Playwrights Company in New York; and in Chicago, where he lived from 1968 onward, he founded the Louis Theatre and School of Drama at the South Side Center for the Performing Arts. Here one must also mention Charles Smith, who grew up on Forty-sixth and Vincennes, and, like August Wilson, "transmutes black history into works of explosive emotional power and intellectual complexity."[1] Among his fourteen plays are *Black Star Line* (1996), *The Sutherland* (1998), *Knock Me a Kiss* (2000), and most recently *Free Man of Color* (2004). David Barr III, a presence on the Chicago acting scene since 1986, has also won several writing awards for his plays, including an Illinois Arts Council Award (1995) and the Black Theater Alliance Award (1997) for *The Death of the Black Jesus.* His adaptation of Walter Mosley's novel *The Red Death* won the Edgar Allen Poe Award (1998), and the following year he began working with Mrs. Mamie Till Mobley on *State of Mississippi vs. Emmett Till,* based on the life and infamous death of her son.

Great history and social analysis, represented here by John Hope Franklin and Lerone Bennett Jr., has always come from Chicago. Along with Franklin and Bennett, Chicago has produced, or has had a major hand in producing, Carter G. Woodson, often called the Father of African-American History, and Sterling Stuckey. The great E. Franklin Frazier received his Ph.D. at the University of Chicago. His controversial *The Black Bourgeoisie* (1957) asserted that the Black middle class had gained status without substance. In addition, the social psychologist Nathan Hare, the first person to direct a Black studies program in the United States, probed the crisis of Black middle-class identity in his *Black Anglo-Saxons,* another work of great interest for anyone who wants to pursue the underlying theme of this anthology further. Mention should also be made of political activist and oral historian Timuel Black, whose recent *Bridges of Memory: Chicago's First Wave of Great Migration* chronicles Chicago's Black history from the 1920s to the present.

As for poets, one of the more widely published in the late 1960s and 1970s was Zack Gilbert, whose forte was the small poem sharply painting a portrait or mini-drama. As early as the late teens and early '20s, there were so many and so distinctive a number of poets from Chicago as to constitute an acknowledged school. Besides Fenton Johnson, W. Allison Sweeney, and Frank Marshall Davis, who *are* represented here, and Arna Bontemps and Margaret Walker, who were mentioned in the introduction, other members of the "Chicago Poets" school included Lucia Mae Pitts, William H. A. Moore, Henry Middleton Davis, Emory Elrage Scott, Edward Smythe Jones, and Alfred Anderson. Of more recent years, one of the most interesting is Sun Ra, who published a small handful of poems and would have fit in wonderfully with the title of this book. Known mainly as the jazz genius of the Sun Ra Solar Myth Arkestra, Sun Ra (Sonny Blount) often insisted he was not of this world, but from Saturn, a part of the mystique Marvin Tate's poem "Soulville Revisited" alludes to. In the middle of one of his signature pieces, a band member exclaims, "It takes too long to become a citizen of this planet, so I am here to proclaim your citizenship in the greater UNIVERSE." Sun Ra may also stand here for Gil Scott-Heron, another Chicagoan who has published good literature (his novel *Vulture*, for example) but is known mainly for his work in other media, in this case music; or Melvin Van Peebles, who wrote—originally in French—the wonderfully odd novel *A Bear for the F.B.I.* but is known more for his work in film.

Even more recent are the Slam and performance poets. Slam champion Regie Gibson says "Mama Maria McCray was the first person to let me on the mic (she's been regretting it ever since)." McCray still reads in Chicago's extraordinary performance and Slam community. This community—represented in this collection by Tate, Jess, Gibson, Green, Betts, and Shannon—was deeply influenced by the ever-present Haki Madhubuti; and Rohan Preston, Michael Warr, Quarysh Ali Lansana, Elizabeth Alexander, even Sam Greenlee, and many others have been greatly nourished by, or come directly out of this community. My list of regrets is particularly long here for the inability to include the fine work of poets Patricia Smith, Kent Foreman, Chuck Perkins, Calvin Glaze, Joffre Stewart, Tina Howell, Sharon Powell, Keith Kelley, Michael Witcher (cofounder of Chicago's legendary Funky Wordsmyths poetry-jazz band), and many, many others.

Sermons and speeches are staples of oral traditions extremely important to Black writing and culture, and Chicago is extraordinarily rich in wonderful preachers and speech-making community activists. Though his words are present in my introduction to Fred Hampton's selection, Jesse Jackson, for example, has made several classic speeches worthy of inclusion here, particularly the "Our time has come" speech delivered at the 1984 Democratic Convention.

Before this collection, there have been two other major anthologies devoted to Black writing from Chicago. Gwendolyn Brooks published *Jump Bad* in 1971 with writing from Carolyn M. Rodgers (who wrote the title piece) and others. Then in 1987, the Organization of Black American Culture published *NOMMO: A Literary Legacy of Black Chicago (1967–1987)*. It would be difficult to exaggerate the importance of OBAC to Black writing from Chicago. Not wanting to duplicate OBAC's efforts, only three small pieces from this key anthology were included here, though of course several writers overlap (Madhubuti, Plumpp, Rodgers, Amini-Hudson, among others). Of the *NOMMO* contributors, I would single out Walter Bradford, who has played many crucial roles in the development of Black writing in Chicago. *Jump Bad* really began when, says Gwendolyn Brooks, Bradford gathered "for me the literary-minded among the Blackstone Rangers, a huge collection of Chicago Youth."[2] I would also highlight the wonderful Nora Brooks Blakely and Daniel Clardy. But why stop here? The rest of the authors in *NOMMO* not represented in this present book are: Abdul Alkalimat (Gerald McWorter), Debra Anderson, Collette Armstead, S. Brandi Barnes, Randson Boykin, Cecil Brown, Pamela Cash-Menzies, Carl Chamberlain, Eileen C. Cherry, Barbara Cochran, Pauline Cole-Onyango, Alfreda Collins, Smalley M. (Mike) Cook, Jim Cunningham, Ronda Davis, Janice Dawson, Ebon Dooley, Eunice Favors, E. Van Higgs, Maga Jackson, Jamila-Ra (Maxine Hall Ellison), Oscar Joseph, George E. Kent, Helen King, Melvin E. Lewis, Johnnie Lott, Denise Love, George Leon Lowe, Antoinette McConnell, Barbara Mahone, Judy B. Massey, Maria K. Mootry, Philip Royster, Sandra Royster, Don Ryan, Adalisha Safi, Omar Shuayb, David Sims, Detmer Timberlake, Jeanne Towns, Andrew Wasaiah (Whitfield), Patricia Washington, Birdie Williams, Tony Williams, Kharlos Wimberli, and Yakie Yakubu. Authors in *Jump Bad* not included or mentioned above are: Linyatta (Doris Turner), Carl Clark, Peggy Kenner, and Sharon Scott.

In his important article "The New Voices Sing of Black Cultural Power," which appeared in the Panorama section of the *Chicago Daily News,* December 7, 1968, Eugene Perkins attempted to survey the entire arts scene in Chicago, including the visual arts, and music—the founding of the AACM (Association for the Advancement of Creative Music), for example, whose main temple, the Velvet Lounge, at Twenty-first and Indiana, is, as I write, on the verge of being bulldozed to make way for luxury condos. Among other sites, Perkins mentions OBAC's Wall of Respect at Forty-third and Langley, and Ellis Book Store at 6447 Cottage Grove. Among the literary/theatrical figures Perkins highlights are Sigemonde Kharlos Wimberli and Mike Cook, both in the *NOMMO* list above. Among those not mentioned anywhere above are James Cunningham, Cecil M. Brown, Val Gray Ward—a dramatist who was known as the "Voice of the Black Writer"—and Harold Johnson, then director of the Stateway Garden Homes and a drama producer and instructor. Perkins quotes him as having said, "A black theater must be completely controlled by black people and attempt to unmask the aberrations and stereotypes created by the white media."[3]

As with OBAC, it would be difficult to overstate the importance of Haki Madhubuti's Third World Press, which, like Madhubuti, has been mentioned time and time and time again throughout this volume. I had, in fact, considered listing the press's entire catalog, from which several pieces for this anthology were drawn. Among those closely associated with the press and of much importance to Black writing in Chicago are Jacob Carruthers and B. J. Bolden. Write Third World Press at P.O. Box 19730, Chicago, IL 60619, for a catalog, or reach them on-line at www.thirdworldpressinc.com. Madhubuti is, at this writing, also assembling the first creative writing program in the country based on Black texts at Chicago State University, an institution of critical importance to Black writing in Chicago, site of the Gwendolyn Brooks Center, and host of the annual Gwendolyn Brooks Writers Conference.

Though not focused solely on Black writing, the Guild Complex, a cross-cultural arts organization, was founded and directed for a decade by Michael Warr and helped nourish a number of Black writers. Tia Chucha Press, the guild's publishing arm, put out several books from which material was reprinted here and in 1999 released the wonderful anthology *Power Lines: A Decade of Poetry from Chicago's Guild Complex*.

Of the many books helpful in compiling this anthology, I would highlight: *The Prentice Hall Anthology of African American Literature*, edited by Rochelle Smith and Sharon L. Jones; and four classic anthologies—James Weldon Johnson's *Book of Negro American Poetry*, Arna Bontemps' *American Negro Poetry*, Abraham Chapman's *Black Voices*, and Addison Gayle Jr.'s *The Black Aesthetic*. Christopher Robert Reed's *"All the World Is Here!" The Black Presence at White City*, Bill V. Mullen's *Popular Fronts: Chicago and African-American Cultural Politics, 1935-1946*, and The Black Public Sphere Collective's *The Black Public Sphere: A Public Culture Book* are also essential works in putting Chicago Black writing in broad perspective.

Finally, no one working on Black writing from Chicago can do without the city's great resources in both texts and personnel. There is the Chicago Historical Society, of course, but I worked mainly at the Chicago Public Libraries—the Harold Washington, certainly, but especially the Carter G. Woodson Regional Library on Ninety-fifth and Halstead, which houses the remarkable Vivian G. Harsh Research Collection of Afro-American History and Literature. Thanks to the Harsh's indefatigable curators Robert Miller and Michael Flug.

Notes

1. Julia Keller, "'Free' from His Past," *Chicago Tribune,* February 22, 2004, sec. 7, 1.

2. Gwendolyn Brooks, introduction to *Jump Bad: A New Chicago Anthology,* ed. Gwendolyn Brooks (Detroit: Broadside Press, 1971), 11.

3. Quoted in Eugene Perkins, "The New Voices Sing of Black Cultural Power." *Chicago Daily News,* December 7 1968, Panorama sec., 4–5.

Credits

Every effort has been made to contact copyright holders of the pieces in this collection. The editor would welcome information concerning any omissions or other inadvertent errors.

Very special thanks to those who graciously donated work to this project, including the following presses:

Third World Press, Chicago, for permission to reprint the selections by Johari Amini-Hudson, from *Let's Go Somewhere,* copyright © 1970; by Hoyt W. Fuller, from *Journey to Africa,* copyright © 1971; by Quarysh Ali Lansana, from *Southside Rain,* copyright © 1999; by Haki R. Madhubuti, from *Black Men: Obsolete, Single, Dangerous?* copyright © 1991; by Eugene Perkins, from *Memories & Images: Selected Poems,* copyright © 2002; and by Sterling Plumpp, from *Horn Man,* copyright © 1995.

Northwestern University Press/TriQuarterly Books, Evanston, Illinois, for permission to reprint the poem by Angela Jackson, from *And All These Roads Be Luminous,* copyright © 1998 by Angela Jackson, published 1998 by Northwestern University Press, all rights reserved; and to Northwestern University Press, Evanston, Illinois, for permission to reprint selections by Leanita McClain, from *A Foot in Each World,* copyright © 1986.

EM Press and Mark Eleveld, Joliet, Illinois, for permission to reprint poems by Regie Gibson from *Storms Beneath the Skins,* copyright © 2001.

And including the following individuals:

Judith Berry Griffin, for permission to reprint selections by Leonidas Harris Berry from *I Wouldn't Take Nothin' for My Journey Now,* Johnson Publishing, 1981.

Margaret T. Burroughs, for permission to reprint her poem from *What Shall I Tell My Children Who Are Black?* M.A.A.H. Press, Chicago, copyright © 1968.

John Hope Franklin, for permission to reprint excerpts from *Racial Equality in America,* University of Chicago Press, 1976.

Ken Green, for permission to reprint his poems.

Sam Greenlee, for permission to reprint excerpts from *The Spook Who Sat by the Door,* Wayne State University Press, Detroit, copyright © 1989.

Bennett J. Johnson and Path Press, for permission to reprint excerpts by Herman Cromwell Gilbert from *The Negotiation,* Path Press, Chicago, copyright © 1983.

Tyehimba Jess, for permission to reprint his poems.

Audrey Petty, for permission to reprint her story.

Carolyn M. Rodgers, for permission to reprint her poems from *We're Only Human Poems,* Eden Press, Chicago, copyright © 1996, and from *A Train Called Judah,* Eden Press, Chicago, copyright © 1998.

David L. Smith, *a.k.a.* D. L. Crockett Smith, for permission to reprint his poem.

Dempsey J. Travis, for permission to reprint excerpts from *I Refuse to Learn to Fail,* Urban Research Press, Chicago, copyright © 1992.

Glennette Tilley Turner, for permission to reprint the poem by Rev. John Tilley.

Thanks also to:

Lerone Bennett Jr., for permission to reprint excerpts from *Before the Mayflower: A History of Black America,* New Millennium Edition, Johnson Publishing Company, copyright © 1988.

Tara Betts, for permission to reprint her poems.

Brooks Permissions for consent to reprint selections by Gwendolyn Brooks.

Broadside Press, for selections by Margaret Danner from *Impressions of African Art Forms,* copyright © 1960, and from Margaret Danner and Dudley Randall, *Poem-Counter Poem,* copyright © 1969.

Coffee House Press, Minneapolis, for permission to reprint poems by Clarence Major from *Configurations: New and Selected Poems, 1958–1998,* copyright © by Clarence Major.

Doubleday, a division of Random House, Inc., for permission to reprint excerpts by William Attaway from *Blood on the Forge,* copyright © 1941 by Doubleday.

Greenwood Publishing Group, Inc., Westport, Connecticut, for permission to reprint excerpts by Richard Durham from *Richard Durham's Destination Freedom,* ed. J. Fred MacDonald, copyright © 1989.

Dick Gregory for permission to reprint excerpts by Dick Gregory from *Nigger!* Dutton, copyright © by Dick Gregory, 1964.

Harcourt, Inc., for permission to reprint excerpts by St. Clair Drake and Horace Cayton, from *Black Metropolis: A Study of Negro Life in a Northern City,* copyright © 1970; and by Ronald L. Fair, from *Hog Butcher,* copyright © 1966, renewed by Ronald L. Fair, 1994.

Harold Ober Associates, for permission to reprint the selection from Langston Hughes, copyright © Langston Hughes, 1946.

HarperCollins Publishers, for permission to reprint excerpts by Clarence Page, from *Showing My Color,* copyright © by Clarence Page, 1996; and by Richard Wright, from *American Hunger,* copyright © 1944 by Richard Wright, and 1977 by Ellen Wright.

Sandra Jackson-Opoku, for permission to reprint her poem "Ancestors: In Praise of the Imperishable."

Scribner, an imprint of Simon and Schuster Adult Publishing Group, for permission to reprint "The Education of Mingo" by Charles Johnson, from *The Sorcerer's Apprentice,* copyright © 1977 by Charles Johnson.

Simon and Schuster Adult Publishing Group, for permission to reprint excerpts by Lorraine Hansberry, from *To Be Young, Gifted and Black: Lorraine Hansberry in Her Own Words,* by Lorraine Hansberry, adapted by Robert Nemiroff, copyright © by Robert Nemiroff and Robert Nemiroff as Executor of the Estate of Lorraine Hansberry, 1969.

Susan Bergholz Literary Services, New York, for permission to reprint excerpts by Sandra Jackson-Opoku, from *Hot Johnny,* copyright © by Sandra Jackson Opoku, 2001.

Three Rivers Press, a division of Random House, for permission to reprint excerpts by Barack Obama, from *Dreams from My Father,* copyright © by Barack Obama, 1995, 2004.

Thunder's Mouth Press, for permission to reprint the story by Cyrus Colter, from *The Amoralist and Other Tales,* copyright © 1988 by Thunder's Mouth Press, a division of Avalon Publishing Group.

Tia Chucha Press, for permission to reprint the selections by Elizabeth Alexander, from *Body of Life,* copyright © 1996; by Sterling Plumpp, from *Blues Narratives,* copyright © 1999; by Rohan Preston, from *Dreams in Soy Sauce,* copyright © 1992; by Marvin Tate, from

Richard R. Guzman is a professor of English at North Central College, where he also directs the Master of Arts in Liberal Studies program and the Master of Leadership Studies program. Over a long career as a community activist, musician, and performing poet, he has worked in a variety forms, and his published pieces include music, poetry, and essays. His most recent book, coedited with David Starkey, is *Smokestacks and Skyscrapers: An Anthology of Chicago Writing.*